Creativity

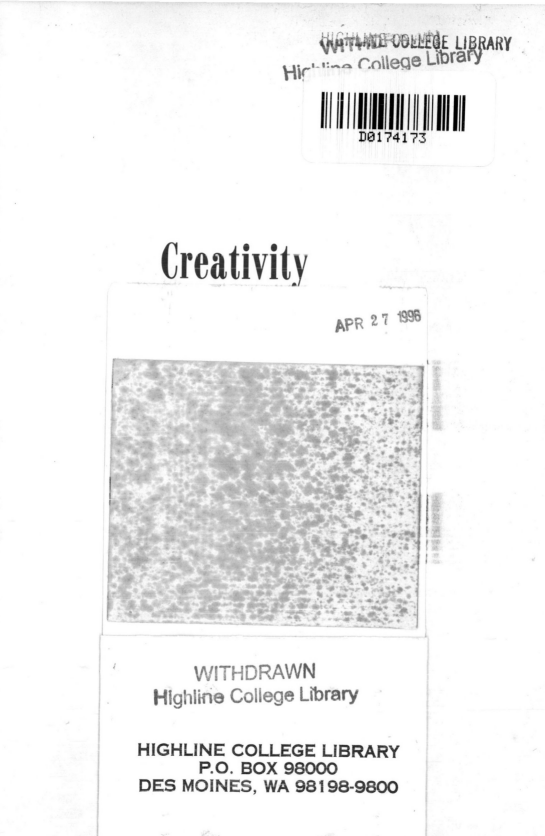

A series of books in Psychology:

Editors:

Richard C. Atkinson
Gardner Lindzey
Richard F. Thompson

CREATIVITY

Beyond the Myth of Genius

Robert W. Weisberg
Temple University

W. H. Freeman and Company
New York

Cover Image:
Pablo Picasso
Interior with Girl Drawing. Paris, February 1935.
Oil on canvas, 51¼ × 6' 4⅝".
Collection, The Museum of Modern Art, New York. Nelson A. Rockefeller
   Bequest.
Photograph © 1992 The Museum of Modern Art, New York.

Library of Congress Cataloging-in-Publication Data

Weisberg, Robert W.
    Creativity : beyond the myth of genius / Robert Weisberg.
      p.   cm.
    Includes bibliographical references and index.
    ISBN 0-7167-2365-4. — ISBN 0-7167-2367-0 (pbk.)
    1. Creative ability.   I. Title.
   BF408.W386   1993
   153.3'5—dc20   92-36442
                                                                  CIP

Printed in the United States of America

2 3 4 5 6 7 8 9 0 VB 9 9 8 7 6 5 4 3

To Nancy, Michael, and Rebecca

You will believe claims about creativity in other areas that you never would about your own.
Laurence Steinberg

Contents

Preface

This is an exciting time to study creativity, and the purpose of this book is to convey the excitement of recent research to the reader. The importance of the topic of creativity in our society is seen in many ways. One gauge of this interest was the recent broadcast of a widely publicized PBS series on creativity, presenting the views of various experts on the origins of creativity and how it can be increased, as well as presenting portraits of corporations that have developed creative methods for carrying out their business activities. Indeed, training aimed at increasing the ability to think creatively is so highly valued that creativity consultants travel the globe, presenting methods for increasing employees' ability to overcome the problems they face in their work.

In education, creativity is a principal component of "critical thinking" courses taught in many institutions of higher learning in the United States. Training in creative thinking also has become a mandated part of the school curriculum for children throughout the world.

This intense interest in creativity reflects a set of beliefs, pervasive in modern society, that I call the "genius" view — that creative thinking is the result of extraordinary thinking processes, processes that are somehow qualitatively different from the "ordinary" thinking that we all use for our daily activities.

Belief in the genius view has led to attempts to specify the thought processes used by creative individuals, such as unconscious thinking and sudden leaps of insight, as well as those psychological characteristics that separate creative individuals from the ordinary, such as the possession of extraordinary flexibility and sensitivity. One needs flexibility to break away from the past and sensitivity to be able to judge the quality of what one has created.

In contrast to the genius view, an alternative view of creativity has developed in scientific circles, which claims that creative thinking and creative persons are extraordinary because of their products, but not because of the processes by which these products are brought about. Various components of this "ordinary" view of creativity have been proposed by psychologists, computer-scientists; and historians of technology, science, and the arts; and it is the synthesis of these views that I see as offering the most excitement in the study of creativity today.

This book is my second on the topic of creativity. The earlier one (*Creativity: Genius and Other Myths*) was primarily a critique of the genius view, in which it was argued that, even though that view is pervasive in our society, the empirical evidence for it is very weak. There is no persuasive evidence, for example, that unconscious processes play a central role in creative thinking. Likewise, there is little evidence that sudden leaps of spontaneous insight are crucial in creative thinking. The same is true concerning the psychological characteristics that are assumed to underlie genius: there is no evidence that flexibility and sensitivity, for example, are necessary for the production of great creative works.

The overall conclusion of my first book was that there is no reason to assume that creativity is based on extraordinary thinking. However, I said little in that book about "ordinary" thinking and how it could serve creativity. Drawing upon evidence from both laboratory studies of creative thinking, and equally important, from historical case studies of the development of important creative works, this book goes beyond the critique of genius presented earlier, to discuss the components of ordinary thinking and how they underlie even the greatest examples of creativity.

The first chapter begins with a discussion of how creativity and related concepts are defined and then presents a sketch of the two views of creativity, "genius" and "ordinary." Two brief case studies are presented as examples of how ordinary thinking can be used to explain creativity: Alexander Calder's development of the first mobiles (abstract sculptures moved by air) and Edison's invention of the kinctoscope. Chapters 2 and 3 expand the critique of the genius view to provide a context for going beyond it. Chapter 2 critically examines a wide range of extraordinary modes of thinking that have been postulated as the basis of creativity, and Chapter 3 critiques attempts to specify the psychological characteristics that cause individuals to be creative.

Chapter 4 uses laboratory studies of creative problem solving to outline the components of ordinary thinking, which then serve to organize the analysis of case studies that follow in later chapters. The chapter emphasizes the importance of "near" analogies in creative thinking; the role of the thinker's expertise and critical judgment; and the role of external events in triggering new directions in thinking.

Creative works begin with what has been done in the past, and they go beyond the past in logical and understandable ways. If one places a creative thinker in historical context, that is, if one attempts to determine what the person knew, then one can understand the development of even the most radically new works. In Chapters 5–7, I provide evidence for this view by describing the development of selected creative work in several different domains. Chapter 5 presents case studies of several seminal inventions, including the steam engine and the Wright brothers' airplane. Chapter 6 presents case studies of scientific discoveries, including DNA and the theory of evolution. Chapter 7 examines artistic creativity in several domains, including two of Picasso's great paintings, the development of Mozart's music, and several works in literature. Finally, Chapter 8 uses the evidence presented in Chapters 4–7 as the basis for a deeper analysis of the processes underlying creative thinking.

This book would not have come into being without stimulation and support of colleagues and students, including Larry Steinberg and Lauretta Reeves. Nora Newcombe and Lynn Hasher deserve special thanks for their years of cogent criticism and unflagging enthusiasm. I would also like to thank Robert T. Brown of the University of North Carolina at Wilmington and Mark A. Runco of California State University at Fullerton for their reviews. I have had the good fortune of working with a number of highly competent people at W. H. Freeman and Company, particularly Jonathan Cobb, who as psychology editor was strong in his support of my vision of this project. Diane Maass, Larry ("We got the fishbowl!") Marcus, and Sarah Polen also deserve special thanks.

Robert W. Weisberg
Philadelphia, October 1992

CHAPTER 1

Two Orientations Toward Creativity

The steam engine [invented by James Watt] had no precedent . . . (it) sprang into sudden existence, like Minerva from the brain of Jupiter.
Cooke-Taylor 1842; cited in Basalla 1988, p. 35)

Watson and Crick relied heavily on inspiration, iteration, and visualization [in formulating the double-helix model of DNA]. Even though they were superb biochemists, they had no precedent from which they could logically derive their structure and therefore relied heavily on left-handed [nonlogical] thinking.
(Adams 1979; pp. 60–61)

In 1907 the young Pablo Picasso painted *Les Demoiselles d'Avignon*. The savage distortions in the faces and bodies of the women were unprecedented in the history of art and are far removed from the traditional concept of "beauty" in painting, which was present in Picasso's own work of just a few years before. Because of its radical break with old traditions, *Les Demoiselles* has been called by several art historians the most important painting of the twentieth century.

Les Demoiselles d'Avignon, by Pablo Picasso. Paris (June-July 1907). From the collection of The Museum of Modern Art, New York.

> [A]t the time of the Wright brothers there was no field of aeronautics. What happens in such cases is that a subset of people from related fields recognize the validity of the new variation [i.e., the new invention] and become identified with the emerging field. . . . [I]n the case of the Wright brothers, it was automobile and bicycle mechanics. (Csikszentmihalyi 1988, pp. 331–332).

The invention of the steam engine, the formulation of the double-helix model for DNA, Picasso's painting of *Les Demoiselles,* and the construction of the first powered airplane—only a few striking examples of creative accomplishment with a profound effect on our lives and our culture. What lies behind these and other examples of human creativity?

Understanding creativity is a challenging task, not only because creative thinking occurs in diverse domains but also because a complex set of psychological and social forces contributes to it. A major difficulty is that, from a distance, the creative processes leading to the accomplishments of inventors, scientists, and artists seem so mysterious. In fact, these processes often seem incomprehensible to the creators themselves.

In our society, attempts to understand the creative process have been dominated by what I will call the "genius" view. This view assumes, as suggested by the quotations beginning this chapter, that great creative achievements must be the result of extraordinary individuals employing extraordinary thought processes. This view has existed in Western society for thousands of years, and can be seen today in the near-veneration of Albert Einstein, for example, and in views such as those presented in Peter Shaffer's *Amadeus*. In that play, Wolfgang Amadeus Mozart is portrayed as an immature, asocial individual who is nonetheless capable of producing miraculous music, as if through the intervention of a higher power. The action is seen from the point of view of Antonio Salieri, a well-known composer of the time who, near the end of his life, went mad and is said to have "confessed" to poisoning Mozart, bringing about the latter's tragically early death, presumably out of jealousy toward Mozart's genius. This portrayal of Mozart as "miraculous" is a modern-day encapsulation of the genius view; it is echoed in a 1989 *Psychology Today* article:

> [T]here *are* extraordinary examples of creativity, for which the only explanation seems to be supernatural intervention (Mozart, the story goes, wrote the overture to *Don Giovanni* in only a few hours, after a virtually sleepless night and without revision).

The evidence supporting the genius view often consists of anecdotes and self-reports — from individuals of acknowledged greatness — concerning how they produced their great works. Examination of this "evidence," however, strongly suggests that "genius" is a myth. In this book, I will argue instead that making sense of the development of creative works requires no elaborate construction, because creativity is firmly rooted in past experience and has its source in the same thought processes that we all use every day.

The term creativity is of course used in various ways. For this reason, it will be useful to begin with a definition of creativity as well as a consideration of the central questions surrounding it. Then, we can look more closely at the genius view and at what other theories might better explain the development of creative works.

Defining Creativity

The steam engine, the structure of DNA, *Les Demoiselles d'Avignon*, and the airplane qualify without question as creative achievements of the first magnitude. Such examples may help to build a working definition of creativity, but to discuss a wider range of phenomena, a formal definition is more useful. I will begin with a characterization that has developed among investigators in different areas of psychology, in which "creative" refers to novel products of value, as in, "The airplane was a creative invention." "Creative" also refers to the person who produces the work, as in, "Picasso was creative." "Creativity," then, refers both to the capacity to produce such works, as in "How can we foster our employees' creativity?" and to the activity of generating such products, as in "Creativity requires hard work."

The primary criterion for calling some product creative is that it be novel, at least for the individual producing it. Some theorists reserve the term creative for products that have resulted in major departures from what was known at the time. This criterion has been called the "degree of transformation" brought about by some creative product. Others make a similar distinction, conferring on products differing degrees of creativity, depending on the degree of apparent innovation in each. However, since the focus of this book is the thought processes underlying creative work, I will not here make any such distinction; one work's being more innovative than another does not mean *a priori* that different cognitive processes brought about the two works.

All who study creativity agree that for something to be creative, it is not enough for it to be novel: it must also have value, or be appropriate to the cognitive demands of the situation. (I will consider these to be equivalent terms.) The classic example of inappropriate novelty is a schizophrenic's free association in a situation that requires problem solving. Value is essential to the definition of creativity, so as to exclude such responses from consideration.

The concept of value is complex, since the value of a creative product depends on what it is. A scientific theory is valuable if it can explain phenomena that individuals in the discipline see as requiring explanation, or if it presents a way of organizing phenomena that is seen as more useful than the current view. An invention is valuable if it can carry out a necessary task. In addition to its value within the immediate scientific or technological context, a scientific theory or an invention can be seen as broadly valuable if it inspires others, as when a scientific theory spawns new research and theorizing. On a still broader scale, a scientific theory or an invention can have influence beyond its domain. For example, Watt's steam engine was a creative invention in the narrow sense because it provided a reliable source of power. On a broader scale, it provided the stimulus for a whole generation of engines. Finally, it played a major role in stimulating the industrial revolution in England.

Similarly, a work of art can be seen to be valuable in narrow and broader senses. For example, a painted portrait is valuable in the narrow sense if it expresses the feelings that the artist wished to express on painting it; it can be seen by the subject as valuable to the degree that it captures the subject's likeness and/or is a sympathetic presentation. In addition, it may be judged by other members of the artistic community — critics, historians, and other artists — to be worthy of study, and to possess ideas that should be carried further. In this case, the broader value of the work is in the influence it exerts on the artistic community. On a still broader scale, a work of art is valuable if it is seen by some of its public to be worthy of inclusion in their heritage, and of being passed down to the next generation.

The judgments of the artistic community do not always coincide with those of the individual artist or of the art-viewing and art-buying public. Paul Cézanne's work, for example, had great influence on painters at the beginning of the twentieth century, without at that time being accorded general acclaim among the museum-going public. By contrast, the works of the painters Norman Rockwell and Andrew Wyeth have been valued by the general public without receiving the same level of respect from the artistic community.

The Central Questions of Creativity

When attempting to understand creativity, we can ask first about the creative process: how a creative work is produced. Second, we can ask about creative persons: what are their psychological characteristics. Finally, we can ask about the creative product: what makes a work great.

One of the most difficult issues for any theory of creative thinking is that of inspiration, or where creative ideas come from. Consider

Picasso's *Les Demoiselles d'Avignon*—how did it come about? This question has two facets: the first concerns the source of the original idea or inspiration for Picasso's painting; the second concerns the development of the work. Regarding inspiration, did Picasso work independently of what came before, or was his work based on his own earlier work and/or on that of others? Concerning the painting's development, did Picasso conceive the painting complete, in final form, in a sudden burst of creative insight, or did it only gradually take final form? If the latter, what factors produced the changes that occurred in Picasso's thinking? These two issues—inspiration and development—are independent. A work might be related to works of others, but the artist might conceive it whole, in a burst of creative insight.

The same questions can be asked about the other examples of creative works noted at the beginning of the chapter. The statement on the steam engine claims that the idea of the steam engine came to Watt whole, in a sudden burst of creative insight, independently of anything that had been done before. James Adams makes a similar claim concerning the development of the double helix: Watson and Crick worked independently of what came before. The quotation about the Wright brothers indicates that there was nothing available on which they could base their work.

Most of us do not produce inventions that change the world, paint revolutionary paintings, make momentous scientific discoveries, or write great novels or poetry. These differences in accomplishment raise the question of the psychological differences among us, the "individual differences" that may play a role in creative achievement. What, if anything, is there about the psychological make-up of some individuals that enables them to produce great creative works? For example, at the same time that James Watson and Francis Crick were successful in developing the double-helix model of DNA, Linus Pauling, Maurice Wilkins, and Rosalind Franklin—very talented and influential workers in the same field—were also working on that problem, but were not successful in solving it. How is it that one scientist can develop a theory, while another scientist, expert in the area, and presumably examining the same facts, does not develop the theory?

All creative products are not of the same degree of importance: Some scientific work is widely influential, and has an effect on every part of our lives, while other work, original though it may be, lies unnoticed for generations, and perhaps forever. It stimulates no research; its creator is not accorded a place of honor in the community of scientists. Similarly, though some inventions have had momentous effects, the files of patent offices around the world are filled with descriptions of inventions with no effect beyond a feeling of satisfaction in their inventors. Then again, two painters may work in obscurity in adjoining studios, both producing unique works, but one painter's work will become crucial to art, while the other's will be ignored. Why are some products of profound importance while others are forgotten?

In the remainder of this chapter, I will give an overview of the "genius" answer to these questions and of another theory arguing that creative works are the result of ordinary thinking. This comparison will set the stage for the discussion of creativity in subsequent chapters.

Genius: The Creator as Hero

There is a long tradition in Western thought, perhaps a vestige of the Old Testament view of God breathing life into Adam, that explains creative achievements by assuming that individuals simply serve as vehicles through which divine ideas are expressed. The individual plays no direct part in creativity; it is carried out by the gods. In Greek mythology, the Muses, the goddesses of song and the arts generally, breathe original ideas into people, which is why we say that we get an "inspiration," meaning the act of breathing in, when we suddenly get a good idea.

Although in our scientific age invoking gods to explain creativity seems farfetched, many people nonetheless believe that to understand creative thinking in its highest forms, a special theory is needed. At its most extreme, the genius view assumes that truly creative acts come about when great individuals, on their own and independently of what has been done before, produce some great achievement in a burst of inspiration. An important component of the genius view is a strong emotional undertone of mystery and wonder at the occurrence of the creative act and its products.

The genius view explains the origin and development of creative works by postulating special thinking processes that allow the individual to break away from the habitual and the ordinary, in what is often called "breaking the set." These processes then enable the creative thinker to weave together ideas that others had seen as unconnected, and to develop an original concept.

The genius has the capacity to leap significantly beyond present
knowledge and produce something new. To do this, a number
of researchers think, he breaks the set—he sees the
relationship between facts or pieces of information in a new or
unusual way. He may also perceive the significance of new
facts when others see them merely as anomalies that don't fit
their set, their way of perceiving information. (Briggs 1984, p. 76)

It is believed as well that great, creative individuals must have
nervous systems different from those of ordinary individuals. In the
same *Psychology Today* article on creativity in which divine intervention was invoked to explain Mozart's creativity, the authors spent
much time discussing recent work that attempts to determine exactly
which parts of the brain are involved in creativity and what could be
the construction of these areas of the brain for them to carry out their
extraordinary functions. Brains of such individuals as Einstein have
even been preserved and examined in an attempt to determine what
areas mught underlie the capacity to be creative.

In the genius view, that some individuals produce great works
while others do not is seen to also be based on a personality structure
that allows such special thinking to flourish. The most important personality characteristics of genius, some argue, are extraordinary sensitivity and flexibility. The sensitivity of genius is seen first in what is
called "problem finding," the ability to focus on artistic or scientific
problems of potential importance. The artist of genius is sensitive to
situations that will serve as vehicles for artistic expression with possibly universal significance. The artist who lacks genius, in contrast,
wastes time dealing with situations that others will not find meaningful.

The scientist of genius is supposed to be extraordinarily sensitive
to the environment, a sensitivity seen in varying sorts of problem
finding. First, such a scientist focuses potentially important scientific
problems. He or she invests time and resources in problems that will
bear fruit, while the "ordinary" scientist spends time working on
problems without solutions or with unimportant implications. In addition, this scientist sees in existing theories difficulties not apparent
to ordinary individuals, which leads to creative work in areas nonex-
istent for the nongenius.

Also, the sensitivity of the genius is assumed to influence the way
that problems of significance are dealt with. It is thought the artist of
genius possesses a heightened sensitivity to the emotional experi-

ences of others, because such artists have more insight into, or are closer to, their own emotional experiences. This insight enables the genius to empathize with the audience, facilitating effective communication of emotion.

In addition to heightened sensitivity, the genius supposedly exhibits a flexibility of personality and of thinking. The artist of genius, due to such flexibility, can continually go beyond earlier work and thereby continue to make creative advances throughout a career. In contrast, the artist lacking genius will continue producing only variants of the same work, and perhaps will never produce anything truly original.

The genius in science can use flexibility of thought to see hidden connections among ideas, which through set-breaking can result in a new theory. Flexible thinking also enables the creative scientist to use unexpected results as the basis for a radical shift in thinking. But the scientist lacking genius, with rigid personality structure and thought processes, may simply respond to unexpected results by more strongly defending the old theory, and thereby make no advance beyond what is already known.

The genius view answers the question of why some works find a lasting place in history while others do not by referring to the personality structure of the genius: immortal works are the result of the extraordinary sensitivity of the person of genius. In the arts, the sensitivity of the genius makes a work universally meaningful. In science, this sensitivity leads the genius to contemplate scientific questions and to propose answers of universal import.

These components of genius are usually assumed to be present in varying degrees in all of us, but most of us do not possess them to a sufficient degree to produce creative work. Some others may produce creative work, but it will not be influential or lasting. However, if all the components are present to an extraordinary degree, one produces work of genius.

The genius view seems so straightforward that we simply take it for granted; we do not even think critically about its basic components. Each of us has had occasion to marvel at some invention; we have all been moved to laughter or tears by a film, been carried away by a novel, been brought to great joy or sadness by music; our lives or those of people we love have been saved as the result of great scientific advances. In the face of such phenomena, it seems obvious that there must be something extraordinary about the people who produce such achievements, or else we would all equal their achievements all the time, and we obviously do not.

Although the genius view in one another of its variants is accepted uncritically by many people as the explanation for the production of creative works, the evidence for it is very weak. The genius view is in fact a myth, fabricated to explain a set of phenomena. In Chapters 2 and 3, I will discuss two foundations of the genius view: (1) that creative thinking involves extraordinary thought processes, and (2) that there is a set of psychological characteristics (the "genius" personality) possessed by all individuals who produce creative works and which allows those thought processes to flourish. It should be emphasized that it is not being claimed that individuals who produce great creative works are in all ways the same as ordinary individuals; the claim at this point is simply that the thinking processes are not different. Later, there will be discussions of the differences between ordinary individuals and the greats. Here, I will briefly outline an alternative to the genius view, an alternative that proposes that creative thinking is based on ordinary thought processes.

Examining Creative Thinking

Many creative products are indeed extraordinary. They are rare; they are sometimes the result of a lifetime of hard work; they can answer questions that have perplexed thinkers for centuries; they can produce new insights into important issues in our lives; and they can have far-ranging influence, beyond even the expectations of their creators. It is often assumed that if a creative product has extraordinary effects, it must have come about in extraordinary ways, but that does not necessarily follow. The creative achievement can be extraordinary because of the effect it produces, rather than because of the way in which it was brought about. As a rough analogy, the straw that breaks the camel's back is not extraordinary *qua* straw, but it is extraordinary because of the effect it has on the camel.

In this book, I examine creative thinking of many sorts, ranging from an undergraduate's solving a simple laboratory problem to the production of revolutionary scientific theories and great works of art. In attempting to understand and explain these phenomena, it will not be necessary to introduce concepts different from concepts we ordinarily use to describe and understand thinking. Ordinary thinking begins with continuity with the past: we use the old to generate the new. Ordinary thinking also goes beyond the past, but does so in straightforward ways, through reasoning and the accumulation of new pieces of information. There are no sudden spontaneous leaps beyond what we have experienced, no unconscious illuminations, no bolts of lightning from the blue (although things sometimes feel that way). Furthermore, the inspirations that start the creative process — when a composer thinks of a melody, or a poet a line or a phrase — come about through the same processes that enable us to describe a scene we have witnessed or to plan how we will carry out our day's errands.

It may be difficult to believe that great works of art or breakthroughs in science or in technology could be the result of the same cognitive processes involved in making dinner or driving to work, since these latter activities are usually thought of as simply the running along of habitual modes of behavior, with no novelty or creativity involved. However, I take the view that there is never simply the "running along" of some "habitual behavior" in our activities; novelty is the norm in all behavior, because the exact repetition of any environmental event is an impossibility. If novelty in environmental events is the norm, then novelty of behavioral products must also be the norm, because we are continually adapting our behavior to fit new circumstances. "Ordinary" thinking processes must then produce novel works of value (even if the work is a salad for dinner). In the following pages, I will argue further that ordinary thought processes must underlie even the most exalted examples of creative thinking, such as Watt's invention of a revolutionary source of power, the Wright brothers' invention of a new mode of transportation, Picasso's development of a new style of painting, and Watson and Crick's formulation of a structure for DNA.

This view will be supported by two sorts of evidence: laboratory studies of creative problem solving and historical case studies of important creative achievements. Although most work in cognitive psychology — the study of thought processes — is based on laboratory research, the study of creative thinking must almost by definition go beyond the laboratory. When one carries out an experiment in the laboratory, the subjects are not Picasso or Mozart. Therefore, making claims about general aspects of creative thinking from results of a laboratory experiment may beg the critical question of whether the results are generalizable. For this reason, I also make use of the "historical case study," a method which relies on historical records — early sketches for paintings, early drafts for poems and novels, and early notes for scientific theories — to make inferences about the creative process. This method is standard in art history, the history of technology, and musicology, among other disciplines in which at-

tempts are made to understand the processes involved in the genesis
of creative works. In psychology, it has been used to great advantage
by Howard Gruber and his students.

A limitation in using historical case studies is that the researcher
cannot carry out experimental manipulations. If the researcher con-
cludes on the basis of historical analysis that, say, exposure in 1906 to
new works by another artist brought about a shift in Picasso's style of
painting, then the research worker would like to be able to obtain additional evidence to support this claim. A way to do this might be to
expose other artists to those same paintings, to demonstrate that such
a style shift does indeed occur. However, since the claim was made
about Picasso, presenting these alleged stimulus-paintings to other
artists — and especially, other artists in the context of today's art
world — would not be relevant. However, in many important cases,
data are available to allow conclusions strong enough to illuminate the
present concerns. There are, as well, data from laboratory studies
(covered in some detail in Chapter 4) that provide a framework to
support and amplify the phenomena to be seen in the case studies.

When using case studies as an important part of the data base for
theory building, other important issues must be discussed. First, how
"representative" are the reported case studies. That is, can the studies
be taken as a reasonable sampling of case studies of creative individuals, or might each case be unique in some way, and therefore of little
general impact? Second, how were the cases selected? Is it possible
that the cases were chosen because they support my view, and that
other cases would not?

Concerning representativeness, we can only know if a given case
study has broadly relevant implications if we have available a large
number of case studies to examine and compare, which is not yet the
case. Even so, we may never be able to make generalizations of the
sort, "All creative individuals are thus and so," because, as Howard
Gruber has argued, each case of creative thinking may be unique. If
Gruber is correct, we should be looking at as many case studies as we
can, to get a sense of the multiplicity of forms that creative processes
can take. Furthermore, the only way to determine if Gruber is correct
is again to examine many case studies.

The case studies presented in this book were chosen according to
three criteria, that they (1) cover the highest level of achievement, (2)
in a broad range of areas, and (3) that some of them provide particularly difficult tests for the view that creative products come about
through ordinary thought processes. If the case can be made that many
highly esteemed products came about through ordinary thought pro-

cesses, such a case would be particularly strong, while coverage of a broad range of achievement makes it clear that no areas are being swept under the rug. Concerning the relationship between the selection of the case studies and the ordinary-thought-process point of view, several of the cases were chosen because they seemed to be especially difficult ones. For example, I felt that it would be very hard to make sense of the development of Jackson Pollock's poured paintings, which seem to have resulted from some volcanic upwelling of unconscious energy, far removed from our ordinary activities. Similarly, because Mozart is reported to have composed in ways very different from ordinary thinking, his case seemed particularly difficult to deal with. Picasso also provides special difficulties, since some of his works were radically different from his own earlier art as well as from that of earlier artists and of his contemporaries.

In order to begin elucidating the "ordinary" processes underlying even radically creative products, I will briefly examine two case studies: Calder's development of mobiles and Edison's invention of the kinetoscope, a device for showing motion pictures. Once these cases are analyzed, it should not be necessary to invoke any concepts beyond those used to describe thinking in ordinary situations.

Calder's Mobiles: A Case Study

Mobiles are everywhere: they soar above our largest public spaces and bob above the cribs of babies, but before the early 1930s there were none. The name "mobile" was given in Paris in 1932 to the work of the young American Alexander Calder (1898–1976), who is given credit for inventing a new form of sculpture. Calder's mobiles are hanging works so constructed that their abstract components rotate about each other, and thereby cut out "chunks" of space, which become part of the work. Tracing the development of the concept of mobiles involves following several important themes present early in Calder's life and that, with some important outside stimuli, came together in his production of mobiles.

Calder came from an artistic family; his mother was a painter, and his father and grandfather were famous sculptors. His manual and mechanical skills were evident very early in the jewelry he made out of wire for his sister's dolls and the toys and other gadgets he made for himself. The use of wire to fabricate objects was a constant avenue of expression throughout his career. Calder's mechanical abilities led

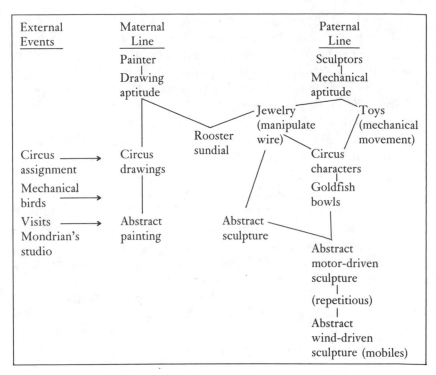

A developmental history of Calder's mobiles.

him to pursue engineering as a career, and he attended Stevens Institute of Technology from 1915 to 1919.

Between 1922 and 1926, Calder attended drawing classes in New York. In 1924, at the age of twenty-six, he began working as an illustrator for the *National Police Gazette*, a periodical. One assignment for the *Gazette* involved attending the circus for two weeks and drawing various circus scenes for publication. At about this time, Calder created his first wire sculpture, a sundial in the shape of a rooster. Though he had made jewelry and toys out of wire, this was his first attempt to represent an animal.

Calder moved to Paris in 1926 to immerse himself more deeply in an art career. By this time, two important streams in his work were already present: his use of wire to sculpt animals and other objects, and his interest in the circus. Soon after arriving in Paris, Calder began what was to become a lifelong project: he began making small movable wood and wire people and animals for a model circus of his own. This interest in making his works move, seen earlier in making toys, was a third factor leading to the development of mobiles.

Calder's circus, which began with a few animal and human performers, gradually expanded until it incorporated tents, multiple
rings, tightrope walkers, bareback riders, an exotic dancer, a sword
swallower, acrobats, a strong man, animal trainers, stands for specta-
tors, and music. In the performances Calder gave of this circus for
friends and acquaintances in the art world, several facets of Calder's
abilities were combined: his manual talent in sculpting with wire and
other media, his artistic ability in creating animals and people, and his
engineering ability to design circus performers that could move and
perform "tricks."

Between 1927 and 1929, Calder exhibited animated toys, wire
animals, and wire portraits of people in galleries in Paris and New
York. For an American company, he also began to design "action
toys," elaborations on the toys he had made as a child. In December
1929, Calder exhibited in a New York gallery that also was showing a
collection of eighteenth century mechanical birds in cages. Sight of
these birds inspired him to produce an analogous work, his first moving sculpture: wire goldfish bowls in which fish were made to swim
about by means of a hand crank operated by the viewer. These goldfish bowls were the result of a straightforward coming-together of his

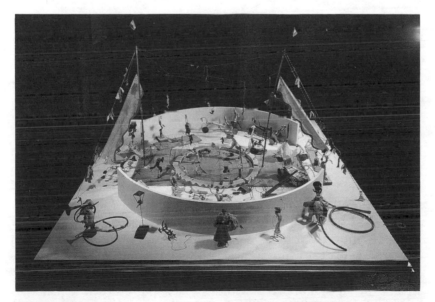

Calder's Circus. From the collection of the Whitney Museum of American
Art, New York. Photograph by Jerry L. Thompson, New York.

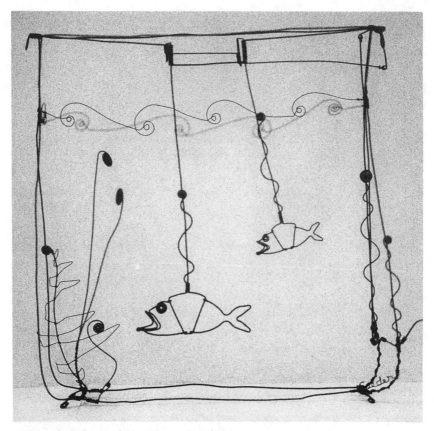

Fishbowl with crank by Alexander Calder.

interest in movement, his construction of circus animals, and the analogy he drew on seeing the mechanical birds.

The final steps in the evolution of mobiles involved the use of abstract shapes in random wind-generated movement, rather than familiar objects in mechanical movement. In the fall of 1931, Calder visited the Paris studio of Piet Mondrian, whom he had met when Mondrian attended a circus performance. Mondrian's work was abstract and strongly geometric in its organization — white canvases, for example, divided by black lines into rectangular blocks, some of which were painted in different primary colors. Mondrian's studio was decorated in the same way — white walls, with rectangular blocks of primary colors on them. This visit stimulated Calder to experiment with abstract painting and drawing. Although he soon returned to materials he felt most comfortable with, those which he could manipulate, the influence of Mondrian was apparent in his new abstract sculpture.

Calder also reports that when he saw Mondrian's blocks of color, he felt that the blocks ought to be in motion. Over the next several years, Calder produced many abstract moving sculptures. These initially were put into motion by hand cranks or motors, as were the goldfish bowls, but without complicated mechanisms, the motion was relatively restricted, and it quickly became repetitive. Calder then turned to a more natural and unpredictable source of movement — the wind. One early mobile is also of interest because it is analogous to a goldfish bowl. Although Calder's sculpture became abstract, it still retained structural elements from his earlier work.

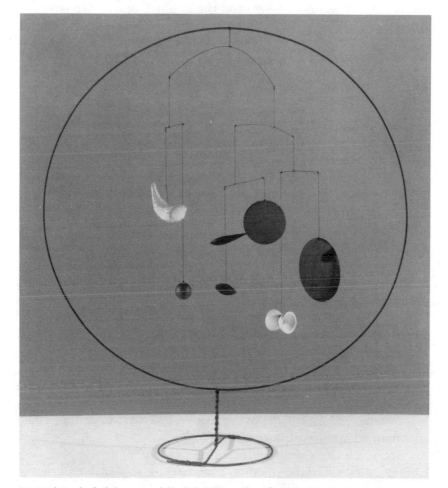

An early wind-driven mobile by Alexander Calder.

In this brief tracing of Calder's development of the mobile, the evolution of the new form can be clearly seen. Calder's enduring interest in movement and wire materials, combined with important external events — the circus assignment for the *Police Gazette*, the exhibition of mechanical birds, and Mondrian's abstract painting — resulted in the development of moving abstract sculpture. The creative thought processes involved here, as they are indirectly observed through the work of the artist, do not seem to be in any way extraordinary. No great leaps of artistic intuition are involved. Rather, Calder seems to have approached everything in art from the point of view of an engineer: could it be made from materials that could be shaped by the hand and could it be made to move? This point of view initially was directly applied to the representation of living objects, as in his circus animals and performers and the goldfish bowls. He later applied the technique to abstract objects, with a new form of sculpture as the result.

Edison's Analogical Thinking in Invention

Thomas Edison is the paradigm case of the great American inventor, producing over a long career a series of devices — among them the light bulb, the electrical lighting system, the phonograph, and the kinetoscope (a device that could present motion pictures) — that are woven into the fabric of modern society. An examination of the invention of one of these, the kinetoscope, based on principles Edison had employed in the phonograph, illustrates the use of analogy in creativity.

The phonograph was invented in Edison's laboratory in 1877. Its public demonstration the next year made Edison world-famous. One preliminary sketch of the phonograph shows a cylinder — with its horizontal long axis — as the central piece of the apparatus. The sound information was carried in a spiral groove cut into the surface of the cylinder, and a moving stylus or needle was used to retrieve that information. A crank at the end of the device was used to turn the cylinder and to make the pointed stylus move down the cylinder, tracing as it moved the path of the spiral groove. The stylus was made to vibrate by the modulations cut in the groove, and these vibrations could be amplified and heard as sound.

About ten years after the invention of the phonograph, Edison's laboratory produced the kinetoscope, a machine that enabled a viewer to see moving images. The kinetoscope served a purpose very differ-

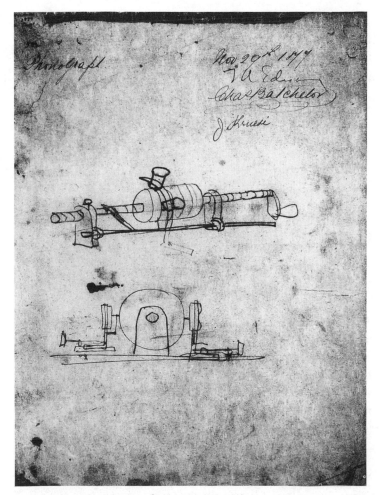

Thomas A. Edison's sketch of the phonograph.

ent from that of the phonograph and was very different in design and appearance from the earlier invention. It consisted of an upright cabinet with a viewing hole and shutter at the top, through which the viewer looked down into the cabinet to see the moving image. Film printed in frames was wound on many rollers inside the cabinet, allowing the film to be drawn under the peephole one frame at a time. If it was drawn under the peephole at the proper speed, a moving image was seen.

Although on the surface the phonograph and the kinetoscope appear to be entirely different devices, Edison's preliminary work on the kinetoscope shows that the former served as the basis for the ini-

The final version of Edison's kinetoscope.

tial development of the latter. Edison's earliest preliminary patent application for the kinetoscope contained a sketch that looked nothing like the final version. This sketch showed an apparatus that had as its central piece a single cylinder that rotated around its horizontally oriented long axis. On the cylinder was a spiral of images viewed through a moving eyepiece as the cylinder rotated. Thus, the earliest version of the kinetoscope was based directly on the phonograph, as Edison makes clear.

> I am experimenting upon an instrument which does for the Eye what the phonograph does for the ear, Which is the recording

and reproduction of things in motion. . . . The invention consists in photographing continuously a series of pictures occurring at intervals which intervals are greater that [*sic*] eight per second, and photographing these series of pictures in a continuous spiral on a cylinder or plate in the same manner in which sound is recorded on the phonograph.

Based on an analysis of Edison's notebooks, including many drawings, Reese Jenkins has concluded that Edison used a small number of ideas or forms repeatedly in attacking many problems. Perhaps the most frequent example is the use of the cylinder, as we have just seen in the phonograph and the kinetoscope; other such forms were the tuning fork and curved ratchet pawl. Jenkins traces the importance of the cylinder in Edison's inventions to his early work experience as an operator in telegraph offices, which contained mechanical devices using cylinders. Edison's later work on newspapers exposed him to printing presses using rotating cylinders. Finally, Edison's work in machine shops gave him much experience with the lathe, which involves a rotating piece of material cut into cylindrical form by a cutting tool directly analogous to the stylus in Edison's inventions.

Ordinary Thinking and Creative Thinking: Toward A Theory

A cornerstone of the concept of ordinary thinking is that it is based on continuity with the past: we deal with new situations on the basis of what we have done in similar situations. This belief leads to the expectation that creative works in all domains, even those works that make the most radical breaks with the past, must be based on what was done before. The new must begin as a variation on old themes, which may come from the work of others or of the individual in question, depending on the specific knowledge and experience available to that person.

Continuity in thought can clearly be seen in the careers of Calder and Edison. Calder's circus sculptures were a development from his early experience making toys and jewelry; his moving sculpture came out of his circus sculpture. The wire circus sculpture, although it incorporated elements of his earlier work, also went beyond it: the circus figures were more sophisticated in appearance and construction, as well as being from a different domain. Thus, although all works are based on the past, there is still room for novelty. Recognizing continuity of creative thought does not imply that there is never anything new produced. One of the main tasks of the present analysis is to describe how work based on the past can go beyond it.

In Edison's case, continuity with the past was based on analogical thinking. Such thinking occurs when we deal with the present on the basis of a situation in the past that we perceive to be similar to the present one. Edison used such thinking when he based the kineto- scope on the phonograph. In Calder, we saw analogical thinking when his exposure to the mechanical birds in cages led to his mechanical goldfish in a bowl. We will see other examples of analogical thinking in later chapters, both when we examine undergraduates solving labo- ratory problems and in the most exalted examples of creative thinking.

We saw also in Calder's history at least one example of a radical shift in his work: the sudden switch from representational (realistic) to abstract forms. This shift, a *discontinuity* in thought, occurs when a change is made to a new direction of work, rather than continuing along the same line. The visit to Mondrian's studio was the event that precipitated the move to abstraction.

A second example of discontinuity in Calder's development, al- though on a smaller scale, was the shift from the use of motors to move the early mobiles to the use of the wind, as Calder's dissatisfaction with the repetitiveness of motor-driven movement drove him to seek new sources. There are thus at least two different types of discontinu- ity: one brought about by an external stimulus (a "trigger"), and one brought about through critical analysis of one's own work. But, in ei- ther case, the processes involved are ordinary.

In this book, the phrase "ordinary thought processes" will refer to continuity of thinking as well as to the discontinuity brought about through feedback and through external triggers; ordinary thinking is thus a term covering a family of activities. The distinction between continuity and discontinuity in thinking is not a sharp one, however. Sometimes an external event can influence an individual's work with- out producing a radical shift in direction, as when Calder used the circus as a source for new drawings and wire sculptures that were es- sentially in the same style as his other work. Similarly, one's critical judgment can sometimes result in a small-scale revision of a work, again without producing a radical shift. The basic mechanisms of con- tinuity and discontinuity are the same: the use of critical judgment to assess — on the basis of one's knowledge — the quality of work pro- duced, and the incorporation of ideas from external sources.

The purpose of this book is to show that creative thinking is based, not on "genius," but on ordinary thought processes. In Chapters 2 and 3, I will examine the evidence for the two basic components of the genius view: that extraordinary thought processes are the basis for creativity (Chapter 2) and that creative individuals possess a special set of psychological characteristics (the "genius personality") that plays a role in causing creativity (Chapter 3). The results of this review will provide the second step in moving beyond the myth of genius.

In Chapters 4 through 7, creative thinking will be examined in a number of areas, ranging from undergraduates solving simple problems in the psychological laboratory to great inventors, scientists, and artists producing works of lasting significance. The results in these domains will be examined with three questions in mind. First is the question of continuity in creative thought; how did the work in question develop out of what was already available? Second is the question of novelty in creative products: how was the antecedent work modified in the creation of the new work? Third is the question of discontinuity in thought: if a new work makes a radical break with past work, how was this new work brought about?

Finally, in Chapter 8, I will use the information from these chapters to outline a general theory of creative thinking. This chapter will bring together conclusions from the various domains examined in the case studies and will suggest answers to questions of where novel ideas come from and how humans produce novel works through ordinary thinking.

But if one wishes to claim that the thought processes that we all possess are the basis for creative thinking, the question arises why we are all not equally productive and influential. There must be some differences among us; we do not all produce great art or great inventions or make great scientific discoveries. It is helpful to think of the differences between ordinary individuals and those who produce works of great significance in terms of levels of specific skills, motivation, and knowledge.

There are many different sorts of activities in which humans can perform creatively, ranging from painting, to cooking, to studying the origins of the universe. A different set of special skills may be required for each of these activities. Painters, as an example, might have to possess great memories for visual information, a visual imagination which would allow them to anticipate what the effect would be of putting paint on canvas in a certain way, a high degree of sensitivity to color, a high degree of hand-eye coordination, and fine control over small-motor movements. On the other hand, sculptors who construct works by carving them out of blocks of stone or wood, or who construct large works out of smaller pieces, might require a high degree of visual imagination of what one could call the transformational sort, involving the ability to anticipate how something will look after it has been modified. As we have seen, Calder, given his inheritance, may have possessed two sets of artistic abilities.

We all possess these various skills to some degree, although usually not to the degree needed to perform at a high level of proficiency in a creative domain. Considering the hypothetical "transformational imagery" needed for sculpture, we all have such imagination, in that we can imagine how our living room would look if we rearranged the furniture. However, we differ in the level of the skill, which would limit our performance as sculptors. Others of us have difficulty carrying a tune, and would do well not to try to become the next Mozart. It is probably also true that these skills can be improved with work and study, although there are inherited limits set to development.

These skills are often not general skills applying across a large set of different domains. It is useful to compare the skills involved in outstanding "creative" performance with those involved in athletic ability. A person who is a great diver, say, may have no aptitude for golf or tennis. "Athletic ability" is not one skill, but many different abilities, some of which have very little in common with one another. "Creative ability" may be similar.

In addition to the possession of a set of skills uniquely suited to some creative field — "talent" — research indicates that there might be some general motivational characteristics that creative individuals have in common. Such characteristics are a strong desire to succeed and a high level of commitment to one's chosen field, which may be the same thing. One particularly impressive characteristic of the most esteemed individuals (and presumably the most creative) in any field is that they are almost always extremely productive. In addition to possessing talent, then, one must be willing to work, sometimes to the exclusion of everything else.

Talent and motivation, although perhaps necessary for the production of creative work, are not sufficient. An interesting study by John Hayes, discussed in more detail later, indicates that years of work are necessary, even for the most talented and motivated individuals, before they produce what are usually considered to be their masterworks. Even Mozart, who began extraordinarily early in composition, did not produce a masterwork (the Piano Concerto No. 9, K.

271) until the twelfth year of his career. Hayes concluded from his analysis that one must become immersed in a field and develop a deep expertise before one becomes capable of going beyond what has already been produced.

I have so far discussed nothing beyond the specific domain and a high degree of motivation, which raises the question whether there are general skills relevant to all creative work, such as the "breaking sets" mentioned in the quote presented earlier. (Teresa Amabile presents a variant of this view.) Do individuals who produce creative works do so by applying specific "creativity-relevant" thought processes that are not used by ordinary individuals in ordinary situations?

Evidence from the case studies already discussed goes against this idea. As one example, one could say that Calder's production of abstract moving sculpture "broke a set," but when we examined how and why this came about, no separate set-breaking process was seen. Rather, when an individual of Calder's particular interests, skills, experience, and sensibilities was exposed to Mondrian's work (and to that of Joan Miro, another painter/sculptor working in abstract materials; as well as to the works of several other artists), abstract moving sculpture was born. Other case studies will support the same conclusion — novel products develop through the use of ordinary thought processes when a particular individual is placed in a particular situation.

CHAPTER 2

The Myth of Genius
INTUITION, UNCONSCIOUS PROCESSING, AND INSIGHT

"Now let's have the 'chicken cheer,'" says the session leader. A dozen managers shed their jackets and stand up. A vice-president from a Midwestern industrial giant glances uneasily around the room, his cheeks glowing pink. The leader starts. One by one, others join in. They flap their arms and scratch at the floor with their feet. Finally, the room fills with crowing sounds a rooster would envy. Strange as it may seem, such sessions are becoming a way of business in the U.S. With the intensity of itinerant evangelists, "creativity consultants" are roaming the corporate landscape preaching an appealing gospel to managers: You can learn to be creative. And business is listening. . . . Participants learn a variety of exercises intended to get their creative juices flowing. Using devices from the "chicken cheer" to flying kites, creativity consultants try to break down rigid thinking that blocks new ideas.

(Smith 1985, p. 80).

There is no such thing as a logical method of having new ideas, or a logical reconstruction of this process. . . . [E]very discovery contains an irrational element, or a creative intuition."

(Popper 1968, p. 32).

Creative thinking breaks the boundaries of what we know, which has led many to assume that it is basically different from ordinary thinking. Theorists from many different viewpoints have tried to make explicit what allows creative thinking to break out of the supposedly rigid structures imposed upon us by our past experience and our ordinary methods of thinking. However, there exists an underlying consistency in this theorizing that can be captured when we consider the difference between logic and intuition.

Logical thinking takes our existing knowledge and uses rules of inference to produce new knowledge. Because logical thinking progresses in a series of steps, each one dependent on the last, this "new" knowledge can be seen as being merely an extension of what we already know, rather than being truly new. It may therefore not be possible for logical thinking to serve creativity. On the other hand, intuitive thinking can seemingly produce a sudden insight or conclusion, without apparent logical reasoning from what we know to that conclusion. Since intuitive thinking is not bound by the rules of logic and the need for step-by-step reasoning, it seems to have a freedom and flexibility, an "irrational" element, that enables the thinker to make connections among ideas to produce something truly new.

In this chapter, I discuss the most important proposals concerning the differences between ordinary and creative thinking — Freudian primary-process versus secondary-process thinking, conscious thought versus unconscious incubation, trial and error versus insight, vertical thinking versus lateral thinking, and convergent versus divergent thinking — all of which can be traced to this distinction between logic and intuition. The basic conclusion from the chapter is negative: there is little support for the notion that creative thinking uses a thought process different from ordinary thinking.

The Freudian Unconscious in Creativity

Although Freud did not formulate a full-blown theory of creative thinking, he attempted to apply his psychodynamic theory to creative individuals, through the method of psychobiography. This method involved retrospective psychoanalytic case studies of a number of great individuals. In turn, these studies enable one to infer Freud's general beliefs concerning the processes underlying creative production. In Freud's view, creative *work* was motivated by unresolved conflicts; creative *thinking* was dominated by primary-process thinking — irrational and primitive and associated with the id and the unconscious — rather than by secondary-process thinking — logical and realistic and associated with the conscious ego.

Human beings are born with a set of instincts, related to the needs for food, warmth, and sex, among others, on which survival of the organism and the species depend. These instincts form the id, which functions through the use of the *primary process*. The id is concerned only with survival. It functions according to the pleasure principle, striving only to achieve pleasure and reduce pain. When an instinctual need is unsatisfied, the id through primary-process thought forms an image of the desired object. According to Freudian thinking, for example, when an infant is hungry, primary-process thought serves to produce an image of the breast in an attempt to satisfy the need.

Image formation can bring temporary relief, but cannot in the long run reduce a need. Due to the accumulation of energy from unsatisfied needs, there develops the ego, which functions through the use of the *secondary process*, and which serves to deal with the real world and to satisfy needs through logical thinking and problem solving. The ego also develops defense mechanisms to block unacceptable id needs from expression in the form of action in the world, which society will punish, or in conscious thought, which the thinker will find threatening. As the ego develops, because it serves to satisfy needs through transactions with the world, the id impulses are blocked and become unconscious, serving as an unknown source of energy that strives to direct behavior in ways often unacceptable to the ego.

This blocked id energy can sometimes become strong enough to find expression, usually in disguised form, in situations in which the ego defenses are momentarily weakened, such as dreaming, daydreaming, under the influence of drugs, or during fever. Primary-process thought can sometimes be experienced during the time just before dropping off to sleep, when one may suddenly experience what appears to be a string of disconnected images.

Because of their different sources and developmental histories, there are basic differences between primary and secondary-process thought. Primary-process thought produces combinations of ideas that strike the thinker and the audience as at least unconventional and perhaps bizarre, because the connections depend on unconscious material, of which the thinker and the audience are unaware. Primary-process thinking is also irrational, in that it does not follow ordinary logical connections among concepts, but finds connections among ideas on the basis of links in sound ("clang" associations and puns), visual similarities, and other primitive bases, rather than through sophisticated conceptual links. These connections were believed by Freud to possess an internal logic, hidden in repressed material and not comprehensible to the untutored individual.

The mechanisms of primary-process thought violate the rules of ordinary logic in other ways as well. Through the mechanism of condensation, a single symbol in primary-process thought can express several different and perhaps incompatible ideas. Through the mechanism of displacement, unacceptable emotions toward one individual, say aggressive impulses toward a parent, are expressed toward another, say the president of the United States. Because of its roots in inherited instinctual needs, this "primitive" thought is unfettered by restrictions imposed by one's experiences in the world, and thus has a freedom about it that is lost when thinking becomes "civilized."

Primary-process thinking has direct implications for the creative process. According to Freud, creative activity begins when some adult experience arouses an unsatisfied childhood need, to which — if the adult is an artist — he or she may respond through a work of art. The creative individual is similar to the neurotic in having strong unfulfilled needs, but unlike the neurotic is able to express those needs through art. Since primary-process thoughts, disguised as they may be, have their origin in instinctual needs, they will carry strong emotional content. One of the skills of the great artist is the ability to develop these very personal ideas in such a way that they will be universally meaningful.

Freud used the work of Leonardo da Vinci to illustrate some of his ideas. In his study of the artist, Freud concluded that Leonardo painted the striking smile on the *Mona Lisa* because of his early experiences and their residue of unsatisfied needs and unconscious conflicts. Leonardo's having been orphaned at an early age left him, according to Freud, searching for a woman to fill the role never filled by his mother. The woman who posed for the *Mona Lisa* struck a chord in Leonardo because her enigmatic smile aroused Leonardo's emotions toward his unknown mother.

Some of Freud's later followers (neo-Freudians) toned down his emphasis on the primary process, by stressing the fact that creative thought occurs under conscious control, and so cannot involve purely primary-process thought. However, for the emotional aspects of creative work, the chief emphasis — especially in the arts — is still placed on the primary process. Some of Freud's followers also modified the concepts of primary- and secondary-process thinking, resulting in more overlap between them. For example, one argument is that the primary-process mechanisms of condensation, displacement, and so forth, develop to serve secondary-process thought, making the distinction between the two types of thought less sharp than it was in Freud's original formulation. The emotionally laden, unconscious associations based on unsatisfied childhood needs are still assumed to be limited to primary-process thinking.

This conceptual modification can change the way in which creative thinking is analyzed. Colin Martindale has recently argued that all nonlogical thinking, such as "associational" thinking, is primary-process thinking. That is, if presentation of some situation causes the recall of some other situation because the two are associated, Martindale would call this primary-process thinking. Similarly, he would label as primary-process Edison's use of the phonograph as the basis for development of the kinetoscope, discussed in Chapter 1. Martindale's is a very broad interpretation of primary process which, as he notes, turns much ordinary thinking into primary-process thinking.

However, the fact that thinking is not strictly logical is not the only reason for calling it primary process. Primary process also depends on the hidden emotional content of the thought and on mechanisms such as transformation, condensation, and displacement, which Martindale's distinction ignores. I will therefore make a distinction between "ordinary" associational and analogical thinking, which involves conscious thought and associative connections of which the thinker is aware; and primary-process thinking, which, even when it serves secondary-process thought, uses mechanisms and associations not available to ordinary thinking.

In recent years, a number of highly acclaimed psychobiographies have appeared that provide provocative analyses of the creative process. For example, in his psychobiography of Beethoven, Maynard Solomon argues that several relatively radical shifts in style in Beethoven's music can be traced to important life incidents, which made themselves known in the music through the influence of Beethoven's unconscious.

Similarly, Mary Gedo has argued that much in Picasso's work can be understood through an analysis of Picasso's early experiences and their residue in his unconscious. As an example, in a preliminary sketch made for the great painting *Guernica*, Picasso painted a woman wearing a kerchief on her head, holding a dead baby. Gedo argues that the woman was painted with a kerchief because the incident which stimulated the painting, the bombing of the Spanish city of Guernica during the Spanish Civil War, reminded Picasso on an unconscious level of a childhood incident. In 1894, when Picasso was three, an earthquake struck his home city of Málaga, Spain, and during this terrifying incident Picasso's mother uncharacteristically wore a kerchief as she led the family to safety.

Gedo argues as well that Picasso's participation in the development of Cubism can be traced to feelings of devastation felt each day by the artist when, as a young child, he was taken from home to school. According to Gedo, the feelings of fragmentation felt by the young Picasso were expressed in the fragmentation of objects in Cubist painting.

Another example of the use of the Freudian primary process in explaining creative thinking is Albert Rothenberg's analysis of the production of a poem by a poet whom he had been interviewing regularly for several years. The poem centers on an encounter the poet and a friend had during a trip to Monument Valley, Utah. While they were having a hurried, unpleasant, wind-blown, sand-infested picnic, a starving horse suddenly appeared and came toward them. The poet was touched by his friend's strong reaction to the dying horse, and thought that he might some day write a poem about the incident. Several years later, he did. In the poem, the incident in Monument Valley is related to a flashback to an earlier experience riding on horseback.

Through his analysis of the poet's dreams and associations to them, in conjunction with the structure of the poem itself, Rothenberg concluded that the poem was a representation of the poet's feelings toward his mother and other important women in his life, and the horse, through primary-process thinking, was a symbol for these women. Determining the "meaning" of the poem requires that one unearth the connections among ideas that have been transformed before they become conscious.

Rothenberg presents several reasons for concluding that the horse symbolizes important women in the poet's life and the poet's relationships with them. In the poem, the horse carries a burden — the poet. In the poet's life, his grandmother, near the end of her life, burdened the poet's mother with her needs for care, which in one case led to the mother's literally carrying the grandmother. Furthermore, at about the time he wrote the poem, the poet reported several dreams in which an old woman is described as having an elongated face, like a horse, as well as growths on her fingers which may have been related to horses' hooves. In one dream, the poet carries the old woman, as the horse carries him in the poem. Also, the inspiration for the actual

Man with violin by Pablo Picasso. From the Philadelphia Museum of Art: Louise and Walter Arensberg Collection.

writing of the poem, several years after the incident in Monument Valley, may have been the impending visit to the poet of a woman friend of the poet's mother, whom the poet had been visiting when the original incident occurred.

Although the Freudian perspective and its offspring are often fascinating and provocative, they are sometimes of limited usefulness in understanding creative thinking. One difficulty with any Freudian analysis is that Freudians usually do not conduct experiments or in any other way attempt to provide independent evidence to support or contradict their analysis, so that the issue becomes whether or not one finds the analysis coherent and compelling. A similar problem arises when one uses historical case studies, as I do, as one source of evidence for a theory of creative thinking, since one is also limited in the degree to which one can produce independent experimental evidence to support one's interpretation of the case study. However, as could be seen from the case studies in Chapter 1, much less in the way of "deep" interpretation is required.

Primary-process thought occurs during daydreams, among other times, and investigators have therefore analyzed the contents of people's daydreams in order to examine support for the Freudian view. One would expect, for example, daydreams to involve expression of unconscious conflicts, and thus to be symbolically sexual and/or aggressive, since these are the types of impulses that often cannot be expressed in ordinary thought. Studies of daydreaming have shown, however, that they are usually neither sexual nor aggressive in content, but rather involve planning for relatively prosaic activities.

The Freudian view postulates unconscious connections to explain the presence of certain elements in creative works. Two examples of this are Gedo's analysis of the presence of the woman wearing the kerchief in Picasso's *Guernica* and Rothenberg's analysis of his poet's deciding to write about a horse in Monument Valley. However, in both these cases, one need not go beyond the ordinary retrieval processes operating in everyday recall of information stimulated by outside events.

According to Gedo, the noise and devastation during the bombing of Guernica reminded Picasso of the earthquake he had experienced as a child, which led him to think of his mother in a kerchief. However, the bombing was not directly experienced by Picasso — he only read newspaper accounts and saw photographs of the event. Picasso has also reported that the earthquake was on the whole an exciting rather than terrifying experience, which raises a basic problem for Gedo's attempt to equate it with the bombing of Guernica in its emotional effect on him.

Even if the newspaper accounts were enough to stimulate Picasso to recall his early experience, this would be a straightforward case of retrieval of one event by another, as happens to all of us when we remember something that happened last week, say, because of a cue occurring today. Furthermore, Picasso commented that his recollection of the earthquake was unique in that his mother had worn a kerchief. This comment indicates that he was able to *consciously* recall the earthquake. Therefore, in order to explain its retrieval by the bombing, we do not need to call on unconscious thinking at all (although given that Picasso was three when the earthquake occurred, one might suspect that he was not recalling directly).

Regarding Gedo's psychobiographical analysis of Picasso's participation in the development of cubism, Picasso was not alone in that enterprise: he worked in close collaboration with the French artist, Georges Braque, and at the beginning of their collaboration Braque even led the way. Since there is no evidence that Braque's childhood was filled with the feelings of fragmentation experienced by Picasso Gedo's analysis leaves us with no explanation for Braque's leading role in the development of cubism.

One can also question Gedo's equation of Picasso's childhood feelings and the conscious attempt of two mature artists to represent objects and space in a particular way. The term "fragmentation" is used metaphorically by Gedo to describe a child's feelings, and its use in that context may not be at all comparable to its use in the description of the aims of the cubists, which were based on deep intellectual analysis of the works of other artists, most notably Paul Cézanne, and on endless discussion.

A similar analysis can be made of the circumstances leading to the poem about the horse in Monument Valley. One can, without resorting to symbolic analysis, explain why the poet chose this subject matter. Rothenberg reported that his poet-subject had been moved during the picnic by his friend's strong response to the approach of the starving horse. He had also been impressed by a poem by another poet about horses, and had noted at the time of the incident that he might at a later time write a poem about it. One could take this to mean that we do not need the deeper analysis, in terms of the horse symbolizing the women in the poet's life, in order to understand why he wrote his poem. Moreover, Rothenberg's poet-subject was familiar with Freudian theory and Rothenberg's elaboration of it, which raises some questions about how one is to interpret his reports.

If the creation of the poem was occasioned by the impending visit by the friend of the poet's mother, this too does not seem to be the result of some extraordinary process, but the kind of memory retrieval that occurs in all aspects of our lives. The poet had visited this friend on the trip that included the picnic in Monument Valley. In addition, he had noted at the time of the incident with the horse that he might at a later time write a poem about it.

Questions have been raised as well concerning the accuracy of Freud's case studies. Freud argued that Leonardo painted the enigmatic smile of the Mona Lisa because the woman who served as the model aroused in Leonardo his need for his mother. However, there are earlier works of Leonardo's in which women possess the same enigmatic smile, indicating that Freud may have been incorrect in his emphasis on the model for the Mona Lisa as a stimulus to Leonardo's unconscious.

Freud also emphasized a report by Leonardo of a dream in which a vulture touched him on the lips with its tail-feathers, which Freud interpreted as symbolizing Leonardo's sexual feelings for his mother, because in mythology vultures have connections between motherhood and sexuality. However, Freud used an erroneous translation of Leonardo's dream report; in the original report the bird was a kite (a hawk), not a vulture, which makes Freud's interpretation irrelevant, because kites do not have the mythological connotations of vultures.

Overall, support for the various components of the Freudian and related views is not compelling. Freud's case studies are of questionable validity, and one can raise questions about the primary-process interpretation of several other more recent case studies. Research studies investigating the content of primary-process thinking have also raised questions about the concept. This general orientation has also led some to theorize that great creative achievements should be related to psychopathology, but again research has not supported the hypothesis.

Genius and Madness

One particularly interesting variation on the theme that creative thinking involves extraordinary thought processes is the hypothesis that creative ideas arise from changes in thought processes brought about by psychopathology. This hypothesis has several roots, one of which is Plato's contention that poets are gripped by madness when in the throes of creation, and another is Freud's emphasis on the neurotic roots of creativity and on primary-process thought. With this view in mind, the thought processes of schizophrenics have been compared to those of individuals of acknowledged creativity, since schizophrenic thought was assumed to be close to primary-process thought. A different — and, presently, more influential — view was proposed by Emil Kraepelin, who in his classic study of "manic-depressive insanity" hypothesized that mania might bring about changes in thought processes resulting in increased creativity of thinking.

The bipolar mood disorders or bipolar affective disorders — e.g., manic depression and cyclothymia — involve cycling between highly elated mood states (mania or, less severely, hypomania) and depression (or, less severely, dysthymia). In mania, the individual feels extraordinarily elated and energetic, and plunges into activities without thinking about possible negative consequences; for example, an individual may make foolish investments or emotional entanglements. In clinical depression, there is a pervasive negative mood, with feelings of worthlessness and sometimes suicidal thoughts. Manic depression involves cycling between full mania and depression, while cyclothymia (literally, "changing mind"), a less severe disorder, involves cycling between hypomania and dysthymia.*

In Kraepelin's view, during mania, thought processes are "loosened," which can result in the production of new ideas that would not be possible during nonmanic states. Kay Jamison, a strong recent advocate of Kraepelin's view, has discussed in detail the relation between mood changes and creativity. Artists and writers studied by Jamison have reported powerful positive mood changes before periods of intense creative activity.

> This period of elated and expansive mood is described by many individuals as their time of inspiration: a time of faster and more fluid thinking, new ideas and connections of thoughts. (Goodwin & Jamison 1990, p. 338)

The changes in thought processes are believed by Jamison to be both quantitative and qualitative. Quantitatively, speed of thought, *per se* is increased during mania; more ideas would be produced, but not necessarily better ones. However, Jamison also believes that this increased output of thought may bring with it a qualitative change in the ideas produced, with the ideas becoming better, that is, more original.

Nancy Andreasen has investigated frequencies of psychopathology in family histories of creative writers. The creative writers were a sample of participants in the Iowa Writers' Workshop, at which well-known writers serve as teachers for students of creative writing. Andreasen found a higher rate of affective disorders in the writers than in controls matched for age, education, and sex, with a large majority of the writers experiencing an affective disorder of some sort at

---

*Diagnostic and Statistic Manual of the American Psychiatric Association, 3d ed. rev. — DSM IIIR — 1987. The relationship between mental health and creativity is discussed in several issues of the 1990 *Creativity Research Journal*.

some time in their lives, and almost half experiencing a bipolar disorder. There were also more affective disorders found in the family histories of the writers than in the controls.

Jamison and her colleagues have examined several different samples of creative individuals for the prevalence of manic-depressive disorder. They have found a high frequency of bipolar affective disorder and suicide in creative individuals, especially in modern poets of great renown. Of the thirty-six poets born in the twentieth century who are listed in *The New Oxford Book of American Verse*, for example, eight (22 percent) exhibited well-documented histories of bipolar illness severe enough to have resulted in hospitalization. The rate of bipolar illness in the general population is 1 to 2 percent. There are, however, other data available concerning frequency of manic-depression in creative individuals which do not support Jamison's.

Frederick Goodwin and Jamison discuss the case of the composer Robert Schumann (1810–1856), who is generally acknowledged to have suffered from bipolar disorder, as additional evidence for the positive effect of mania on creative thought processes. Schumann may have exhibited suicidal tendencies when he was only twenty; after making at least two unsuccessful attempts at suicide, he died in an institution at forty-six. In addition to a diagnosis of manic-depression, he probably also suffered from syphilis, which in the last years of his life resulted in severe physical and mental decline. Schumann's family was also troubled psychologically: his older sister became mentally ill at seventeen and drowned herself at twenty-nine, and one of his sons spent thirty years in an institution.

From biographical information, medical records, and Schumann's correspondence, Eliot Slater and Alfred Meyer concluded that there was a single dominant mood for a number of years in his career. The relationship over Schumann's career between his output and his mood is presented in the table below. The compositions tallied for each year are based on dates of completion rather than publication. There is a strong positive relationship between the quantity of Schumann's output and his mood; the three years with by far the greatest numbers of compositions are those during which Schumann was hypomanic; those of low productivity are the years of depression.

Significant differences in the frequency of bipolar affective disorder between creative samples and the general population provide no actual support for Kraepelin's hypothesis that mania is the *cause* of the creativity exhibited by the samples in question. The studies just reviewed are all of necessity correlational in nature, not experimental,

Schumann's Productivity as a Function of Mood: Summary for Years with Single Dominant Diagnoses

Year	Number of compositions
Depression	
1830	X
1831	X
1839	XXXX
1842	XXX
1844	
1847	XXXXX
1848	XXXXX
Mean	2.7
Hypomania	
1829	X
1832	XXXX
1840	XXXXXXXXXXXXXXXXXXXXXXXXXX
1843	XX
1849	XXXXXXXXXXXXXXXXXXXXXXXXXXXXX
1851	XXXXXXXXXXXXXXX
Mean	12.3

and a significant problem in any correlational study involves determining cause and effect.

A high level of bipolar affective disorder in a creative sample might indeed mean, as Kraepelin believed, that mania results in changes in associative processes that facilitate certain sorts of creative thinking. A second possibility, however, is that just the opposite is true: being creative might make one pathological. For example, an individual who is successful could be pushed to extremes of mood by success and adulation from others, as well as by positive or negative criticism. Third, it might be that some other factor both makes one creative and produces psychopathology, and there would then be no causal link between creativity and psychopathology. For example, stressful events in childhood might facilitate creative thinking and also dispose one toward psychopathology.

Problems of interpretation of data also arise concerning the relationship between Schumann's affective state and his creativity. No attempt was made by either Slater and Meyer or Goodwin and Jamison to analyze the *quality* of Schumann's compositions for the various years in his career, and only an analysis of this sort would enable one to draw conclusions relevant to Kraepelin's hypothesis that thought becomes more creative during manic periods. I have carried out such an analysis, and the results do not support Kraepelin's hypothesis.

I assessed the quality of Schumann's compositions using the number of recordings available for each of his compositions, a measure proposed by John Hayes in an often-cited examination of the development of musical composition. This measure seems reasonable, since it represents the combined judgments of musicians, recording companies, and record-buying public. Quality of composition was assumed to be represented by the number of recordings available.

If Schumann's mania increased his creativity, then his best works should have been produced during manic periods. Statistically, the highest proportion of compositions of high quality should have occurred during such periods. However, two different statistical analyses of data from both the Schwann and Penguin record catalogues indicated that there was no significant relationship between Schumann's mood and his creativity: the proportion of frequently recorded works did not systematically change over his career. This result is consistent with the finding that over a career there tends to be a constancy in the probability that an individual will produce great works. During the years in which relatively large numbers of great works are produced, large numbers of minor works are also produced, resulting in a constant proportion of great works to minor.

I also used the data from Schumann's career to examine the hypothesis that mood state increases motivation, but has no effect on creativity of thinking. If affective state were related only to motivation, and not directly to creativity, then during Schumann's manic phases his total output should have increased, but the quality of work, i.e, the proportion of high quality works during a given year, should not have changed. This unchanged proportion was found for both measures of quality, indicating contrary to Kraepelin that mood affected only the quantity of Schumann's work.

There are several possible explanations for the high frequency of affective disorders in creative individuals who have achieved eminence, explanations that do not assume that mania increases creativity of thought. First, the frequency differences might be artifactual, that is, not real but due to flaws in the methods used to collect them, and therefore should be disregarded. Second, the differences in frequency might be real, but might be due to factors other than the disorder's increasing the creativity of the individual. Third, the disorder could be related to increased creativity, but not because it influences the quality of thought processes.

In order to demonstrate that the psychopathological state contributed to the quality of creative production, it is necessary to first use a comparison group in the same field, but without achieved eminence. Such controls are not usually used, and in studies which have attempted to use them, the sizes of the various groups are so small as to make any conclusions problematic. As an example, Jamison's investigation, described above, used a comparison group of biographers, which may be reasonable, but only examined five individuals.

Thus, the high frequency of affective disorders in creative samples may be an artifact of the comparison group used. Furthermore, the eminent individuals are given detailed scrutiny by historians and critics, which could result in the uncovering of "symptoms" of psychopathology, not seen in the noneminent control group, due only to a lack of similar scrutiny.

Also, an inordinate number of poets may exhibit manic-depression because — in our society — poetry is assumed to be the refuge of individuals with such problems, so those individuals may tend to gravitate toward poetry. The accumulation of manic-depressive individuals in poetry may mean nothing more than that such people can function in that field, once they have found it. In order to function creatively as a chemist, for example, one usually has to have an academic or industrial position, which someone suffering from bipolar affective disorder might have trouble holding.

Manic depression might also affect the eminence of an individual in a creative field without directly affecting that individual's thought processes. If the manic or hypomanic individual produces three or four or ten times as many works as does the nonmanic, then even assuming equal quality of work, the manic individual will have a much higher probability of becoming acknowledged within a career. Thus, positive affective states may be causally related to productivity, and through productivity to eminence, and not be related to creativity at all. Being labeled as having suffered from manic depression may in itself produce eminence, and when depression leads a poet to commit suicide, his or her work may be seen thereafter as great work.

Bipolar illness might also result in increased creativity because of the emotional experiences that it produces, rather than through its effect on thought processes. That is, extremes of mood may bring with them changes in the intensity and quality of emotional experience, which can provide the artist with potent inspiration. There is some evidence that the novelist Virginia Woolf, who suffered from severe depressions, used her experiences during those states as the basis for her writing. I do not wish to claim here that emotion is independent of cognition; it may be true that emotional experiences are based at least in part on the interpretation of the situation, and thus on cognition. However, the processes that mold emotional experiences into works of art can be conceptualized independently of the experiences themselves.

The Cognitive Unconscious in Creativity: Incubation and Intuition

The role of unconscious processes in creative thinking has also been emphasized outside the Freudian tradition, mainly as a result of the writings of Henri Poincaré. This viewpoint could be called the "cognitive unconscious," to differentiate it from the classical Freudian view. Poincaré, a world-famous mathematician early in the twentieth century, wrote — late in his life — about the thought processes in his creative work. He believed that creative ideas came about through the combination of old ideas in the unconscious, in a process of "incubation." In this way, carrying out numerous combinations would not put a burden on our conscious processes. If a potentially useful combination occurred, the thinker would experience an "illumination," or an "Aha!" reaction, accompanied by the sudden appearance in consciousness of the new idea. Arthur Koestler, who studied many historical examples of creative thinking, presented a conception of unconscious incubation based on that of Poincaré, but broadened to include unconscious thought of the sort postulated by Freud.

On the basis of his historical analysis, Koestler concluded that while ordinary thinking used habitual associations, creative thinking used *bisociative* thinking to combine two previously separate associative streams to produce a new idea. As an example of bisociative thinking, Koestler discussed Johannes Gutenberg's invention of the printing press, which reportedly came about when Gutenberg realized that a wine press could provide a principle to be used to print letters on a page. Combining these two previously separate streams of associations or knowledge — one organized around printing letters on a page, and the other around pressing grapes to make wine — resulted in a new stream of thought and a revolutionary invention.

According to Koestler, Gutenberg's insight was helped along by wine that he drank; alcohol presumably works to lower conscious inhibitions, and can thereby facilitate primary-process thought.

One main source of support for the cognitive unconscious comes from a number of anecdotes about acknowledged creative geniuses, and these people's own reports of how their work was carried out.

Mozart's productivity, precocity, and early death under somewhat mysterious circumstances have combined to make him the epitome of the intuitive creator, and many stories chronicle his near-legendary creative feats (see, for example, the quotation on page 3). A letter attributed to Mozart has often been taken as evidence for the operation of unconscious process in creative thinking.

> When I am, as it were, completely myself, entirely alone and of good cheer — say, travelling in a carriage, or walking after a good meal, or during the night when I cannot sleep; it is on such occasions that my ideas flow best and most abundantly. *Whence* and *how* they come, I know not; nor can I force them. Those ideas that please me I retain in memory, and am accustomed, as I have been told, to hum them to myself. If I continue in this way, it soon occurs to me how I may turn this or that morsel to account. . . . All this fires my soul, and, provided I am not disturbed, my subject enlarges itself, becomes methodized and defined, and the whole, though it be long, stands almost complete and finished in my mind, so that I can survey it, like a fine picture or a beautiful statue, at a glance. Nor do I hear in my imagination the parts *successively*, but I hear them, as it were, all at once. . . . All this inventing, this producing, takes place in a pleasing lively dream. Still the actual hearing of the *tout ensemble* is after all the best.

The poet Samuel Taylor Coleridge wrote a description, now also well known, of the circumstances leading to his writing the poem "Kubla Khan." Coleridge had been ill and was living in the country; one afternoon, because of "a slight indisposition," he took "an anodyne" (a painkiller — in actuality, a dose of opium) and fell asleep while reading a book describing Kubla Khan's capital city. According to Coleridge, the following events occurred.

> The Author [Coleridge] continued for about three hours in a profound sleep, at least of the external senses, during which time he had the most vivid confidence that he could not have

composed less than from two to three hundred lines; if that indeed can be called composition in which all the images rose up before him as *things*, with a parallel production of the concurrent expressions, without any sensation or consciousness of effort. On awakening he appeared to himself to have a distinct recollection of the whole, and taking his pen, ink, and paper, instantly and eagerly wrote down the lines that are here preserved. At this moment he was unfortunately called out by a person on business from Porlock, and detained by him above an hour, and on his return to his room, found, to his no small surprise and mortification, that though he still retained some vague and dim recollection of the general purport of the vision, yet, with the exception of some eight or ten lines and images, all the rest had passed away like the images on the surface of a stream into which a stone has been cast, but alas! without the after restoration of the latter!

An entire poem thus seemingly appeared full-blown, just waiting to be written, with no conscious work on Coleridge's part. He had begun to write it down when an interruption made him lose the rest.

Poincaré also reported an experience which he and others have interpreted as an observation of his own unconscious at work. He was attempting to prove that a certain sort of mathematical function, which he called Fuchsian functions, could not exist. He worked on a proof without success for fifteen days. One night, after an unsuccessful day, he drank black coffee and went to bed. As he lay awake, "[i]deas rose in crowds; I felt them collide until pairs interlocked, so to speak, making a stable combination." After this sleepless night of thinking, Poincaré established that his original idea was incorrect—one example of a Fuchsian function could be shown to exist. Poincaré was obviously conscious when these ideas arose, but he felt that the thinking was of an extraordinary sort, since it occurred during sleeplessness induced by coffee. Because he felt himself to be an inactive participant, he concluded that he was essentially observing the workings of his own unconscious.

Poincaré then went on a geological expedition, and made another mathematical discovery. During a conversation on another subject, he suddenly realized that the Fuchsian functions were identical to the transformations of non-Euclidean geometry.

The incidents of travel made me forget my mathematical work. Having reached Coutances, we entered an omnibus to go some place or other. At the moment when I put my foot on the step, the idea came to me, without anything in my former thoughts seeming to have paved the way for it. . . . I did not verify the idea; I should not have had time, as, upon taking my seat in the omnibus, I went on with a conversation already commenced, but I felt a perfect certainty. On my return to Caen, for conscience' sake, I verified the result at my leisure.

These examples are often cited as support for the importance of unconscious processes in creative problem solving. This interpretation was proposed by Poincaré himself, who said that the sudden "illumination," was "a manifest sign of long, unconscious prior work. The role of this unconscious work in mathematical invention appears to me incontestable."

Based on the reports of Poincaré and others, Graham Wallas proposed that there are four stages in all creative acts. The first stage, *preparation*, involves a long period of intense conscious work, without success. (Poincaré, for example, worked for fifteen days.) This is the stage in which potentially useful ideas are considered. The problem is then put aside and not thought about consciously. (Poincaré goes on an expedition.) During this time, according to Poincaré, Wallas, and others, *incubation* occurs, as the potentially useful ideas from the preparation stage are combined in new ways in the unconscious. If the incubation stage is successful, the person experiences a sudden *illumination*, a sudden insight into the solution of the problem. (Poincaré steps on the omnibus.) The illumination stage usually produces only a glimmer of the solution, however, with *verification*, Wallas's final stage, being worked out later. (Poincaré verifies "for conscience' sake" the accuracy of his insight.)

The term incubation is sometimes used to refer simply to a period of time spent away from the problem, whether or not it ends with illumination. Based on this interpretation, incubation occurs simply if the person performs better with a break than without it. Poincaré and Wallas did not use the term in this sense — by their definition, incubation involves active unconscious processing, and the time away from the problem must end with a sudden illumination that produces a method for solving the problem that is new and unrelated to what preceded it.

Robert Olton has discussed what he calls "creative worrying," which refers to brief episodes of mulling over a problem while one does something else during a break. If one then found that a break produced progress in such a situation, it would be the result of the conscious work on the problem, not of incubation. In addition, even if the person does no conscious work at all on the problem during the break, the fact that a break facilitates problem solving does not necessarily mean that true incubation has occurred. There are several psychological explanations, which have nothing to do with the idea of incubation, that have been proposed to explain why breaking away from a problem might help in solution of problems. One possibility is that a break might simply provide a rest that results in better performance afterwards.

Anecdotes and self-reports, although fascinating reading, are of questionable value in the study of creativity, because of their potential unreliability. In many cases the "evidence" concerning the creative process is based solely on one person's report, and even if the individual in question is the one who produced the creative work, one must be very cautious in accepting anecdotes and self-reports. There is strong evidence that a number of them are at least inaccurate and there is also circumstantial evidence that several self-reports are fabrications.

Musicologists who have studied "Mozart's letter," presented earlier, in which his wondrous methods of composition are described, for example, have concluded that it is a forgery. Furthermore, objective evidence, to be discussed in Chapter 7, indicates that compositions did not come to him complete, simply waiting to be written down.

Coleridge's self-report of the creation of "Kubla Khan" is at least inaccurate, because a version of the poem exists that was written earlier than the one actually published. Such a manuscript indicates that Coleridge carried out revision before publication, which brings into question his claim that the poem appeared whole and was published just as it appeared to him. "Kubla Khan" is in actuality an unfinished fragment, and at least one critic believes that Coleridge fabricated the story of his opium-inspired inspiration to make the fragment more interesting to his audience.

In another example of what is at least an inaccurate self-report, Charles Darwin wrote in his autobiography that when he began formulating a theory of evolution, he simply sifted through facts until he hit upon an idea to work with. However, Howard Gruber's detailed examination of Darwin's own notebooks indicates that his autobiographical report was incorrect. Gruber has found that Darwin began his theorizing early in the enterprise, with a theory very different from the final one based on natural selection.

Finally, there is no independent support for Poincaré's conclusion that he was actually "observing his own unconscious at work" during his sleepless night. All he reports is that he was consciously thinking while unable to fall asleep and he believed that he was not consciously directing the thought process. It is a very large step from a nondirected conscious thought process to the conclusion that one is observing one's own unconscious, but many have not hesitated to take that step with Poincaré.

Accepting Poincaré's claim for unconscious processing during the ride on the omnibus depends on another critical assumption: that Poincaré did not think about his work while away on the expedition, which strains credulity. Before he left for the expedition, Poincaré worked persistently for more than two weeks trying to devise a proof. He seems not to have gone on vacation to get away from his work; rather, the work was interrupted by a trip that had been planned earlier. Under these circumstances, it seems unlikely that such a person would forget his work. Poincaré's report was produced many years after his discoveries took place; it is quite possible that he forgot what had actually happened.

In conclusion, several of the reports often cited as evidence for the operation of unconscious processes in creative thinking are of questionable credibility. Of course, these problems with self-reports do not mean that all self-reports are of no value, but they raise questions about building a theory of creative thinking on them.

In addition to anecdotes and self-reports, laboratory studies have been conducted in an attempt to provide more objective evidence for incubation, but with little success. In early work often cited as supporting the notion of incubation, Catherine Patrick studied creative thinking in artists and poets, by questioning subjects about their working methods. Most of the artists and poets reported that Wallas's four-stage process (preparation, incubation, illumination, and verification) described their work. They said that an idea for a painting or a poem was not worked on immediately, but was first "carried around" for a period of time. However, Patrick also found that the idea was thought about occasionally during the incubation period, so that there is no need to assume that unconscious thought occurred.

Patrick also attempted to study Wallas's postulated four stages of creativity directly in experiments. In one study, poets were given a picture of a mountainous landscape and asked to write a poem in response to it. Artists were given a poem as a stimulus for a painting. The typical sequence of production began with general impressions and recalling of relevant memories in response to the stimulus, but no concrete work was done. This was followed by a few lines of poetry or the blocking out of a picture; these products were subsequently revised and elaborated. Such behaviors seem to correspond reasonably well to Wallas's stages of preparation, illumination, and verification. (In this case, verification is *revision*, when an early idea is modified or elaborated.) However, these poets and artists did not take a break from the problem; thus, by definition, incubation could not have occurred. Furthermore, the stages were not completely separate, and overlapped in time. Jan Eindhoven and Edgar Vinacke conducted a similar study with artists and found, because of overlap, that it was impossible to identify separate stages at all.

In an interesting and important series of studies, Robert Olton and his associates tried to replicate the important factors involved in a situation such as that described by Poincaré. They hoped to find evidence of incubation by observing expert chess players trying to solve a chess problem, since the domain was thoroughly familiar to the subjects and the problem was the sort that the subjects would ordinarily do on their own, which roughly corresponds to Poincaré working on a mathematical problem. The chess players were divided into two groups, each of which had several hours to work on the problem, but one group was given a break while the other worked continuously. The group given the break was asked not to work consciously on the problem during the break, in order to give unconscious incubation a chance to work.

Much to Olton's surprise, the study uncovered no evidence for unconscious incubation: on the whole, the group given a break performed no better than the group without one. This experiment and negative findings from several others led Olton, despite his initial belief in the existence of incubation, to question whether it actually occurs. Olton was also unable to replicate other studies that had reported finding evidence for it.

A supporter of incubation could of course raise several questions about Olton's studies. For example, Olton's chess-player subjects were not as motivated as was Poincaré, since he was working on problems which were central to his professional career. Also, Olton's subjects did not work on their problems for as long as Poincaré did before they took their break, and the break was not as long as Poincaré's. However, given that the designs of Olton's studies are among the best in the literature, and that there is no compelling evidence from other laboratory work to support the occurrence of incubation, the most reasonable conclusion is that incubation is, at best, very difficult to demonstrate in controlled situations. When this fact is combined with the negative conclusions from examination of self-reports of incubation, there appears to be no evidence for the occurrence of the phenomenon.

This conclusion is important because theorists are still using self-reports of spontaneous insights as evidence on which to base theories of creative thinking. As one example, R. E. Ochse has recently proposed a model to account for incubation and illumination which does not postulate unconscious processes. Ochse concentrates on what is called the "bed, bus, bath" syndrome, the fact that many reported spontaneous illuminations occur just before sleep or during rides in buses, which according to Ochse are states of low cortical arousal. It is assumed that illumination occurs during conscious states of low cortical arousal, because during such states multiple streams of thoughts can be activated simultaneously, in contrast to states of high arousal, when only a single stream of thought can be activated. When multiple streams are activated, combinations of thoughts from the two streams can occur.

Ochse's view is interesting, but it rests on several questionable assumptions. The first is that self-reports are useful as evidence for theories of creative thinking, but people do not have privileged access to their thought processes, and any person's report of his or her own cognitive activities may provide little useful information. Many things are occurring during situations in which "inspiration" comes about, including strong emotional responses, which means that the thinker may have great difficulty in making an accurate report. (There is much experimental evidence available to support the claim that individuals have great difficulty in accurately reporting on their own cognitive processes.) Furthermore, these self-reports are not *protocols*, or on-line verbalizations, but retrospective reports, and are sometimes constructed long after the event.

A second questionable assumption behind this broadened-attention theory is that illuminations occur during periods of low cortical arousal. Let us reexamine Poincaré's two examples in this context. First was his sleepless night, when he "observed the workings of his own unconscious," and discovered the existence of Fuchsian functions. When one has had coffee too close to bedtime and is kept awake, that is anything but a state of low cortical arousal. Poincaré's second example involves the mathematical discovery made while boarding the bus, and he was not dozing or daydreaming on boarding the bus: he was engaged in conversation, which again does not seem to be a state of low arousal.

The cognitive unconscious is a concept that has received much discussion in the literature on creativity, but solid evidence to support it is very difficult to find. Thus, if there is any truth in the popular belief that "sleeping on it" is helpful in solving problems, it is probably not because of unconscious processing during sleep.

The Myth of Leaps of Insight

1. A man in a certain town in the United States married twenty women from the town. All the women are still alive, none has been divorced, the man is not a Mormon, and yet the man broke no law. How is that possible?
2. Yesterday, when I went to sleep, I turned off the light and then got into bed. My bed is located twenty feet from the light switch, and yet I got into bed before the room got dark. How is that possible?

Over 60 years ago, the Gestalt psychologists proposed the distinction between problem solving based on trial-and-error methods versus insight. In trial and error, we attempt to use what we know in order to deal with some new situation, and, consistent with *trial* and *error*, we make mistakes until we discover what is to be done. Insight, on the other hand, like intuition can produce a sudden solution to a new problem without trial and error, and it can be independent of our specific knowledge and experience concerning the problem.

The two problems just presented are examples of what are called "insight" problems, because solving them is assumed to require a leap of insight. The solutions to the problems are: 1) the man is the minister who married the women to their husbands; and 2) I went to sleep when it was still daylight. When given the solution to an insight problem, especially after trying unsuccessfully to solve it, one may experience a sudden "Aha!" reaction as one sees that the situation can be interpreted in more than one way. So long as one stays with one's initial interpretation, based on past experience, the problem is unsolvable. Upon changing the way one interprets the problem, however, it becomes trivially easy. Thus, in these cases, past experience interferes with creative thinking.

In their analysis of problem solving, Gestalt psychologists made a distinction between *reproductive* thought, which involves the reproduction or recall of past experience, and *productive* thought, which involves creation of something truly novel, by going beyond one's past experience to work out each new problem as an independent entity.

These psychologists wished to show that one could solve problems for which one had no specific knowledge or experience, simply by considering what the real difficulty was and how to overcome it.

An important example of the Gestalt view of thinking is Wolfgang Kohler's work on problem solving in apes. Kohler set out to show that animals could demonstrate intelligence while solving novel problems, and that they were not limited to associations previously acquired in similar situations. In one situation, Kohler found that apes could use a stick to rake in a banana from outside the cage; in another situation, an ape piled several boxes on top of each other, ladderlike, in order to reach a banana hanging from the top of the cage.

According to the Gestalt view, if a stick is in the animal's field of view while it looks for a way to reach a banana beyond its grasp, the visible length of the stick will cause the animal to realize that it can serve as a means of lengthening its arm. This realization is thought to occur because of the way in which the situation is perceived, which is assumed to be relatively independent of past experience. According to the Gestalt view, if the situation is set up in the right way, things "click" and even a naive subject would suddenly see the solution to the problem.

The Gestalt psychologists thus believed that creative problem solving is similar in important ways to perception. If you look at a Necker cube, for example, you are likely to see it in a specific orientation. If you continue looking, the cube may suddenly reverse itself in depth and flip inside out, in what is called *spontaneous restructuring*. The Gestalt psychologists claimed that, in a similar way, spontaneous restructuring may occur in problem solving. The problem solver sud-

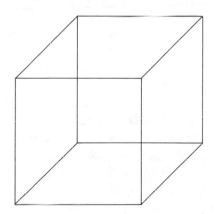

The Necker cube.

denly achieves a new understanding of the parts of the problem and their relations, a feeling of "Aha!" occurs, and the new solution is produced smoothly, not in fits and starts.

In the Gestalt view, we are all capable of productive thinking, and the question to be answered is why we do not think productively more often. According to the Gestaltists, restructuring and productive thinking often do not occur because problem solvers tend to become *fixated* on attempting to apply past experience to the problem, and thus do not deal with each problem on its own terms.

There is no question that all of us have "Aha!" experiences at various times in our lives. The issue here is whether such experiences are the result of leaps of insight that are independent of, and that can be disrupted by, past experience.

The animals in Kohler's experiments were captured, not raised from birth in captivity, leaving open the possibility that past experience played a role in their "insightful" behavior. Some researchers have raised apes from birth and thus have been able to control their experiences with sticks. Herbert Birch, for example, presented five naive animals with a "hoe" problem, in which the hungry animal could simultaneously see an out-of-reach piece of food and a potentially useful stick. Even though the various visual elements in the situation were thus "properly" arranged, Birch's apes made no insightful use of the stick. He then gave his subjects access to sticks in their cages for several days. The apes gradually learned to use the sticks as an extension of the arm and then could solve the hoe problem effortlessly.

Additional evidence also indicates that the capacity to behave insightfully in some situation depends on extensive experience in that sort of situation. Harry Harlow studied the ability of monkeys to solve two-choice discrimination problems. Monkeys perform very poorly, in a fumbling, trial-and-error manner, when first given such a problem. The animal may choose one stimulus and get food, but then may pick the other stimulus; it only gradually learns always to choose the correct stimulus.

Harlow gave his subjects a series of more than 300 discrimination problems, in which the stimuli were changed from problem to problem. By the time the animals finished the series, they were solving problems insightfully: Once the first choice was made, the animal never made a mistake. If the initial choice was correct, the animal picked that stimulus exclusively from then on; if it was incorrect, the animal immediately picked the other stimulus and never returned to the incorrect stimulus. Harlow's work indicates that problems that

Harlow's two-choice discrimination problems. From Harlow and Harlow, 1949. Learning to think. Copyright © 1949 by Scientific American, Inc. All rights reserved.

appear trivially simple may only be so because of the knowledge we bring to them; if we are inexperienced, we may confront great difficulties in solving even a seemingly "simple" problem.

Psychologists have studied the performance of humans on a number of "insight" problems, the best-known of which is called the

The 9-dot problem. Connect all nine dots with four straight lines, without lifting your pencil from the paper.

nine-dot problem — the problem being to connect all the dots without lifting pencil from paper or retracing any lines. The results parallel those obtained in the animal studies: one needs detailed knowledge in order to perform with insight. According to Gestalt theory, most people fail to solve the nine-dot problem because they make false assumptions about the problem, based on their past experience. They assume that the lines they draw must stay within the boundaries of the square formed by the dots, although nowhere in the problem is this restriction implied. Fixation on the square formed by the dots makes it impossible to solve the problem. If this fixation could be broken and the problem approached on its own terms, however, the solution would be trivially easy, or so the Gestalt theory claims.

Two studies, one by Clarke Burnham and Kenneth Davis and the other by Joseph Alba and me, tested this assumption and found no support for the Gestalt view. Subjects were told that the only way to solve the nine-dot problem was to draw lines outside the square. This instruction was designed to break the fixation on the shape of the square, which should have resulted in direct and smooth solution, as connoted by the term insight. However, in contrast to the Gestalt view, the problem did not become trivially easy — only 20 to 25 percent of these subjects actually solved the problem, although they all went outside the square. Furthermore, the few subjects who did solve it after receiving the hint took a long time to do so, and used trial and error.

Weisberg and Alba also showed that performance on the nine-dot problem could be improved by giving subjects experience solving simple dot-to-dot problems that required them to go outside the pattern of dots. These results were extended by Ching-Tung Lung and

Roger Dominowski, who gave subjects detailed strategy instructions about the nine-dot problem: they had to draw lines outside the square formed by the dots, at least one of the lines drawn outside the dots would have to end at an imaginary dot, and the next line would begin from that same imaginary point. Subjects also were given extensive practice before working on the nine-dot problem, through six dot-to-dot training problems, each of which required that the subject draw at least one line outside the dot pattern.

Lung and Dominowski's strategy instructions plus dot-to-dot training facilitated solution of the nine dot problem, but still only a little more than half of the subjects solved the problem, and they did so not smoothly in a sudden burst of insight, but only after a number of tries. This study provides particularly graphic evidence that insightful behavior, contrary to the Gestalt view, is the result of expertise. (The role of expertise in creativity will be discussed in Chapters 4 and 7.)

Other researchers have experimentally examined "intuitive" judgments and have shown that, contrary to the idea that intuition de-

"Intuition" Problem from Bowers, et al

Read down the following list of clues and try to guess the word that they refer to. Make a guess after each clue. Your guess does not have to change after each clue. If you think you have solved the problem, stay with your guess.

1. times
2. inch
3. deal
4. corner
5. peg
6. head
7. foot
8. dance
9. person
10. town
11. math
12. four
13. block
14. table
15. box

Solution: Square

pends on a sudden realization of a conclusion with no antecedents, such judgments are also the result of a gradual process. Kenneth Bowers and his colleagues had subjects generate "hunches," and then rate their confidence that the hunch was correct, about solutions to problems that had stumped them.

The results showed that these hunches were dependent on accumulation of information from the problem, and that the subjects made good predictions of how close their hunches were to solving the problem. These findings support the claim that intuitive judgments depend on the same sorts of processes that underlie logical judgments, in the sense that one needs to acquire information before one can produce a "hunch," and are also in accord with findings that indicate that insight during problem solving is not the result of an intuitive leap.

Remote Associations and Intuition

Dean Keith Simonton has recently proposed a theory of creative thinking that assumes that the basis for production of original ideas is the chance combination of "remotely-associated" mental elements. Simonton's theory builds on work by Donald Campbell and Sarnoff Mednick. Campbell proposed that creative thinking is based on "blind" trial and error, a process that in his view is analogous to biological evolution: it requires two mechanisms, one for producing many novel ideas and a second for determining which ideas should be retained for further development. (This distinction between idea-generation and idea-evaluation was also a feature of Poincaré's theory.) One important aspect of Campbell's theory is that new ideas are generated by randomly combining mental elements; Simonton calls this "chance permutation."

The second component of Simonton's theory is that the creative genius is able to generate combinations of elements that are more original than those produced by ordinary thinkers. This occurs because the genius possesses a "looser" set of associative connections, and is less tied to habitual associations, than the ordinary person, and is thus more likely to think original thoughts. Mednick theorized that the ability to form "remote associations" is important in creativity and developed the Remote Associates Test (the RAT) to assess this ability. The test consists of triplets of words, and the subject is asked to supply a fourth word that is related to all the others. An example would be: Surprise, Line, and Birthday. (The answer is party —

surprise party, party line, and birthday party.) The answer to each item is a word that is only weakly associated to all three words. In order to answer the item correctly, one would have to be able to break away from the frequent or dominant associations to each word, and generate "remote" associations. According to Mednick's theory, people who score highly on the RAT are able to generate such associations, and therefore should produce novel responses in other situations, which should result in their exhibiting creativity of thought.

Simonton likewise believes that creative geniuses (those who have made extraordinary contributions) do so in part because they possess many mental elements, which enable them to form many permutations. In addition, these elements in the genius are not strongly interassociated, so that more remote combinations can be produced more easily. Simonton has applied his theory to a wide-ranging set of phenomena, including the changes in creative productivity in age and the relationship between quantity and quality of creative output over a career.

Several questions can be raised concerning the chance-permutation view, however. According to Campbell and Simonton, chance permutation means that each novel idea generated by a thinker who would solve a problem is independent of the ideas that precede it and also of the environment in which the thinker is placed. That is, although the thinker's previously acquired associations participate in the idea-generation process, each combination of ideas has nothing to do with the combinations which have already been produced. Production of a new idea is like a mutation in genetic material: random and independent of other material. Successive solution attempts should therefore be independent of each other and of feedback from the environment concerning errors. This prediction is contradicted by much evidence from studies of laboratory problem solving, as will be seen in Chapter 4, which show that successive attempts at solving problems depend on each other and are affected by feedback. It is also contradicted by the case studies presented in Chapter 1 and Chapters 5 through 7. We have already seen in Chapter 1 that Calder's career went forward by building on what he and others had done before, as did Edison's. If these cases can be considered problem solving, they contradict the chance-permutation view.

The concept of remote associations as the basis for creative thinking also has not received strong support. First, Mednick's RAT has not had great success in predicting creative ability in individuals. Second, as we have already seen in the case studies presented in Chapter 1 and will see further in Chapters 5 – 7, creative thinking seems not to be based on remote associations. Calder's production of abstract sculpture can be analyzed in a straightforward manner without assuming that it was the result of remote associations. The same is true of Edison's kinetoscope.

Techniques of Training Creativity: Do They Work? Divergent Thinking, Lateral Thinking, and Brainstorming

Our society has a great interest in self-improvement, and one area in which many of us seek improvement is the area of creative thinking. Not only are courses available that claim to teach creative thinking, but also consulting companies provide seminars in creativity for government and industry (see the "Chicken Cheer" episode described at the beginning of this chapter). Much of the interest in such training programs stems directly from the genius view and the belief that creativity requires a special kind of thinking. Each of the various training programs claims to have discovered the secret and to have developed methods for teaching it.

The creativity training industry developed largely independently of scientific psychology, partly because most psychologists in the 1950s and 1960s were not interested in creative thinking, and were therefore not in a position to assist business leaders wishing to increase employee creativity. An exception to this fact was the mental-testing movement, led by J. P. Guilford, whose presidential address to the American Psychological Association expressed dismay over the "appalling" neglect of creativity by psychologists, and attributed much of this neglect to their interest in studying learning in lower animals. Historically, training creativity and testing for it have gone hand in hand.

In order to help stimulate interest in the subject of creativity, Guilford presented a set of hypotheses concerning the specific abilities important in creative thinking, and proposed tests that could be used to determine if an individual possessed them. Since Guilford's ideas are representative of the genius viewpoint on the creative thought processes, these abilities will be familiar.

Guilford hypothesized first that individuals differ in how sensitive they are to problems. Two research scientists might examine a report, but only one might see a problem in the results, and thus have a chance to produce a creative solution to that problem. In the set of

Problem 1 List all of the questions you can think of concerning the figure shown below. Ask all of the questions you need to know for sure what is happening. Do not ask questions that can be answered just by looking at the drawing. (Give yourself three minutes to list your questions.)

Problem 2 Suppose that all humans were born with six fingers on each hand instead of five. List all the consequences or implications that you can think of. (Give yourself three minutes.)

Problem 3 List as many white, edible things as you can in three minutes.

Problem 4 List all the words that you can think of in response to *mother*. (Give yourself 3 minutes.)

Problem 5 List all the uses that you can think of for a *brick*. (Give yourself 3 minutes.)

Some creativity problems. Adapted from E. P. Torrance, 1968, "Examples and rationales of test tasks for assessing creative abilities," *Journal of Creative Behavior* 2 [3], published by The Creative Education Foundation, Buffalo, New York. Used with permission.

problems shown, similar to those Guilford suggested using to test for creativity, Problems 1 and 2 test for sensitivity to problems.

Guilford also hypothesized that individuals differ in "fluency," or the ease with which they produce ideas. Problems 2 and 3 test for fluency, scored by counting the number of different responses produced. In addition, the creative thinker, by definition, produces original or novel ideas. Problems 4 and 5 can be scored for originality, by giving the person more credit for acceptable responses not produced by others in response to the same test item.

Creative thought is assumed to involve attacking a problem from a new direction, which implies flexibility of thought. One way to test this possibility is by counting the frequency with which an examinee switches response categories when, for example, listing uses for a brick (i.e., building material, weight, missile, and so on). A second measure of flexibility is the total number of different categories the examinee uses. The flexible thinker switches categories frequently and uses many different categories (see Problem 5).

Based on such tests, Guilford identified a large number of abilities contributing to human intellect. Those important to creativity involve two kinds of thinking or "production": divergent and convergent, as well as an ability to evaluate information and draw conclusions. Divergent thinking uses fluency, flexibility, and originality to "diverge" from what we know, to produce many original ideas; convergent thinking, the logical mode of thought, uses information to "converge" on a single solution or idea. In a situation demanding creative thinking, convergent thinking would be useful only after divergent thinking had been used to produce new ideas.

A related concept was developed by Edward deBono, one of the leaders of the creativity-training movement, whose theorizing is often cited by psychologists and others who have written about training creativity. According to deBono, solving many problems, especially the most important ones, requires a fresh viewpoint, one not provided by ordinary "tried and true" logical thinking. This different mode of thought (the intuitive mode) is what deBono calls "lateral" thinking since it moves "sideways," to a new way of looking at a situation.

> Everyone has come across the type of problem which seems
> impossible to solve and then turns out to have an obvious
> answer. These are the problems that elicit the remark: "Why
> didn't I think of that before?" Many inventions are obvious
> once someone else has thought of them. . . . Lateral thinking
> seeks to get away from the patterns that are leading one in a
> definite direction and to move sideways by re-forming the patterns.

Although they have different histories and come from different backgrounds, deBono's notion of lateral thinking seems to be very similar to Guilford's concept of divergent thinking. Both have as a central idea that overcoming old habits (that is, being flexible, moving laterally), is the crux of creative thinking. There also are similarities between Guilford's and deBono's ideas and Mednick's remote-associative theory of creative thinking discussed in the last section, since the latter theory is also based on the idea that creative ideas are more remote (more divergent, more lateral) than are ordinary ideas.

Many investigators followed Guilford's lead, developed tests to measure divergent-thinking abilities in adults and children, and used the results to study creative thinking in other situations, producing a voluminous literature, but a number of investigators in the field have concluded that divergent-thinking tests do not measure either creative thinking or the capacity to become creative.

Studies have shown that creativity tests have little or no predictive validity: children's test scores are of marginal help in predicting creative performance several years later. Lack of such validity led one of the leaders in this area to conclude that the tests that he had helped develop were scarcely relevant to creativity. In other studies, workers in various fields were independently rated for creativity, using such criteria as the number of important publications produced by scientists. They were then tested for creativity, using divergent-thinking tests. It was found that creative individuals in a given field were not necessarily those who score highest on the tests.

In another study, scientists were given descriptions corresponding to different modes of thought — one which described divergent thinking and another which described convergent thinking — and were asked to choose the description that best matched the way they carried out their thinking during research. Contrary to Guilford's theory, the scientists picked convergent thinking as the description of the way they thought. Since the scientists in this study were asked to choose the mode of thinking that *best* matched their own mode, the results do not necessarily mean that divergent thinking is completely irrelevant; it may simply be less important. However, a number of detailed reports of scientific discovery, artistic creativity, and invention are available, including Darwin's notebooks on the development of his theory of evolution, Watson's report of the discovery of the structure of the DNA molecule, Picasso's preliminary sketches for several of his most famous paintings, and Edison's notebooks on the invention of the kinetoscope. These examples are covered in detail in later chapters, and nothing like divergent thinking is evident in any of them. Thus, although it seemed reasonable to Guilford that producing many and varied ideas through "divergent" or "lateral" thinking ought to be a cornerstone of creative thinking, this idea does not seem to be correct.

The concepts of divergent production and lateral thinking are closely related to "brainstorming," an extremely influential group–problem-solving method elaborated over 40 years ago by Alex Osborn in a series of books, speeches, and seminars. This method was designed to help thinkers produce many new ideas by enabling them to diverge from their habitual ways of approaching problems. Brainstorming can—from my perspective—be looked upon as a method to bring about increased flexibility and perhaps also increased fluency in thinking, and would therefore be expected to contribute to divergent production. If one believes that divergent thinking is important in creativity, then one would expect brainstorming to increase creativity. Osborn begins his analysis with the assumption that all people possess creative capacity. He divides the thinking mind into two now-familiar components: *judicial mind*, which analyzes, compares, and chooses, and *creative mind*, which visualizes, foresees, and generates ideas. Although we all have both capacities, especially when we are young, the creative capacity can dwindle over the years as one becomes increasingly judgmental. Most importantly, *premature* judgment can interfere with creativity when it causes one to reject as useless those ideas that might solve the problem if given the chance. The importance of deferral of judgment has been accepted by many of those who seek to facilitate creativity.

The brainstorming technique is designed to offset the inhibiting effect of premature judgment and to make it possible for problem solvers to produce many wild ideas in order to maximize the chance of producing a potentially useful idea. Four basic rules govern any brainstorming session:

1. *Criticism is ruled out*: no judgment is made of any idea until all ideas have been produced.
2. *Freewheeling is welcomed*: because it is easier to tame down than to think up, the wilder the idea the better.
3. *Quantity is wanted*: the more ideas, the greater the likelihood of winners.
4. *Combination and improvement are sought*: participants may suggest how the ideas of others can be made better, because one may see implications in the ideas of others that were not apparent to those who produced them.

In addition, each brainstorming group must have a leader who structures the situation in such a way that the rules are used most effectively.

To give the reader a more concrete idea of how creative thinking is supposedly fostered, we can outline a well-known how-to book on creativity, James Adams's *Conceptual Blockbusting*. Adams's purpose is to make the reader conscious of the various aspects of the creative process, most importantly, the various "blocks" that inhibit creative thinking — perceptual, emotional, cultural, and intellectual and expressive — in order to overcome them.

Human perception is strongly influenced by what the perceiver expects to see, and these perceptual expectations can interfere with creative problem solving in various ways. Adams uses the nine-dot problem (see p. 54) as an example of the effects of a perceptual block. According to Adams, experience causes one to delimit the problem too closely; that is, one assumes that the square's boundaries cannot be crossed, thereby making it impossible to solve the problem.

Another example of a perceptual block occurs when one's past experience makes it difficult to look at a problem from various viewpoints. In this context, Adams refers to deBono's distinction between vertical and lateral thinking. To use deBono's analogy: vertical thinking involves making an old hole deeper, while lateral thinking involves digging a new hole. Sometimes, according to deBono, to find treature, you may have to dig a new hole.

According to Adams, one emotional block to creative thinking is fear of taking a risk, since production of a creative idea involves taking risks. In order to overcome such blocks, Adams suggests that one try to assess the consequences realistically and recognize that they may not be that terrible. What will *really* happen if one proposes an idea that others think is foolish and/or does not work?

Another important emotional block involves judging, rather than generating, ideas. Judging is safer than attempting to generate something new, and people often concentrate on judging ideas, to the exclusion of generating them. A difficulty can arise when one judges a newly formed idea too early and rejects it before all its implications are considered. Adams here discusses brainstorming.

Adams believes that our culture's emphasis on logic and reasoning stifles creative thinking, which depends more on intuition, and he presents various methods for thinking through such cultural blocks. Intellectual blocks occur when a thinker is unable to approach a problem in the most efficient way. He or she may be inflexible in the use of problem-solving strategies, or may not have adequate information before beginning the problem. Expressive blocks interfere with one's ability to communicate ideas during problem solving.

Adams proposes many different "blockbusting" methods to help spur creativity. He first considers a general class of methods that enable the thinker to produce thoughts he or she would not produce ordinarily. One method is simply to adopt a questioning attitude, because it enables one to be sensitive to questions and "problems" that others never see. Furthermore, if one begins to ask questions, questioning soon becomes habitual.

In order to increase fluency of thinking, or the production of ideas, Adams recommends making lists. These help a person to concentrate on the problem at hand, making it easier to produce a larger number of ideas. Since one's thought must be flexible as well as fluent, Adams suggests listing the attributes of the critical object in one's problem, and then attending to each attribute in turn, which will insure that the object will be considered in different ways.

In the area of invention, another way to increase idea production involves listing the attributes of the object you wish to improve, and then listing alternative forms for each attribute. One then randomly connects the various values of the attributes, to produce a new "object" which may be potentially valuable. As an example, if a person were considering how to improve a pen, he or she would list the attribute of cylinder for shape, and then would list other possibilities, such as cube or sphere; he or she would also list the material, say plastic, and list other possibilities, such as metal, glass, or paper. Might a cubic or spherical pen made out of glass or paper be an improvement over current versions?

A second general type of blockbusting method concerns "freeing the unconscious." Adams accepts the view that creative thinking depends on the unconscious as discussed in Freudian and neo-Freudian work, and that we sometimes are not creative because we are unable to give our unconscious free rein. Adams suggests learning about psychological processes to loosen the control of one's ego over the unconscious, and he also recommends brainstorming. He also mentions in passing less practical techniques, such as undergoing psychoanalysis and learning Middle-Eastern psychologies.

Adam's program for increasing creative thinking is organized around the notion that all people are capable of thinking creatively if they are not blocked from doing so, a residue of the Gestalt view of "insight" and "fixation" discussed earlier in this chapter.

Adam's analysis has been very influential; although he presents no evidence that his various proposals are effective, a number of more recent guides for increasing creative thinking follow his outline. As one example, here is a selected list of skills that purportedly have been found in creative adults and children, from a book by Teresa Amabile for parents who wish to foster creativity in their children.

1. "Breaking set": breaking out of your old patterns of doing something
2. Keeping options open as long as possible
3. Suspending judgment
4. Thinking broadly: trying to see as many relationships as possible between different ideas
5. Breaking out of "scripts": breaking out of well-worn habits of doing things
6. Perceiving freshly: trying to see things differently from the way you or other people normally see them
7. Using tricks, or little rules of thumb that can help you think of new ideas: for example, "make the familiar strange and the strange familiar"; "play with ideas"; "investigate paradoxes."

John Bransford and Barry Stein have developed a program for teaching problem-solving skills called the IDEAL model, which is an acronym of: identify the problem; define and represent the problem; explore possible strategies; act on strategies; look back and evaluate effects of your activities. Bransford and Stein include a separate chapter on creativity and discuss blocks and how to overcome them. They recommend — among other techniques — asking yourself if you are making implicit assumptions that limit your ability to find solutions.

Bransford and Stein present several methods for generating new ideas, such as analyzing the components of objects, brainstorming, and incubation, which they define simply as time away from a problem, which is not quite Poincaré's definition. They present various interpretations of what might be happening during the time away from the problem, including unconscious processing, and they seem to accept the possibility that keeping a problem in the back of one's mind leaves one open to external triggers.

Marvin Levine's "*Effective Problem Solving*" is another guidebook along the same lines, with a discussion organized around the topic of lateral thinking. In Levine's view, much of the difficulty in solving problems can be attributed to staying with a habitual strategy when it is not useful. He presents a number of methods to facilitate lateral thinking, such as brainstorming, random associations (pick out a word in the dictionary and associate to it), and incubation, although he too deviates from Poincaré's definition and defines incubation as simply the facilitation of problem solving by the passage of time. Le-

Summary of Methods for Increasing Creative Thinking Discussed in Several Recent How-to Books

Method	Author(s)			
	Adams	Amabile	Bransford & Stein	Levine
Questioning assumption	x		x	
List-making	x			
Attribute list	x		x	
Heuristics (Polya)	x	x		x
Brainstorming	x	x		x
Analogies	x	x	x	x
Lateral thinking	x	x	x	x
Incubation	x		x	x
Set-breaking	x	x	x	
Random association	x			x
Exercises	x		x	x

vine says that when we return to a problem after the passage of time, we are less dominated by an earlier incorrect set.

The high degree of agreement among authors is impressive; all are agreed that in order to produce creative ideas, it is necessary to move away from the habitual (that is, break the set — use divergent or lateral thinking) and that one can do this through brainstorming and related methods, if only informally by suspending judgment and keeping your options open. These how-to methods point to a domination of this area by the genius view.

But is brainstorming effective? Osborn presents varied evidence to demonstrate what appears to be remarkable success using brainstorming as a technique to generate useful ideas. Many organizations have adopted the method to foster employee creativity — the list reads like a who's-who, from Alcoa, DuPont, and IBM, to RCA, US Steel, and the U.S. government. In one forty-minute session, a group of U.S. Treasury personnel brainstormed the question of how to encourage federal employees to sell more U.S. Savings Bonds, and produced 103 ideas. However, this report is impressive only if a comparable control group without brainstorming training produced fewer valuable ideas, since only controlled experiments can determine if the method is effective. Osborn's results therefore say nothing about whether brainstorming is effective, because the necessary control groups were not tested. The fact that many institutions enthusiastically adopted brain-storming may mean nothing more than that Osborn was an excellent salesman.

The critical assumption underlying brainstorming is that by de-ferring judgment, many ideas are elaborated that otherwise would be rejected too soon. A number of experimental studies have compared the performance of subjects given brainstorming instructions to that of subjects told to criticize their own ideas in various ways, and the results raise difficulties for those who argue that deferring judgment facilitates creative problem solving.

In one study, problem solvers received one of four different types of instructions, including brainstorming and "criteria-cued" instruc-tions, in which subjects were told how their responses would be eval-uated for "creativeness." The criteria-cued subjects produced fewer responses overall but the largest number of superior responses. Simi-lar results were reported in another study, where subjects were told beforehand what the criteria for a good solution were for five differ-ent sorts of problems. Criteria-cued subjects again produced fewer solutions overall, but produced more high-quality solutions. A rea-sonable conclusion from these studies is that, contrary to the assump-tions behind brainstorming, the more one knows about the criteria a solution must meet, and the greater role these criteria play in the ac-tual generation of solutions, the better the solution will be.

Does Creative Thinking Depend on Extraordinary Thought Processes?

The overview in this chapter indicates that the evidence for extraor-dinary thought processes in creative thinking is very weak. First, negative evidence was found for components of the Freudian and neo-Freudian views, and for madness as a cause of genius. There is also no evidence save subjective reports that unconscious incubation occurs, and questions of several sorts can be raised about the value of subjective reports as evidence for theories of creative thinking. Ex-perimental studies have found no evidence for the postulated stages of creative thinking or for the occurrence of illumination based on un-conscious incubation. Furthermore, there is no convincing evidence for the occurrence of insight during creative thinking. The Gestalt psychologists and their followers postulated leaps of insight, which were assumed to result in the sudden appearance of complete solutions to problems. Contrary to the Gestalt view, scientific attempts to study insight have found that solution of insight problems depends on detailed knowledge about the type of problem being solved. There is also little evidence for the claim that creative thinking is based on the generation of many associative combinations, perhaps at random, until a sufficiently original combination is produced.

Many methods of teaching creativity have been developed over the years, based on the concepts of divergent or lateral thinking and brainstorming, both of which are offspring of the genius view, specifically the idea that creative thinking is extraordinary in its capacity to break out of our past experience. Research has indicated that creativity tests based on divergent thinking do not predict creativity in real-life situations, and scientists do not believe that their own thinking process correspond to divergent thinking. Brainstorming, a method developed to facilitate divergent thinking, has been shown to be ineffective in promoting creativity.

Based on these uniformly negative results, a basic assumption of the genius view can be seriously questioned. The next chapter will discuss the second cornerstone of genius view, the notion of creative personality.

CHAPTER 3

The Myth of Genius
THE CREATIVE PERSONALITY

*There is good reason for believing . . . that
originality is almost habitual with persons who
produce a really singular insight. The biography of
the inventive genius commonly records a lifetime of
original thinking, though only a few ideas survive
and are remembered to fame. Voluminous
productivity is the rule and not the exception among
individuals who have made some noteworthy
contribution. Original responses, it would seem,
recur regularly in some persons, while there are other
individuals who never depart from the stereotyped
and the conventional in their thinking.*

*If, then, some persons are regularly original,
whereas others are regularly unoriginal, it must be
the case that certain patterns of relatively enduring
traits either facilitate or impede the production of
original acts.*

(Barron 1955, 478).

*What we mean by creativity is the achievement of
something unique, or at least very rare. There is no
reason at all to think that any two creative people
are alike in those key respects that lead us to label
them as creative: what is most evident about each
one is the uniqueness of his or her achievement. We
will need a new scientific strategy to cope with this
issue, a way of constructing for each creative person*

> *(indeed, for each living person) a "theory of the*
> *individual." There are, in all probability, infinitely*
> *many ways of being organized for highly effective*
> *work. What we need is a general approach that*
> *grasps this individuality without disregarding the*
> *social nature of every human being. Such a theory*
> *would not be composed of sentences of the form "all*
> *creative people are XYZ," but of the form "this*
> *unique configuration interacts with that unique*
> *configuration thus and so."*
>
> *(Gruber 1981, p. xx).*

Some individuals produce numerous works of genius over long careers; others produce one or two great works in an otherwise undistinguished career; and others never produce anything noteworthy throughout their careers. According to the genius view, one important component underlying these differences in productivity and influence (or differences in "genius") is differences in personality: there is a set of psychological characteristics that facilitate creativity, and individuals who produce many great works over long careers possess those characteristics to an extreme degree. Much research over many years has been directed toward isolating those characteristics, and there is a voluminous literature in this area. The purposes of this chapter are to explore the validity of the assumptions underlying the search for the creative personality and to examine significant research studies that bear on those assumptions.

There are three main assumptions behind the search for psychological characteristics that underlie creative genius. The first assumption is that "genius" is a measurable psychological characteristic, or trait, of people, or a set of characteristics, much like having an I.Q. of 115, say, or being a hypochondriac. Providing support for this assumption requires more than isolating a group of creative individuals and assessing their personalities. One must also compare any resulting personality traits with those of an appropriate control (or noncreative) group.

A second assumption is that any personal characteristics unique to creative individuals, whatever they turn out to be, are causally related to creativity. The fact that creative individuals are different psychologically from noncreatives in the same field, however, does not necessarily mean that those differences cause the differences in creativity. (This is the issue of correlation versus causation discussed in

Chapter 2 concerning the relation between genius and madness.) If creative scientists, say, are found to be more autonomous than non-creative ones, such results can support any one of several conclusions concerning the relation between autonomy and creativity. Being autonomous may make one creative, as the genius view would argue. However, the opposite might be true—being creative might allow one to be autonomous. Finally, to make matters even worse, there might be no causal relation at all between autonomy and creativity, even though the two are correlated. For example, more creative individuals often come from better economic backgrounds than do less creative individuals, which may mean that being well-off economically is the cause of both creativity and autonomy.

Third, the quality of "possessing genius" is assumed to be a permanent, or at least relatively permanent, characteristic of an individual. Differences in creative production are assumed to be enduring qualities of people, and to exist because of comparably enduring differences in personality traits. However, the concept of genius, as we will see, is much more complicated than this view assumes. The genius possessed by an individual can wax and wane over time, and is a funtion of factors outside the individual, raising serious questions about just what is meant by genius. This in turn raises doubts about the usefulness of searching for genius through measurements of personality.

Measuring Genius

The Study of Values scale measures six kinds of traits individuals are assumed to possess to varying degrees: theoretical (interest in truth); economic (interest in things for their usefulness); aesthetic (a search for harmony); social (altruistic love); political (power); and religious (belief in an all-encompassing unity). Using results from this scale, one can compare the strengths of an individual's values with those of various groups for which normative data are available.

Several personality inventories, the most well-known of which is the Minnesota Multiphasic Personality Inventory (MMPI), are used to assess broader aspects of personality than does the Study of Values. Inventories are long questionnaires in which respondents are usually asked to respond to general statements about themselves rather than to concrete situations. An individual's responses to the MMPI items are analyzed by grouping them together into a small number of scales

A.
Which of the following branches of study do you expect ultimately
will prove more important for mankind? (*a*) mathematics; (*b*) theology.

Which would you consider the more important function of modern
leaders? (*a*) to bring about the accomplishment of practical goals; (*b*) to
encourage followers to take a greater interest in the rights of others.

When witnessing a gorgeous ceremony (ecclesiastical or academic,
induction into office, etc.), are you more impressed: (*a*) by the color
and pageantry of the occasion itself; (*b*) by the influence and strength
of the group?

Which of the following would you prefer to do during part of your
next summer vacation (if your ability and other conditions would
permit) —
a. write and publish an original biological essay or article
b. stay in some secluded part of the country where you can appreciate
   fine scenery
c. enter a local tennis or other athletic tournament
d. get experience in some new line of business

Do great exploits and adventures of discovery, such as Columbus's,
Magellan's, Byrd's, and Amundsen's, seem to you significant because—
a. they represent conquests by man over the difficult forces of nature
b. they add to our knowledge of geography, meteorology,
   oceanography, etc.
c. they weld human interests and international feelings throughout the
   world
d. they contribute each in a small way to an ultimate understanding of
   the universe

B.
Do you agree or disagree?
   Sometimes I think I may kill myself.
   My greatest troubles are inside myself.
   I certainly have little self-assurance.
   I wish I were not so awkward.
   I am shy.

A. Values questionnaire. B. Items similar to those on the MMPI. Sample
items from G. W. Allport, P. E. Vernon, and G. Lindzey, 1960, *A Study of
Values*, Boston, Houghton Mifflin.

(such as those for depression and masculinity-femininity), each of
which contains items that are related to other measures of behavior
(such as psychiatrists' diagnoses).

Comparisons of creative and noncreative individuals have yielded
a small number of characteristics shared by all creative individuals.

Among these characteristics are broad interests, independence of judgment, self-confidence, intuition, and a firm sense of the self as "creative." In addition to these core characteristics in common, some critical differences are thought to exist between creative individuals in the sciences and those in the arts.

Creative scientists are believed to be different from noncreative scientists in their need to be free of rules (flexibility), in their need for recognition by their peers, and by the possession of strong aesthetic feelings about their work. Creative scientists consistently talk about their desire to produce theories or to design experiments that are simple, elegant, and beautiful, which is taken to be evidence for an aesthetic component in scientific judgment. Creative scientists have also been found to differ from the noncreative in their sensitivity or in their ability to be open to new experiences. This latter characteristic is particularly important because it makes creative scientists more sensitive to scientific problems than are their noncreative colleagues. Artistic genius includes the ability to move others emotionally through one's work, and those who can do so are more sensitive and open to feelings. Frank Barron and David M. Harrington comment in a review of the literature on the creative personality that the research has brought no surprises, in that the findings correspond to the general beliefs our society has concerning the characteristics of creative scientists and artists.

Richard Mansfield and Thomas Busse have raised an important critical note concerning many of the studies of personality characteristics. The subjects typically complete many different measurements, which results in a large number of scores accumulated for each subject. The investigators then compute correlations among these measures, and between each of them and a rating of each subject's creativity, to determine if there are any relations among them. This results in the computing and interpreting of a large number of correlation coefficients, which raises the serious possibility that some significant correlations occur just by chance. That is, when one carries out large numbers of statistical tests, there is a strong likelihood that some apparently significant results will occur just because so many tests were done, and for no deeper reason. Thus, some of the personality differences are derived from questionable statistical procedures and may have little to tell us about creativity.

Also, in some studies, the creative and control groups are not treated identically during data collection. As an example, in one study, the creative individuals filled out personality inventories as part of several days of interviews, while the control groups were mailed questionnaires and asked to fill them out at their leisure at home.

These differences in setting could produce differences in responses that would have nothing to do with creativity. In addition, in some of the studies of personality, the "creative" versus "noncreative" groups are defined by scores on "creativity tests," for example, tests of divergent thinking ability. It was pointed out in the last chapter that many investigators now believe that such tests are not valid measures of creativity, therefore bringing into question the results of such studies.

In order to test the hypothesis that individuals who exhibit genius in a particular field possess a unique set of characteristics, it is crucial to choose a relevant comparison or control group. If we compared the personality characteristics of creative mathematicians with those of the general population, for example, any differences could be related to either or both of two factors: creativity versus lack of creativity, or a career in mathematics versus no career in mathematics. To draw conclusions concerning the personality characteristics underlying genius in mathematics, one must compare creative mathematicians with noncreative mathematicians. The noncreative mathematicians should be as similar as possible to the creative in other ways, such as work experience and education.

Though the need for such a comparison group seems obvious, some studies in this area fail to include them, which may severely limit the usefulness of their conclusions. In these studies, the characteristics of creative individuals are measured and compared with norms for the general population or are simply examined on their own, with no comparison group at all. In addition, in many of the studies which have used control groups, the match between creative and noncreative subjects has not been very close, which renders the conclusions problematic.

The study that contains the best match in terms of demographics between creative and comparison groups is an often-cited one by Donald Mackinnon, which produced negative results concerning differences between creative and noncreative individuals. Mackinnon's study examined the personality characteristics of forty of the most creative architects in the United States in the 1950s, as nominated by a panel of professors of architecture. The findings from this sample of unquestioned creativity were compared with those from two control groups. The first or noncreative control group, chosen from the 1955 *Directory of Architects*, was matched with the creative group by age and location of practice. Each of the members of the second or associated control group, in contrast to the first, had worked with one of the architects in the creative group for at least two years. These associates of the creative architects were much closer in measures of creativity to the noncreative comparison group than they were to the creative group.

The creative architects were significantly different from the noncreative comparison group on many of the personality scales. On the Study of Values, for example, the creative group scored much lower on the economic scale and much higher on the aesthetic scale. On the MMPI, the creative architects scored as more feminine than the noncreative comparison group, which in this context means a sensitivity to feelings and emotions, especially one's own. On thirteen of the eighteen scales of the California Psychological Inventory, the creative group's scores were significantly different from the noncreative group's. Overall, the creative group was less social, more sensitive, and less self-controlled, among other things.

These findings seem to support claims about the personality characteristics underlying genius in architecture except for one complication: the architectural associates were remarkably similar to the creative group on all but one of the numerous measures mentioned above. Out of nearly forty scales on three instruments, the creative group differed from their associates on only one — they scored lower on the economic scale on the Study of Values, which means that they were less concerned with economic considerations in their work. As noted earlier, one difference out of forty comparisons could very well have been due to chance, and I will assume so henceforth.

The study just reviewed casts considerable doubt on the assumption that creative individuals possess some unique set of personality characteristics. Other questions can also be raised about the notion of a "genius personality," specifically whether the characteristics obtained from research studies have relevance to the actual behavior and attitudes of scientists. Conclusions about personality traits are derived from the analysis of subjects' responses on personality inventories. No actual measures of behavior are made. It is simply assumed that responses made by subjects reflect their actual behavior. While there is no reason to question subjects' honesty, there is good reason to question exactly what traits are being measured in such studies.

For example, in some cases the traits attributed to creative individuals are based on adjectives the subjects check as describing themselves. Thus, if creative scientists check "independent," it is taken to mean that they are independent. But such a response does not mean anything of the sort. All that one can reasonably conclude is that the group thinks that such an adjective applies to them. The trait in question, thus, is not "independent," but rather "believe themselves to be independent."

Evidence that scientists possess a strong aesthetic sense comes from studies using the Barron-Welsh Art Scale, which asks subjects to select their preferences among several stimulus pictures that range from simple symmetrical line drawings to complex asymmetrical "abstract-expressionist" paintings. In such investigations, creative scientists have been found to prefer asymmetrical and complex works over those that are simple and symmetrical.

However, this seems to be in opposition to the judgments that creative scientists give about their own scientific work, where they say that they strive for and appreciate a "sense of beauty," which includes simplicity, symmetry, and elegance. This sense of aesthetic appreciation in scientific work does not seem to be the same sense of aesthetic appreciation measured by the Barron-Welsh Art Scale, although it is asserted that aesthetic sensitivity, as measured by that scale, is an important characteristic of creative scientists. There is thus a question of whether the characteristics measured by personality scales are valid measures of the personality characteristics that play important roles in creative work.

A similar problem arises in interpreting the trait of flexibility, which in personality studies has been found to be an important characteristic of creative scientists. Other research finds that scientists most admired by their colleagues for their contributions to their discipline (presumably the most creative scientists) are often strongly committed to proving cherished hypotheses, rather than objectively searching for "truth". A commitment to proving cherished hypotheses is antithetical to the description of the creative scientist as a searcher after truth, ready to adapt flexibly to new information. Thus, once again, one can raise questions concerning the relevance to the real world of responses on personality inventories.

If we ignore for the moment the methodological questions that can be raised about the studies of the creative personality, examination of the results reveals that many of the isolated "personality" characteristics of genius have no content; they are basically motivational in nature. They are not traits such as paranoia or altruism, but are, rather, related to interest in and commitment to work. As noted in Chapter 1, the most influential individuals in a given discipline are almost always extremely productive, which supports the view that a high degree of motivation may be causally related to creativity. On the other hand, of course, the high level of productivity may be the result of creativity: if a person is successful early in a career, he or she may become highly motivated, which would then result in high levels of output.

Some evidence supports the idea that a high degree of motivation is present early in the careers of those individuals who do creative work. For example, a good predictor of productivity in a research career is the level of an individual's productivity in graduate school. Similarly, high levels of performance in high school (for example, winning The Westinghouse Talent Search) predict later success, indicating that interest and motivation may be present early and may cause later productivity. There will be many examples of the importance of motivation in creative production in the case studies.

Correlation, Causation, and Genius

Most studies of the genius personality have measured the personality characteristics of creative adults, with these findings then used to support the claim that certain personality characteristics facilitate genius. However, in order to demonstrate that some personality characteristic or characteristics play a part in causing genius, one must assess the personalities of individuals who have not yet demonstrated creativity. One can then examine the relation between possession of various characteristics and the later development of creativity, which allows one to infer that the personality characteristic(s) played a causal role in the creative development.

The relationship between personality characteristics and the development of creativity was investigated by Jacob Getzels and Mihalyi Csikszentmihalyi, who followed a group of artists from their art-student years through the beginnings of their careers. A total of 205 students, 94 men and 111 women, at the School of the Art Institute of Chicago were tested during their second or third year in the Institute's three-year program. The fine-art majors were contacted several years later, after they had had a chance to establish their careers, which allowed Getzels and Csikszentmihalyi to examine the relationship between certain personality characteristics and later creative performance.

When tested in art school, the students differed from the general college population in some ways, but not in others. On conventional measures of intelligence, the art students as a group scored close to college norms, but on two tests of perceptual abilities, they scored, not surprisingly, far above their peers, indicating that they possessed a specific set of skills. When psychological characteristics were assessed, the art students scored extremely high on the aesthetic scale of the Study of Values, apparently indicating strong commitment to their chosen careers. They also scored very low on the economic and social scales, indicating that the commitment to art as a career was not an unrealistic choice, since it is notoriously insecure financially and involves intense work, often with an accompanying sacrifice of social relationships.

On the Sixteen Personality Factors Questionnaire, a questionnaire measuring various aspects of personality, the following composite portrait emerged when the art students were compared with college norms. The art students were more socially aloof, introspective, self-sufficient, nonconforming to society's norms, radical, and experimental. They were also more subjective and imaginative, rather than conventional, in their outlook. This pattern corresponds reasonably well to the popular stereotype of the artist.

Getzels and Czikszentmihalyi located thirty-one of the male fine-art students seven years later, when they had been out of school five or six years, and examined the relationship between career success and scores obtained on various measures when the men were students. Although this length of time is obviously too short to determine which students, if any, would become artists of lasting reputation, large differences in success, as defined by the judgments of two art experts and by the students' judgments of each other, had already been achieved. Of the thirty-one students, fifteen had severed all connections with the art world. Seven others were in careers only peripherally related to art, such as art teachers and model builders for architects. The remaining nine subjects had succeeded in establishing places for themselves in the art world. Though most of them showed their work only sporadically, one artist had already achieved unqualified success.

Getzels and Csikszentmihalyi found that essentially *none* of the measures obtained in art school related to career success. No standardized test of intelligence, cognition, or divergent thinking (see Chapter 2) related to later success. The same was also true of the students' values — none of the scores on the Study of Values obtained in art school related to later success. Finally, only one of the Sixteen Personality Factors Questionnaire factors was significantly related to career success: the successful artists scored lower on the scale measuring conformity and concern with social approval. Given the large number of measures involved, however, a significant difference on a single factor could very well be due to chance. Csikszentmihalyi has recently reported an eighteen-year follow-up of those student artists, and his interpretation has not changed.

A similar result was reported by Stephen Segal, Thomas Busse, and Richard Mansfield, who tried to predict the development of creativity in a sample of biologists by using several different sorts of developmental measures, and found that the best predictor of later scientific creativity was performance in graduate school. Here too, measures of characteristics from earlier in life were not useful predictors.

The results just reviewed raise serious questions about the assumption that there is a small core of personality traits that characterizes creative individuals, and that such characteristics play a causal role in creativity. Many of the studies that have tried to isolate a set of characteristics in creative individuals have not compared the creative individual with an appropriate comparison group. Those studies that have used an appropriate comparison group have not been successful in isolating a set of core characteristics possessed by creative individuals; the occasional differences that are sometimes found could be due to chance. In addition, one well-designed developmental study that has followed artists from art school through the beginnings of their careers found that only one personality characteristic measured in art school predicted later career success. Again, that one difference out of the many examined could have occurred by chance.

Is Genius Constant?

As a result of an unquestioning acceptance of the genius view, our society tends to view great scientists and artists in a heroic light, which leads to the belief that such individuals can do no wrong in their professional judgments. Contrary to this assumption, there are great fluctuations in the "genius" of a given individual, which indicates that attempting to measure the personality characteristics that form the basis for genius is a mistaken enterprise, because the same characteristics are related to both genius and nongenius production. The discussion that follows can be viewed as raising questions about some individuals of high reputation. However, the individuals in question have never claimed that they were perfect; that attribute has been given to them, based on society's belief in genius.

One characteristic believed to be associated with scientific genius is a greater sensitivity to potentially solvable problems of great import. The nongenius may waste time on problems that have no solution or, if solvable, are not important in the long run. Studies of the lives of great scientists, however, including Leonardo da Vinci and Isaac Newton, provide much evidence that many of them spent significant portions of their careers working on problems that similarly turned out to be of little import, and which may have not had solutions.

Leonardo da Vinci, a renaissance man literally and figuratively, is the classic example of the type of individual Frank Barron was referring to in the excerpt that begins this chapter, as living "a lifetime of original thinking." The common version of Leonardo's life centers on his wide-ranging investigations and insightful commentary on all areas of human study.

This view of Leonardo has recently come under revision based on modern analyses of his notebooks and their relations to the works of others. Many ideas in Leonardo's notebooks he copied or paraphrased from others, sometimes without acknowledgment. In addition, the breadth of interests revealed in his notebooks, ranging from painting to military engineering and anatomy, were subjects that trained artists of the time often studied and were not peculiar to Leonardo. Furthermore, many of the projects described in his notebooks were never put into practice, a parallel to his tendency not to complete artistic works.

Leonardo also made his share of mistakes, some of them major. In his speculations on human flight, for example, he spent years considering a flying machine that flew by flapping its wings, a design that was not successful. In addition, he developed a new method of painting on plaster that allowed him to paint his fresco of the *Last Supper* at a more leisurely pace, but unfortunately this method resulted in the paint's fading prematurely, so that the *Last Supper* is in relatively poor condition today. Examples of this sort simply indicate that even the greatest scientists and inventors among us are nonetheless human, and as such are fallible.

In Charles Hope's opinion, Leonardo's chief claim as a theorist of art was the idea that the artist should strive to reproduce as accurately as possible the external world. In Leonardo's view, painters were unique in their ability to move the audience because of the vividness with which they could depict scenes, which places painting above poetry in effectiveness. Hope notes that Leonardo was not the first Italian artist to attempt to represent the world as realistically as possible, but he did so at a high level of energy and commitment. This indicates that one of the unique aspects of Leonardo's personality may have been a commitment to his work, which has already been mentioned as an important characteristic of genius, and which we will see other examples of in subsequent chapters.

Isaac Newton is universally acknowledged to be one of the greatest scientists who ever lived. He developed the laws of physics that bear his name, produced seminal work on light, and invented the calculus, among other accomplishments. In addition, however, Newton also spent twenty-five years in the study of alchemy, searching in secret for mysterious elixirs and forces to influence nature. This alchemical work led to no outcome of value, although Newton wrote thousands of pages on it.

There are other examples. Alfred Russell Wallace independently of Charles Darwin developed the theory of evolution through natural selection and stimulated Darwin to present their similar ideas in public. Wallace later in his life became interested in communicating with the dead, and attempted to prove that "messages from the dead" were communications from spirits, and not the work of fraudulent mediums. He also published papers claiming that the spirit world had helped bring about the rapid evolution of humans from apes.

Franz Joseph Gall was one of the pioneers in the study of the structure of the brain. However, Gall went on to develop phrenology, the theory that mental development influenced the shape of the brain and that the bumps on one's head were clues to one's mental capacities. Phrenology was found to be totally unfounded and was dismissed as quackery. Gall is now usually limited to a footnote in the history of neurological science, an example of a genius gone astray, even though he stayed within his own discipline.

The astronomer Urbain Jean Joseph Le Verrier discovered the planet Neptune in 1846. Upon studying the irregularities in the orbit of the planet Uranus, Le Verrier predicted that they were the result of another planet's gravitational influence, which was soon confirmed, and the discovery brought him great honor. Several years later, after studying irregularities in Mercury's orbit, Le Verrier predicted the presence of another unknown planet. In this case, however, his prediction was incorrect; no planet was ever found, and his stature received a crippling blow.

Perhaps the most striking example of a scientific genius making the wrong choice on a scientific problem is Albert Einstein's reaction to the uncertainty principle of quantum mechanics. One of Einstein's most profound insights was his postulation in 1905 of the particle nature of light, or the light quantum. His elaboration of this idea led to great developments in physics, one of the most important of which was quantum mechanics, the study of the laws governing the behavior of light quanta and other particles.

As work progressed on the laws of quantum mechanics, several of the most important physicists in the first quarter of the twentieth century came to the view that it was impossible to measure precisely the behavior of particles, because the very act of measuring the position and velocity of a particle changed the quantities one wished to measure, making it impossible to ever measure those quantities precisely. This was the uncertainty principle of Werner Heisenberg, and it meant that the laws of quantum mechanics had to be statistical laws, rather than precise deterministic laws. The best one could do was to say that with a certain probability the particle was here, or there, or wherever.

Although probabilistic laws are accepted today, Einstein was among the many physicists of his time who resisted the notion of statistical laws, and throughout his life he believed that eventually a way would be found to develop strictly deterministic laws governing the behavior of particles. Einstein encapsulated his strong opposition to the probabilistic view in December 1926, in a famous statement made in a letter to Max Born, a fellow physicist.

> Quantum mechanics is certainly imposing. But an inner voice tells me that it is not yet the real thing. The theory says a lot, but does not really bring us any closer to the secret of the Old One [i.e., to understanding how God created the world]. I, at any rate, am convinced that He does not throw dice.

The important point about Einstein's rejection of the statistical laws of quantum mechanics is that these laws are now accepted as the basis for the modern physicists' conception of the universe. Einstein's rejection of quantum mechanics can thus be seen as a failure of his "sensitivity to problems," since quantum mechanics became an area that led to fruitful work. As Einstein himself elsewhere put it, this rejection resulted in his being moved from the forefront of theorizing in physics and becoming "a genuine old museum piece."

It should be noted that Einstein's rejection of quantum mechanics was not because his personal characteristics had changed in any fundamental way from the time when he did his revolutionary work. His basic belief in determinism and in strict causal laws motivated both his earlier work and his rejection of quantum mechanics. This indicates that the same characteristics can be those of genius or of an "old museum piece." Einstein exhibited genius in an area that was amenable to the sort of deterministic analysis with which he was comfortable. When theorizing in physics shifted to laws of a statistical nature, however, he was left behind.

The case of Einstein makes clear that the crucial personal characteristics determining genius in a scientist depend upon the problem being considered, and there are many types of problems in science. There must then be many ways to be creative in science, and many different sorts of characteristics must be relevant to scientific genius, although none of these may be relevant in a wide range of situations. The idea of a set of core characteristics common to all creative scientists thus seems to have little merit.

Artists of the highest levels of accomplishment also do not exhibit constancy of genius throughout their careers: no artist produces only masterpieces. As discussed in the last chapter, Wayne Dennis's analysis of the careers of well-known composers reveals an essentially constant relationship between the production of major and minor works, classified on the basis of their being discussed in music reference works. This has been formulated by Dean Kieth Simonton as the constant-probability-of-success model. In the periods in which composers produced relatively large numbers of major works, or works of genius, they also produced large numbers of minor works.

This finding raises a question about the alleged sensitivities of genius. If a genius makes public a piece of work, presumably he or she would believe it to be worthy, and not simply a quick way to earn some money (although the latter may also be the case). If posterity deems the work a minor work, however, then the artist's judgment is mistaken. This raises the possibility that the artist of genius, contrary to our culture's beliefs, is not always particularly sensitive to the responsiveness of the audience.

An example of this can be seen in the "London" symphonies of Franz Joseph Haydn, his last twelve, composed for two extended visits to England, in 1791–1795. Haydn was then the most famous living composer, at the height of his powers, and his visits were met with great enthusiasm by performers and audiences alike. Haydn composed twelve symphonies for use in subscription concerts in London, and they were well received when premiered. Since all are of the same form and on the same scale, Haydn seems to have worked on all of them with the same level of commitment. And yet there are large discrepancies in the reputations of these symphonies: several are universally admired as high points of Haydn's symphonic output, while others are not considered to be at the same level. Assuming that Haydn meant all these symphonies to reach the same level, he did not succeed — he had better and worse days. This does not mean that one does not want to listen to some of the London symphonies, but that some are more memorable than others, which indicates that Haydn's artistic judgment was not infallible.

The Relative Nature of Genius

One of the unarticulated assumptions motivating the genius view is that "genius" is a psychological characteristic of an individual that can be measured as can any other. However, a number of recent theorists have come to the conclusion that genius is not a psychological characteristic, and therefore one cannot measure genius. The genius view assumes that the greatness of an individual (that is, the ability to produce works of great value and influence) is the result of cognitive and personality characteristics, but if genius is not a psychological characteristic, then the greatness of an individual does not reside in that individual. The genius view also assumes that a product becomes great (that is, valued and influential) because of the extraordinary characteristics of the individual who produced it. If, however, the creator does not possess extraordinary characteristics, it follows that the greatness of a product does not reside in the product, either. Finally, these two conclusions imply that "greatness" is not something that is "put into" the product by its creator.

The view that the greatness of a creative achievement resides in that achievement is challenged by cases in which — over time — there is changes in the evaluation of an achievement and, therefore, of the individual who produced it. There are a number of important cases in the history of the arts and sciences in which the evaluation of the work of some individual underwent a relatively radical shift over time.

The music of J. S. Bach, today acknowledged as one of the high points in the history of Western music, was ignored for over fifty years after his death. Furthermore, it was not until recently that Bach's music and that of his contemporaries have been taken as valuable on their own terms, and have been performed in the style in which they had been composed. This indicates that Bach's "genius" was not universally recognized in the time following his death.

Before Bach could become a genius, changes had to occur in the sensitivity of the musical community. Clearly, these changes were independent of Bach himself, since they occurred after his death. These changes resulted partly from political pressures, such as the rise in German nationalism in the nineteenth century, which stimulated interest in the music of German composers but had nothing directly to do with music. This fact means that Bach's genius did not reside in his music, because the music did not change after Bach died. Furthermore, it is possible that future changes may come about in musical sensibilities, such that Bach's music might become uninteresting and of no value. There is nothing sacred or permanent about our judgments.

In order to understand why Bach is labeled a genius, one must analyze Bach's music in its historical context. If one measured Bach's personality characteristics, that would not help one understand how he became a genius, since Bach possessed the same personality characteristics when his music was ignored (i.e., when he was not considered a genius) and when his music was celebrated as one of the high points of western culture. If one day Bach's music again becomes uninteresting, his personality characteristics will have become those of a nongenius.

As another example of a shift in judgment concerning the quality of an individual's work, during their lives the work of the Dutch painter Jan Lievens was held in higher esteem than that of his contemporary Rembrandt. At present, only a few art historians know of Lievens, while Rembrandt is held to be one of the seminal figures in Western Art. A similar story is told of Botticelli, whose painting of women was held to be coarse and crude until the nineteenth century, when art critics and historians came to appreciate the "modern" qualities of his figures.

George Basalla, a historian of technology, has proposed a similar analysis concerning genius in the area of invention. According to Basalla, an invention is made great, and an inventor is made a genius, by the significance of the invention for the society in which it is produced. Eli Whitney's cotton gin (see Chapter 5) was acclaimed a product of genius because it served an important role in the economy of the antebellum South and spawned a whole family of newer developments, as others tried to make improvements on it. In Basalla's view, if the same device had been invented in a society in which cotton had been a crop of minor importance, the invention would have been of little significance, and Whitney would not warrant entries in encyclopedias.

It might be thought that this discussion of the relative nature of genius is not relevant to scientific creativity, because science depends on "facts" and "truth," which are very different from the subjective judgmental phenomena important in the arts, perhaps also in invention. However, the situation in science is not very different from that in the arts, because, as scientists know, "facts" are not absolute entities, and are subject to revisions of several sorts. In many cases, "facts" turn out to be incorrect, because facts are only as good as the methods used to collect them. In scientific investigations, facts are often collected through complicated procedures that can sometimes be flawed, making the data from them flawed as well. In science, all facts are accepted subject to replication: other investigators must carry out the same procedures and obtain the same results. When a set of facts is brought into question because of the flaws in the method used to obtain it, questions are raised about the greatness of the scientist whose reputation rests on having obtained what was thought to have been an important result. In turn, it also raises questions about any scientist whose reputation has depended on developing a theoretical interpretation of those now-flawed facts.

The opposite can also occur in science, with previously ignored facts becoming important because of changes in theoretical orientation. An example of this is Gregor Mendel, whose now universally acclaimed work on inheritance languished for fifty years in an unread report, until the development of Darwinian theory made those facts important in understanding the mechanism of transmission of inherited characteristics. This historical change, occurring fifty years after the data were made public, brought Mendel an important place in the history of science and acknowledgment as a genius.

In the area of theorizing, there can be the greatest changes concerning judgments of the greatness of scientific work and of the individual producing that work. An individual can produce an interpretation of a set of facts that may be ignored or even actively rejected by scientists in the mainstream of the field, resulting in the individual's receiving at most a footnote in scientific discussions. However, changes in the direction of scientific thought may make scientists enthusiastic about a theory actively rejected by preceding generations.

For example, Sir Frederick Bartlett in 1932 published a theory of memory which, due to the sway of behaviorism, had almost no influence on psychology in the United States for more than thirty years. With the development of cognitive psychology in the late 1960s and early 1970s, however, Bartlett's perspective was seen as being very much in accord with modern theorizing, and a large amount of research was carried out under the influence of his work.

A similar transition occurred concerning the work of Jean Piaget, whose theorizing was rejected as incomprehensible by most American psychologists until the 1960s. However, by that time, changes had occurred in the way many psychologists viewed psychological theory, and Piaget's work became by far the most important cognitive-developmental theory in the 1970s.

If we could somehow extract a creative work from the historical context in which it was produced and put it into another context, the value and influence of that work — and, hence, our estimation of the genius of its creator — might change radically. If we took a piece of Mozart's music and played it for people of a non-Western culture with a different musical system, they might find it a curiosity of no importance or even unpleasant to listen to. One does not even have to go outside our culture to find lack of universality in judgments of genius. Some people do not like classical music at all, for example, and among those who do, there are great divergences in taste, with one person not appreciating modern music while another does. There are probably no universally appreciated works of art of any sort, and therefore no universal geniuses, much though we may believe that what we look upon as the work of genius must be appreciated in the same way by everyone.

In order to appreciate something as the work of genius, one must be able to place that work in a context, which means that one must know something about works of that type. For example, artistic works from another culture may be brought to ours and a great fuss made over them. But then we learn that what we are exclaiming over in such ecstasy is looked upon as very poor work in the culture from which it came. One cannot tell solely from observation of a work whether or not the author of the work was creative, because that judgment depends on criteria external to the work.

If the creative genius has no intuitive sense of how to make a work meaningful and lasting to an audience, and "greatness" is not something that the creator puts into a work, then how might it be that some works last and others do not? There might not be anything that the genius does in order to make a work "great." An individual committed to a career in a field demanding creativity simply produces work which he or she believes is good; sometimes such work is acknowledged as great by others and sometimes it is not, and the creator has essentially nothing to do with these judgments. Whether or not the audience will acknowledge the quality in a creator's work is not simply chance, because the creator is influenced by factors that also influence the audience, such as the works of others familiar to the members of a cultural group. This means that there will probably be some constraints on what works that the audience will acknowledge as great, as well as constraints on what works artists will attempt to produce. There are, however, some random components in the process, because factors influence the audience that do not influence the creator, such as events that occur after the creator dies.

In a comment to Mozart's father, Franz Joseph Haydn called the young Mozart a great composer, and said of him that he had "profound knowledge of composition," and "taste." In the present context, this compliment is to be interpreted as saying nothing about Mozart. Rather, all that it meant for Haydn to say that Mozart had taste is that Haydn judged that Mozart's music was tasteful.

Genesis of the Genius Myth

The genius view developed out of two assumptions concerning creative thought processes and creative achievements. First, in order to explain how humans can produce novel behaviors, the genius view postulated extraordinary thought processes. This assumption, critiqued in Chapter 2, is based on the premise that ordinary thought processes cannot produce novel behaviors. But the premise is not necessarily true, as the case studies presented in Chapter 1 demonstrated, and as the research and case studies to be presented in Chapters 4 through 7 will make clear. Second, in order to explain how some creative achievements can have wide-ranging influences, the genius view postulated a set of personality characteristics possessed by creative geniuses. This assumes that the greatness of an achievement is "put into" the product by the creator, a concept shown in this chapter to be at the very least an oversimplification of what occurs.

The concept of genius, in the sense of a postulated set of specific personality characteristics and related thought processes determining whether or not one achieves greatness, is thus based on assumptions of questionable validity about how great creative works come about. Based on the point of view to be elaborated in the rest of this book, we all possess the thought processes underlying creativity. Actual production of creative works, on the other hand, involves much more than cognitive processes — among other things, very high degrees of persistence and motivation, which we do not all possess. In addition, once a creative work is produced, other factors, mostly out of the creator's control, determine whether or not the creator will be considered to possess genius.

In the next chapter, I will move away from the critique of the genius view that occupied the last two chapters, and will begin to present evidence concerning how creative thinking actually comes about, by reviewing research on creative problem solving. This research will provide a framework for analyzing case studies of creativity in a variety of domains, to be presented in Chapters 5 through 7.

CHAPTER 4

Creative Problem Solving

THE CHARLIE PROBLEM

Dan comes home from work and finds Charlie lying dead on the floor. On the floor is some broken glass and some water. Tom is also in the room. Dan takes one look around and immediately knows how Charlie died. How did Charlie die?

The last two chapters have reviewed the assumptions and supporting evidence underlying genius, with consistently negative conclusions. In this and the succeeding chapters, I will explore the possibility that creativity is instead based on "ordinary thinking," the second view outlined in Chapter 1. To understand the ordinary thought processes underlying creative thinking, I begin with some laboratory studies of problem solving, for example, how people attempt to solve the Charlie problem. The subjects in these investigations are almost always college students, individuals who by definition carry out "ordinary" thought processes.

Laboratory problems are useful for this purpose because a well-chosen laboratory problem is simple enough to allow the isolation of the variables one wishes to investigate, but complicated enough to engage complex cognition. Since the problems are novel for the subjects, any solutions that are successful are the result of creative thinking. Because of the similarities between the performance of undergraduates on laboratory problems and creative thinking in other situations, one question we will explore is how far the concepts developed here can be extended to creative thinking in other domains.

Although they have approached the question from various perspectives, psychologists have long believed that the study of problem solving would provide insight into creative thinking. We have already examined the theoretical views of the Gestalt psychologists, early advocates of the study of human problem solving (see Chapter 2). More recently, Herbert Simon, Allen Newell and others have studied problem solving from the perspective of computer models of human thinking. Their work has been of seminal importance in the "cognitive revolution" that has taken place in psychology.

One of the cornerstones of Newell and Simon's view is that creative thinking is a form of problem solving. The main differences between "ordinary" problem solving and the creative thinking that characterizes great accomplishment is the high degree of motivation and expertise involved in the latter.

This chapter begins with a discussion of different types of problems studied by cognitive psychologists, and the basic terminology helpful in analyzing problem solving. I then turn to a consideration of responses to two simple problems, to examine continuity and discontinuity of thought and how one goes beyond past achievement. The third section of the chapter discusses the findings from research on domain-specific expertise in creative problem solving. This research raises important questions about the extent to which creative thinking is independent of past experience, and has important implications for understanding creative thinking beyond the laboratory. The fourth section of the chapter discusses the role of memory in creative thinking, and whether the knowledge we use to solve problems is abstract or concrete in form. Finally, we will examine—in the light of research—how one might attempt to facilitate problem solving.

Problem Types and Creativity

A *problem*, as psychologists define the term, occurs when the present situation, or *problem state*, is not the one that the individual wants to be in — the *goal*. The problem solver can carry out moves or *operators* to try to change the problem state into the goal. If the problem takes more than one step to solve, then applying operators will produce intermediate states. Carrying out a sequence of operators that changes the problem state into the goal produces a solution to the problem.

Psychologists who study problem solving classify problems based on how precisely specified are the problem state and goal state, and the moves. In a *well-defined problem*, all the relevant aspects of the problem are specified, as in the Missionaries and Cannibals problem.

Missionaries and Cannibals

Three missionaries and three cannibals come together to the bank of a river. The only method of transportation across the river is a boat that holds at most two people. The missionaries and the cannibals wish to use the boat to cross the river, but there is one difficulty: if at any time the cannibals outnumber the missionaries on either bank of the river, the outnumbered missionaries will be eaten. How is it possible to get all the missionaries and all the cannibals across the river without losing anyone?

Missionaries and Cannibals and other well-defined problems, such as chess and checkers, are sometimes called "move" problems, because in order to solve them one must construct a sequence of moves leading from the initial state to the goal.

A well-defined problem can be contrasted with an *ill-defined problem*, such as "How can I better my life?", in which the initial state (my life at present) is not well-defined, since all the potentially relevant aspects are not yet specified. The goal, "a better life than I have now," and the operators available for reaching the goal, are also not at this point specified further. The Charlie problem is also not well-defined, because neither the goal state nor the operators are specified in precise terms.

One can analyze a well-defined problem by examining all the possible combinations of legal moves starting from the initial state, which produces the "problem space" for the problem. An example of a problem space is shown for the Missionaries and Cannibals problem.

Theorists analyzing performance on move problems have utilized the notion of searching the problem space, or examining the various paths from the initial state, until a path is found that leads from the initial state to the goal state; that is, a path that solves the problem. Algorithms are methods for exhaustively examining all the paths in a problem space, and such methods assure that if a solution exists to some problem, it will be found. Some problems, however, such as winning in chess and checkers, even though well-defined, are so complicated that it is not feasible to exhaustively search their problem spaces.

To get a feeling for the immensity of the problem space in chess, one simply has to contemplate how many possible combinations of moves there are in the game. The first person to move can make any of twenty moves, to each of which the other individual can also make any of twenty moves. The first person can then respond to each of those moves with any of a similarly large number of moves, and so forth. It has been estimated that there are more possible moves in the problem space of chess than there are seconds in a century. In order to deal with such mammoth problem spaces, it is necessary to cut them down to manageable size.

Heuristic search methods assist in the reduction of a large problem space to a size that can be searched in a reasonable amount of time, without exhaustively searching the space. Therefore, heuristic methods do not guarantee that a solution will be found; they are like rules of thumb that make it possible to begin to attack a problem. In chess, one possible heuristic to use in choosing a move is to determine if the move helps you to control the center of the board, because, all other things being equal, a move that results in control of the center is better than one that does not.

Based on the study of move problems, Newell and Simon concluded that there might be a relatively small number of heuristics used in many different problems. Newell and Simon developed several computer models of problem solving that incorporated heuristics, with the most ambitious of these models being the General Problem Solver (GPS). This computer program could solve several different sorts of move problems by searching the problem space, using any of several heuristics that were stored in its memory. One heuristic

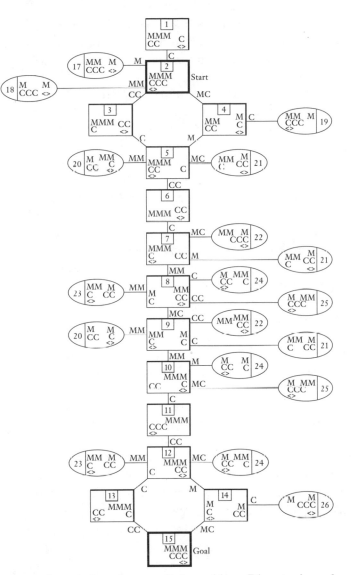

Problem space for missionaries-cannibals problem. Diagram is read as follows: The Ms in each box represent the missionaries on the left-hand and right hand banks of the river, and the Cs represent the cannibals. The symbol <:> represents the boat. Thus, in state 2, there are three missionaries, three cannibals, and the boat on the left bank; in state 21 there are two missionaries and one cannibal on the left bank, and the boat is on the other bank. The letters on the lines between states represent the move made in changing from one state to another. So, for example, from state 2 to state 3, two cannibals are moved. From R. W. Weisberg (1980) Memory, Thought, and Behavior, Oxford University Press, New York.

method incorporated in GPS is to work backward from the goal state rather than forward from the initial state. Another is to break the problem into smaller problems, attempt to solve those separately, and then combine the solutions.

This viewpoint was also applied to creative thinking by theorists who argued that creative thinking was searching a problem space, and the creative thinker could be viewed as someone who knew "better ways of searching." However, more recent work has raised questions about the usefulness of general heuristic methods in solving problems. Effective problem solving in domains that are rich in information, such as chess, physics, and medical diagnosis, depends on possession of deep knowledge or expertise in the domain. Most move problems, such as Missionaries and Cannibals, are not rich in information, and there is therefore usually nothing specific that subjects will know about them. As an example, we are told nothing about the characteristics of the missionaries and cannibals in the problem of that name; indeed, we could solve the same problem with any two classes of participants, so long as it were impossible to have one class outnumber the other. This means that problem solvers facing a move problem must rely on very general knowledge about solving problems, such as not to follow a move with its opposite because that cancels out the first move.

Thus, solutions to move problems may come about in ways different from solutions to problems in domains in which problem solvers have expertise. Furthermore, as we saw in the case studies discussed in Chapter 1, expertise is relevant to creative work in a variety of domains. In this chapter, I shall therefore concentrate on problem-solving situations in which the individual's knowledge plays an important role.

Creative Problem Solving

The candle problem requires that the subject attach the candle to the wall using only the objects available in the picture. (It is assumed that the wall is penetrable.) This problem, first studied by Karl Duncker, provides information about how thinkers use their knowledge to solve novel problems, and how one can go beyond what one has done in the past. In the first of a series of studies using the candle problem, Jerry Suls and I asked individuals to mentally solve the problem with-

The candle problem.

out actually manipulating the objects, and, to the extent that they could, to think aloud while working on the problem. This produces a record of the subject's verbalized thoughts, or a *problem-solving protocol*.

In response to the problem instructions, all subjects started by attempting to attach a candle directly to the wall. A large majority proposed using the nails; the others said that they would start with wax as glue. These responses derive relatively directly from the subjects' knowledge combined with what the problem asks them to do: since the candle is to be attached to the wall, people attempt to use their knowledge about how things can be attached to walls. Although these initial solutions are based on continuity of thought, they go beyond what most individuals have done in the past (most of us have not attached candles to walls or to other vertical surfaces). Thus, even with a simple laboratory problem, we immediately face the question of how we can go beyond what we know.

Although most of us have not done exactly what this problem requires, many have some knowledge that is relevant. Experience using melted wax as glue to get a candle to stand in a candlestick or on a tabletop can be useful in solving the problem, because it involves attaching a candle to a horizontal surface, and the candle problem asks that the object be attached to a vertical surface. If one ignores "vertical" versus "horizontal," the two situations are the same, i.e., "attach candle to surface." Therefore, in this case, the problem solver would think of trying to "glue" the candle to the wall. Based on a match between the problem and the individual's knowledge, a solution may come to mind. In the unlikely event that there is no match between the problem and the individual's knowledge, he or she may simply give up without attempting anything.

In the examples just discussed, solutions were brought to mind as the result of what is called "analogical transfer" in problem solving. Attaching a candle to a vertical surface and attaching one to a horizontal surface are analogous situations, since they have the same structure (attaching a candle to a surface), which means that information from the already familiar situation can be retrieved when the problem is presented, and can then be *transferred* to the problem, to serve as the basis for behavior. We saw in Chapter 1 an example of analogical thinking in Calder's construction of mechanical goldfish bowls after his exposure to mechanical birds in cages. In that instance, Calder's exposure to one type of mechanized animal in a cage stimulated him to construct mechanized sculpture of another animal in its "cage."

Transfer based on analogy depends on the similarity between two situations, and it therefore does not involve an explicit reasoning process; presentation of the problem retrieves the past situation from memory, much like attending a baseball game may remind one of an earlier game. This does not mean that the thought processes underlying the transfer are mysterious; they simply are based on *analogical* thinking, not on *logical* thinking, with its explicit series of steps leading from premises to a conclusion.

The use of analogical thought in problem solving has important implications for our understanding of creative thinking. If one were to ask the problem solver why he or she thought to use the wax as glue, say, the response might be that the thought simply popped into mind, intuitively. The thinker might be tempted to assume that if a solution came to mind suddenly, with no logical reasoning involved, it must have been brought about by unconscious thought processes, but that does not follow. The lack of explicit steps of logical reasoning only supports the conclusion that logical reasoning was not involved; it provides no direct evidence for unconscious or any other processes. Furthermore, analogical thinking explains retrieval of a solution without assuming that either logical thinking or unconscious thought processes were involved. Analogical thinking is not unconscious, since the thinker is obviously conscious when it is carried out and it does not use "primary-process" associations, but it does not utilize a string of explicit steps that can be reported.

Analogical transfer results in retrieval of a potential solution, which is followed by the attempt to carry it out in imagination, which may result in recognition that the proposed solution will not work. In the candle problem, some subjects contemplate attaching the candle with fasteners, but then reject it because they conclude that the fasteners will not pass through the candle without its breaking. This necessitates an attempt to resolve mentally the just-discovered difficulty in the solution. If this mental attempt at repair is successful, the solution can actually be tried. Of course, unanticipated difficulties may arise during the actual solution process, which then will have to be dealt with.

This mental and physical effort depends upon detailed knowledge about objects and what can be done with them. We know, for example, that to use a fastener to attach some object to a wall, the object must be soft enough to allow the fastener to pass into it; the fastener must be significantly longer than the object is thick, and so on. When one begins to contemplate all the details involved in even so simple an operation, the wealth and depth of human knowledge begins to make an impression.

Furthermore, this knowledge can be used to go beyond what we may have done in the past. If, for example, a problem solver decides that the candle is too brittle to be attached with a fastener, knowledge about candles can help the individual out of this difficulty: a burning candle becomes soft and pliable. One could therefore make the candle soft with a match, and then a fastener might pass through.

The conclusion that one uses one's knowledge to go beyond the known is contradictory to a basic assumption of the proposals examined in Chapter 2, which is that extraordinary thought processes are necessary to allow the creative thinker to break away from past experience. Human thinking may go beyond past experience by building on the past, rather than by rejecting it. We can go beyond what we have done because our memory processes work so that knowledge becomes applicable beyond the specific situation in which it was acquired. One does not need a perfect match between knowledge and a situation for that knowledge to be retrieved by the situation. Presentation of the candle problem, for example, retrieves information about other dealings with candles because of a partial overlap of information between the problem and the other situations, and for the same reason also retrieves information about attaching "things" to other things.

One solution to the candle problem — using the box from the fasteners as a platform or holder for the candle — comes about through a discontinuity in thought: the problem solver switches from attaching the candle directly to a vertical surface to constructing a shelf for it. This "box" solution is produced infrequently and late, after attempting other solutions. In analysis of the verbal protocols from the candle problem, the box solution did not usually develop out of a simple extension of the subject's knowledge about attaching candles or other objects to surfaces; it was found to develop out of attempts to correct the inadequacies discovered in the initial attaching proposals.

If a subject is not able to deal with an inadequacy through modification of an attempted solution, that can lead to a discontinuity, as any other possible approaches will be considered as alternatives. A subject faced with the problem of a nail's splitting the candle, for example, might decide that attaching the candle is not feasible, and therefore would discard that method. The subject might then try to find something with which to hold up the candle, and the box would serve that purpose. The subjects who provided the following protocols arrived at the box solution in this way, as did the few other subjects in our study who used the box to solve the problem.

> *Subject 1.* "Candle has to burn straight, so if I took a nail and put it through the candle . . . (ten sec) . . . if I took several nails and made a row and set the candle on that. If I took the nails out of the box, nailed the box to the wall . . ."
> *Subject 2.* "Put a nail into the candle so it supports the candle, so as the candle burns it won't fall. But the nail won't go through the candle, so put some nails around the side of the candle to hold it. Use the box . . ."
> *Subject 3.* "Drive a nail through the candle—a long nail. One problem—a long nail might split the candle. Therefore use a thin nail. You might be able to put up some nails next to each other and burn the candle on them. Or put nails into the wall along the sides of the candle. . . . There don't seem to be enough nails large enough so you could. . . . Another way, take the box, etc.

The box solution to the candle problem has been of particular interest to investigators over the years because it seems "more creative" than, and seems to involve going considerably beyond, such typically attempted solutions as trying to "glue" the candle directly to the wall. However, we have seen that the box solution arises as the result of a new search of memory, in response to difficulties in earlier solutions, which means that it comes about in exactly the same way as do all the other solutions to the problem. A change simply occurs in the information available to the subject, as a result of working on the problem, and this new information cues a new solution type.

There is a parallel between the development of the box solution, arising as a result of the problem solver's dissatisfaction with an earlier solution, and Calder's decision to use wind power for his early mobiles (see Chapter 1), which arose from his dissatisfaction with the overly repetitive motion of his early motorized mobiles. In both cases, the discontinuity arose from the individual's critical analysis of the solution to a problem.

Responses to the Charlie problem (stated at the beginning of the chapter), provide more detailed information concerning how discontinuities develop from initial attempts to solve a problem. In our studies of this problem, the solution we were looking for is that Tom, Dan's pet cat, killed Charlie, Dan's pet goldfish, by knocking over the fishbowl, which caused it to shatter, leaving water and pieces of glass on the floor and Charlie to die on the floor of lack of oxygen. To produce this solution, several discontinuities in thought must occur, since the way the problem is presented suggests to subjects that Charlie and Tom are humans and that the pieces of glass and the water come from a broken drinking glass. This analysis is reasonable, since the characters are referred to by human names, and no hint is given that the use of human names in this situation is in any way out of the ordinary.

In our first experiment with the Charlie problem, fifteen college students were given as much time as they needed to solve the problem. They were instructed that they could at any time either propose a possible solution or ask anything they wished about the situation; the only restriction was that their questions be framed so that the experimenter could answer them with yes or no. Under these conditions, the problem proved to be very difficult, with a median solution time of 47 min., and individual subjects taking as much as 59 min. All subjects initially proposed as solutions numerous typical scenarios whereby a human could die. These proposals, like the initial proposals in the candle problem, were continuous with subjects' knowledge, and based on analogical situations with which they were familiar, and which transferred to the new problem.

When the obvious proposals did not produce a solution, subjects began to include some of the specific aspects of the problem situation in their proposed solutions. As one example, they tried to incorporate the water, and asked if Tom drowned Charlie. When these solutions as well were not successful, subjects began in earnest to ask questions about the situation, and this questioning led to discontinuities and ultimately solution to the problem.

There were two, equally good modes of obtaining the Charlie-is-a-fish discontinuity. *One-step* subjects went in one step from their initial belief, that Charlie was human, to Charlie was a fish, without any intervening inferential steps. Analysis of the protocols indicated that two pieces of information were particularly important in this discontinuity: the glass was from a fishbowl and Charlie died of lack of oxygen. Once subjects had acquired both these pieces of information, it became highly likely that they would propose that Charlie was a fish.

Two-step subjects first went in a separate step from Charlie was human to Charlie was not human, and then to Charlie was a fish. Protocol analysis indicated that they had acquired information which was inconsistent with Charlie's being human, but which was not part of any specific solution, and so this led only to the realization that Charlie was not human. One subject, for example, asked if Charlie was very old, in an attempt to determine if he could have died of old age. After a series of questions about Charlie's age, it was discovered that Charlie was probably between one and two years of age, which led the subject to ask if he was an infant. The experimenter responded no, which led the subject to deduce that Charlie must not have been human, although at that point the subject did not know what he was. It was again obvious from the protocols just what information triggered this inference. Two simulated protocols, which capture the essence of these two modes of discontinuity, are presented in the table below.

Example Protocols

Abridged protocol of a subject who produced the one-step "Charlie Is a Fish" discontinuity

Q. Did Charlie die of natural causes?

A. Yes.

Q. Did Charlie die of lack of oxygen?

A. Yes.

Q. Did he choke?

A. No.

Q. I am picturing a house and everything in it. Was it a fish bowl?

A. Yes.

Q. Did Tom knock over the fish bowl?

A. Yes.

Q. Did the fish bowl get knocked over before Charlie fell?

A. No

Q. At the same time?

A. Yes.

Q. I just figured it out—Charlie is a fish.

Abridged protocol of a subject who produced the two-step "Charlie Is Not Human" discontinuity

Q. Did Charlie die of lack of oxygen?

A. Yes.

Q. Would his age have something to do with it?

A. Why?

Q. If he was old, perhaps when he had fallen, he might have suffocated on his own.

A. No.

Q. Was he young?

A. Yes.

Q. Was he about one year old?

A. Yes.

Q. Ok, we have established that Charlie was an infant.

A. Charlie was not an infant, but he was young.

Q. He is not a baby or an infant?

A. No.

Q. And he was one year old. He was a man or human, wasn't he?

A. No.

Q. A cat?

A. No.

Q. A fish?

Giving new subjects the information that Charlie died of lack of oxygen and that the glass was from a fishbowl should bring about the one-step discontinuity. We tested this prediction using a modified version of the problem.

THE CHARLIE PROBLEM: ONE-STEP VERSION

Dan comes home from work and finds Charlie lying dead on the floor. On the floor are some broken glass and some water. The broken glass is from a fishbowl and Charlie died from lack of oxygen. Tom is also in the room. Dan takes one look around and immediately knows how Charlie died. How did Charlie die from lack of oxygen?

Subjects took 9 min. to solve the one-step version, compared to 47 min. in the first experiment, and fourteen of the fifteen subjects in this experiment produced the one-step discontinuity, compared with only six of fifteen subjects in the first experiment, a significant increase.

In another experiment, subjects were given information which eliminated the entire class of scenarios involving humans, to produce the two-step discontinuity. Each of seventeen new subjects was tested individually with one of two protocols, one of which is shown in the table.

The subjects were first given the original version of the problem, and then one question/answer pair at a time, and were instructed to think along with the subject in the hypothetical protocol, and to suggest a solution or make any comment at any point in the protocol. Almost all of the subjects (15/17) produced two-step solutions, and none produced the one-step solution.

Implications

Presentation of a problem initiates a search of memory for relevant information, which results in the retrieval of possible solutions, based

Example Protocol to Produce the Two-Step Discontinuity in Thought that Charlie is Not Human

1. Q. Was Charlie a perfectly normal human being?
   A. No.
2. Q. Was he mentally disturbed?
   A. No.
3. Q. Was Charlie physically handicapped?
   A. No.
4. Q. Was Charlie retarded?
   A. No.
5. Q. Charlie was not a normal human being. Was he malformed?
   A. No.
6. Q. Was Charlie very smart?
   A. No.

on continuity of thought, that is, the match between the problem and the person's knowledge. This match is often based on analogical relationships between the problem and information already in memory. Assuming that this initial solution proposal is unsuccessful, the newly discovered inadequacy and any still-relevant information from the problem serve once more to retrieve information from memory, which may result in an attempt to modify the initial solution.

Discontinuities from the initial mode of solution are brought about by pieces of information that problem solvers acquire as they work through the problem. This new information triggers new memory searches, which then result in changes in the way the individual approaches the problem. Two types of discontinuities were found: one in which new information itself retrieved a new solution type, and a second which resulted in rejection of the initial mode of solution, without a replacement at that moment. At this point, the subject recycled the now-modified problem through memory to determine if there were any other possible solutions. We were able to produce these types of discontinuities by providing the problem solver with specific pieces of information.

The study of these problems indicates that problem solvers do not make leaps away from the information that they have acquired. New information can trigger what looks like a "leap," but the leap is a function of the new information that is now directing memory search. The finding that retrieval of possible solution types is often based on analogical similarities is supported by recent research that has examined analogical transfer in problem solving. Second, if the initial solutions proposed to a problem, and any subsequent modifications to them, are based on detailed knowledge about the objects in question and what one can do with them, then the more one knows about some domain, the better one should solve problems within that domain. The role of expertise in problem solving has also been supported by recent research.

Analogical Transfer in Problem Solving

Many anecdotal reports have emphasized the role of analogies in creative thinking. An example of this is Friedrich August von Kekulé's report of his discovery, in a dream of whirling snakes, of the structure of benzene — the organic chemical compound made up of a ring of six carbon atoms. He reported the dream in the following words many years after it took place, in a speech at a dinner commemorating his discovery.

> I turned my chair to the fire [after having worked on the problem for some time] and dozed. Again the atoms were gamboling before my eyes. This time the smaller groups kept modestly to the background. My mental eye, rendered more acute by repeated vision of this kind, could now distinguish larger structures, of manifold conformation; long rows, sometimes more closely fitted together; all twining and twisting in snakelike motion. But look! What was that? One of the snakes had seized hold of its own tail, and the form whirled mockingly before my eyes. As if by a flash of lightning I awoke. . . . Let us learn to dream, gentlemen.

Arthur Koestler called this incident "probably the most important dream in history since Joseph's seven fat and seven lean cows". It is of interest to students of creativity for two reasons, first, because of the nonconscious state in which it is alleged to have occurred; second, because of the novel "remote" analogy that Kekulé used. A connection between snakes and atoms had not been made before in the scientific literature, by Kekulé or anyone else, and there is no obvious similarity between snakes and atoms. And yet, in his thought, Kekulé used one to stand for the other. This is basically different from the uses of analogy seen in the candle problem; in that case, the analogies were not remote, since subjects used knowledge about attaching things in order to attempt to attach the candle. This could be called a "near" analogy, or one from the same domain as the problem.

Given the purported importance of remote analogies in creative thinking, there have been a number of laboratory studies of analogical transfer, in which one first provides problem solvers with information, called the "base" analogue, that can be useful in solving some "target" problem. The base analogue and target problem share the same underlying structure, although they may be very different as regards "surface" details, that is, the objects involved. One then examines how easily problem solvers make use of the base information. A number of investigations of analogical transfer have used the radiation problem as the target.

THE RADIATION PROBLEM

Suppose you are a doctor faced with a patient who has a
malignant inoperable tumor in his stomach. Unless the tumor
is destroyed the patient will die. There is a kind of ray that
can be used to destroy the tumor. If the rays are directed at
the tumor at a sufficiently high intensity the tumor will be
destroyed. Unfortunately, at this intensity the healthy tissue
that the rays pass through on the way to the tumor will also
be destroyed, which will kill the patient. At lower intensities
the rays are harmless to the healthy tissue but they will not
affect the tumor either. What type of procedure might be
used to destroy the tumor with the rays, and at the same time
avoid destroying the healthy tissue?

Consider the following two situations — one concerning a general and the other, Red Adair — which are analogous to each other. In
both situations, the individual must provide a force of sufficient intensity (the army or the fire-fighting foam) at one specific point (the
fortress or the fire). The goals are achieved by using a "simultaneous
convergence" solution: the force is broken into parts, the parts are
sent through the surrounding material, and the entire force is then re-
constituted at the target.

A general was trying to destroy a fortress which was situated at
the center of a country with roads leading in to it, by using his
army. He needed to use his army as a complete group in order
to destroy the fortress. However, he could not march his army
down a road to the fortress because the roads were mined to
explode when large groups of men passed over them.
    After considerable thought he knew just what to do. He
divided his army into small groups of men, and, by sending
these groups simultaneously from a number of different
directions, they converged on the fortress, making up a
sufficiently powerful army to destroy it.

Red Adair was called upon to fight an oil-well fire on a
platform in the middle of the Gulf of Mexico. When he
helicoptered in, he found the fire raging, and a plentiful supply
of fire-retarding foam in a tank. He knew that if he could get a
lot of foam on the fire at once, he could put it out. However,

he did not have a hose big enough to provide enough foam. Based on his experience, he knew what to do. He took several small hoses, and hooked them up to the foam tank. He then had these hoses all trained on the fire, and he turned them on at the same time. The total amount of foam reaching the fire at once from the combined action of the hoses was enough to put it out.

These situations are also analogous to the radiation problem, and the simultaneous convergence solution is used to solve that problem as well. The solution to the radiation problem is to take two weak beams of rays and direct them at the tumor from different angles, so that they converge at the tumor, and summate there to sufficient intensity to destroy the tumor.

Students of analogical transfer postulate several steps in using a base analogue to solve a target problem. The base analogue must first be *stored* in memory, and *retained* so that it is potentially retrievable. When the target is presented, the problem solver first attempts a solution, the initial step of which is constructing a *representation* of the problem, which means interpreting the instructions and elements in the problem, and determining what must be done. The next step, as we have seen, is *retrieval* of information from memory. Here, one important question is what factors determine whether the base analogue is spontaneously retrieved ("Say, this problem reminds me of . . ."), which means that no outside direction is given to the problem solver; nothing is said explicitly or implicitly about the possible usefulness of the base analogue in solving the target. This is done because in situations involving creative discovery outside the laboratory, in which analogical transfer is assumed to occur, the thinker is given no direction.

Once spontaneous retrieval of a possibly useful base analogy has occurred, the problem solver must then *apply* the base to the target, which requires that he or she *map* the objects and relations from the base analogue to the target so that the solution from the base can be transferred to the target. In trying to solve the radiation problem, if the base analogue were the story about the general's strategy, then the problem solver would have to make explicit the correspondence between the tumor and the fortress, the rays and the army, and so forth. The solution to the analogue (simultaneous converging of small groups of soldiers at the fortress) would then serve to guide the construction of the solution to the target (simultaneously converging weak beams of the rays at the tumor).

Researchers have investigated the factors that influence spontaneous retrieval of the base analogue by the target problem. If the target and the base have no elements in common, as is the case with the radiation problem and its analogues, then retrieval can only be through their common abstract structure. Thus, studies of analogical transfer have relevance to the question of the abstractness of thought during problem solving. In addition to theoretical interest in understanding creative problem solving, research on transfer also has direct educational applications, since the educational process can be looked upon as an attempt to maximize transfer from one situation (the classroom) to other situations ("real life").

In a pioneering set of studies, Mary Gick and Keith Holyoak used the radiation problem as the target and gave transfer subjects prior experience with base analogues — such as the one concerning the general's strategy — while control subjects were not given exposure to the base analogue. Gick and Holyoak first investigated spontaneous transfer using a single base analogue and found very little. However, when the transfer subjects were given a hint that the base analogue could help solve the target problem, most of them solved it, which indicates that the difficulty was in spontaneously retrieving the base analogue, not in applying it to the target. This lack of spontaneous transfer indicates that people do not automatically process information at a very abstract level. Assume that subjects have stored in abstract form the results of their encounter with the base analogue, something like "If you need to overcome some obstacle, but you cannot use your force at full intensity, then divide the force and unite the separate parts at the obstacle." If the target problem was then analyzed at a similarly abstract level when the subject ran into difficulty, something like "I have an obstacle I have to overcome, but I cannot apply my force at full strength. How can I solve my problem?" the target would then retrieve the analogue, and positive transfer should occur. The fact that such transfer did not occur indicates that subjects did not spontaneously analyze at an abstract level either the base story or the target or both.

Gick and Holyoak hypothesized that abstract analysis of a base analogue was necessary for transfer, because only in this way would the base information be in a form that would be retrievable by the target. The subjects would need to form an abstract "schema," or general description of the base analogue, as outlined above: if you cannot apply a needed force at full value, then try to break up the force and simultaneously apply the weaker forces to the target. Since the target radiation problem also fits this schema, its presentation might retrieve the schema and produce transfer.

In order ensure production of an abstract solution schema, Gick and Holyoak in another experiment gave transfer subjects two base analogues, the General and Red Adair, and asked them to summarize how the stories were similar to each other in structure, especially as regards the problems facing the protagonists and how the problems were overcome. This resulted in each subject's producing a written schema that described the structure of the base analogues. With two base analogues and the schema description, some spontaneous transfer was seen, although it was not nearly complete: 45 percent of the transfer subjects solved the radiation problem, compared to 10 percent of the controls. Still more transfer was produced by giving subjects a hint to use the two analogues to solve the target, indicating again that there had been some retrieval failures. Gick and Holyoak also analyzed the quality of the schemas produced by their individual subjects, and found that those subjects who produced the most complete schemas also produced the most spontaneous transfer, which also supports the notion that formulating the abstract schema is sufficient to bring about remote transfer.

There is one potential difficulty in interpreting Gick and Holyoak's studies, because the base stories and the target were presented in one session, closely in time, by a single experimenter. There is the possibility that the subjects may have been trying to figure out why they were given two tasks to do in the same session, which may have led them to try to relate the stories to the radiation problem, which led to positive transfer. According to this interpretation, overlap of context, rather than analogical thinking, is the primary cause of the solution to the tumor problem brought about by prior exposure to the stories.

In a test of his hypothesis, Mason Spencer and I replicated Gick and Holyoak's study, except that the context was changed from the base analogues to the tumor problem, by having the stories presented at the beginning of a class as part of an experiment, conducted by an experimenter who was a visitor unknown to the students. After the visitor left, the instructor presented the target radiation problem as part of a class discussion of problem solving, without making any mention of a relation between the base analogues and the target. No transfer was found, even for subjects who had formed adequate schemas as the result of their exposure to the stories, unless subjects were explicitly informed of the relation between the base analogues and the target. The results provided no support for the idea that remote analogical transfer will occur once subjects formulate the abstract schema for the base analogues. Richard Catrambone and Keith Holyoak and Mark Keane have reported very similar results.

Keane carried out a further study of analogical transfer in which the context was changed, and he also varied the similarity between objects in the base analogue and the target radiation problem. The two base analogues used by Keane were the general's story and a medical story involving a patient with an inoperable brain tumor. There was no spontaneous transfer from the general's story alone, but 88 percent of the subjects who studied only the brain-tumor base analogue solved the radiation problem, indicating that spontaneous transfer can occur from only a single analogue — even when the context is changed — if the base and the target problem contain identical elements (destruction of *tumors* with simultaneously converging bundles of *rays*). In still another experiment, Keane found that absolute identity of elements in the critical material and target problem is not needed — similar elements are enough.

Another demonstration of positive transfer across contexts was carried out by Keith Holyoak and Kyunghee Koh, who, in a reversal of the usual procedure, used as their target problem the lightbulb problem and used the radiation problem as the base analogue.

THE LIGHTBULB PROBLEM

In a physics lab at a major university, a very expensive lightbulb that would emit precisely controlled quantities of light was being used in some experiments. Ruth was the research assistant responsible for operating the sensitive lightbulb. One morning she came into the lab and found to her dismay that the lightbulb no longer worked. She realized that she had forgotten to turn it off the previous night. As a result the lightbulb overheated, and the filament inside the bulb had broken into two parts. The surrounding glass bulb was completely sealed, so there was no way to open it. Ruth knew that the lightbulb could be repaired if a brief, high intensity laser beam could be used to fuse the two parts of the filament into one. Furthermore the lab had the necessary equipment to do the job.

However, a high-intensity laser beam would also break the fragile glass surrounding the filament. At lower intensities, the laser would not break the glass, but neither would it fuse the filament. How could she use the laser to repair the filament without breaking the bulb?

(Solution: Use two weak lasers and combine them just at the filament.)

As in Keane's experiment, spontaneous transfer was obtained with a single base analogue, and again there was similarity between the base and the target — the lightbulb involves use of lasers, and the radiation problem involves use of rays.

One might be tempted to dismiss these demonstrations of transfer as trivial, since the base and target were so similar. However, it is significant that the two situations had to be made so similar in order to obtain spontaneous transfer, especially when contrasted with the studies that have found no transfer with base analogues that do not have objects in common with the target. In addition, these studies of Keane and of Holyoak and Koh are particularly important because the context was changed between the presentation of the base analogue and the target. This is not always done, and if it is not, then no conclusions can be drawn about the role of analogical structure in spontaneous transfer, because any transfer could be brought about by the context, with the analogical structure playing no part.

The importance of similar objects, or "surface features," in transfer has been demonstrated in a series of studies by Brian Ross, who has examined the learning of statistics by undergraduates. There was no attempt to control context in these studies, since Ross was investigating the factors that influence transfer in educational situations, in which one is trying to teach something to a student, so one hopes that they will use previously-presented material.

Ross provided a worked-out example for each statistical formula that the students were to learn. He then examined whether the students were able to apply the formula to a new target problem. Even though the formulas were presented in abstract terms, surface features of the example problem were found to be important in transfer; when the target problem had a story line and objects in common with an already-studied example problem, the students applied the formula from that example to the target. Furthermore, if the objects were the same as in an earlier example, but their roles were changed in the target problem, the change resulted in large amounts of interference. Thus, not only retrieval but application of an analogue to a new situation are strongly influenced by surface features.

The present analysis has provided little support for the idea that creative thinking is based on the spontaneous use of novel remote analogies. If one assumes that the same thought processes are at work in laboratory problem solving and other examples of creative thinking, this assumption leads to the expectation that analogical transfer in domains such as invention, scientific discovery, and the arts will be based on common surface features in the base analogue and the target — that is, "near" rather than "remote" analogical transfer.

The negative findings from laboratory studies also raise questions specifically about Kekulé's report of his dream of whirling snakes. There is some question about whether he was actually dreaming. In addition, a question can be raised about whether, dream or no dream, he was contemplating snakes. In Kekulé's report of the incident in his address, quoted earlier in this chapter, he used the term "snakelike" to describe the motion of the imagined strings of atoms. This is a strange choice of words to describe the motion of a snake. That is, if Kekulé had been *watching* a snake, then it would have been at least redundant to call its motion snakelike. One only uses such a term to describe the motion of something that is not a snake but whose motion reminds one of the motion of a snake. Thus, perhaps Kekulé was simply imagining strings of atoms, represented in some way, in various configurations, and he used "snakelike" to communicate this to his listeners.

Expertise in Problem Solving

Much recent research in several domains has converged on the conclusion that high-level problem solving is based on detailed and highly structured knowledge, or expertise, within that domain. These results have been shown to have relevance for the understanding of creative thinking in domains not considered to be problem solving, such as musical composition and painting. Interest of cognitive psychologists in the study of expertise was stimulated by Adrian DeGroot's analysis of problem-solving skills of master chess players. DeGroot was investigating the factors that enabled a chess master at any point in a game to choose the best available move. One might think that this comes about because the master is able to examine more possible moves and combinations of moves than are less-skilled players; the master might search more widely and more deeply. That is, if I choose a move as a result of analyzing a few combinations of the form "Well, I could try this move, then he might do that, then I could do this, then he could do that," then the chess master could carry out many more of these possible combinations than I, and do it faster.

DeGroot examined this possibility by having a chess master think aloud during a game as he decided on the next move and, contrary to the expectation that the master searches more widely and deeply than less-skilled players, if anything, the master searched less. At each choice point, the master considered only one or two moves that seemed best, and simply ignored other moves that a less-skilled player would examine. DeGroot found that the crucial difference between the master and less-skilled players was that the master was able to focus on the right move, without much search. DeGroot argued that the master's selection of a move was the result of perception, rather than analysis and decision making. On looking at the board, the master simply "sees" the best move.

How did the correct move become so obvious to the master? Results from a study of chess-players' memory performance provided some answers. DeGroot gave chess players of different levels of skill five seconds to examine a chess board with pieces on it from the middle of a master-level game. The board was then covered and the subjects tried to reconstruct the just-seen position on an empty board. DeGroot found that a master-level player was able to replace all the pieces (approximately thirty pieces) after this brief exposure, while players of less skill were able to reconstruct less.

One might dismiss these results as trivial: chess masters have great memories; that must mean that in order to play great chess, you need to have a great memory. That is not true; chess masters have great memories only for *chess positions*. If you randomly place chess pieces on a board and ask the master to try to recall them, performance will be at ordinary levels. DeGroot concluded from these findings that chess masters perform well in the memory task because they are able to analyze a chess board into meaningful groups of pieces, or "chunks," and these serve as the basis for recall. Where the ordinary individual sees a group of five separate pieces, and thus has five things to recall, the master sees one familiar pattern, and thus has only one thing to recall.

DeGroot theorized that the master's ability to choose the best move is based on the same analytical skill. On examining the board, the master finds familiar patterns, and these lead to retrieval of possible moves that have been successful in analogous situations in the past. These few possible moves then are analyzed in order to deal with the particular situation now being considered, but much of the preliminary work has been done.

DeGroot's results were replicated and extended by William Chase and Herbert Simon, as they tried to analyze in more detail the knowledge possessed by the chess master. In one study, subjects were to construct a chess board to match another visible board, which relieved the subject of the memory burden. The master placed the pieces on the board not singly or as a whole, but in groups of three to seven pieces, defined by the relationships among the pieces, such as a rook, bishop, and pawns of the same color defending one another.

This type of chunking was also found when Chase and Simon analyzed the way the pieces were put on the board during the memory task, and, in accord with DeGroot, the researchers concluded that the same knowledge was being used both in memory and perception. They then estimated how many chunks the chess master must have stored in memory in order to be able to recall perfectly all the pieces after one brief exposure. They concluded that it is something on the order of 50,000 patterns. While this is a large number, it is not out of the range of ordinary human capacity. The average receptive reading vocabulary for college students is more than 20,000 words, which, although smaller than the chess masters' knowledge, is of the same order of magnitude. Furthermore, chess masters do little more than play and study chess, which would provide time to learn those patterns. For example, if a 45-year-old chess master had spent an average of five hours a day playing and studying chess for thirty years, he or she would have to learn only one pattern an hour in order to perform well on DeGroot's memory task.

Expertise in Other Domains

DeGroot's work led to much interest in the study of expertise in other domains, such as physics, computer programming, medical diagnosis, and political problem solving. Results in these areas have supported the conclusions from chess: master-level problem solving depends on the acquisition of domain-specific expertise. Studies comparing problem-solving performances of experts and novices have indicated that experts are able, because of their knowledge, to focus on the important aspects of a novel problem. The expert is able to relate a novel problem to something already known and to use this knowledge as the basis for performance.

Studies of physics professors reveal that they solve problems differently than do undergraduates who have had only an introductory physics course, and these differences may be due to different ways of analyzing problems. The novices examine the elements in the problem and immediately try to set up equations and undertake a solution. The experts, on the other hand, first analyze the problem and determine what physics principles it embodies (e.g., Newton's second law, or conservation of energy). Only then do the experts begin to set up equations and move to actually solve the problem. Quantitative solution attempts, in other words, only occur after extensive qualitative analysis of the problem, based on detailed domain-specific knowledge about physics principles and how they are embodied in problems.

Michelene Chi, P. J. Feltovich, and Robert Glaser asked eight advanced graduate students in physics and eight undergraduates who had just completed their first physics course to sort a set of twenty-four physics problems into groups based on how they would solve them. The novices tended to group together those problems that were similar on the "surface," that is, that had similar objects, such as inclined planes, or springs; or the problems were grouped on the basis of similar physical terms, such as "friction."

The groups set up by the relative experts, on the other hand, were not similar on the surface; rather, they were structured around the underlying physical laws applicable to the problems. Since these laws are not usually mentioned in the problems, the subjects must have done an analysis of their underlying structure.

A particularly interesting set of studies on expertise, carried out by Allen Lesgold and his colleagues, has examined the development of skill in X-ray diagnosis, using as subjects experienced radiologists and medical residents with differing degrees of expertise in radiology. Lesgold and his colleagues estimate that their experts had examined between 10,000 – 200,000 X-rays in their clinical practices. The basic research procedure was to first present a to-be-analyzed X-ray for a brief (2-second) exposure, and to have the subject describe aloud anything that was seen. Subjects were then given unlimited time to examine the X-ray, again thinking aloud, and were asked to make a formal diagnosis, as would be done in their offices.

The experts first quickly attempted to determine the type of problem that the X-ray presented, and then searched for additional information to confirm or reject that initial diagnosis. The experts had available many possible diagnoses, based on their extensive knowledge, and relatively easily switched from an initial diagnosis to another that better fit the information on the film. The residents, on the other hand, took longer to establish an initial diagnosis and were more reluctant to give it up. The residents often shaped what they saw on the film to fit their already-made diagnosis, while the expert's diagnosis was shaped by what was on the film.

Creativity and Expertise

These conclusions have direct relevance to understanding creativity. As James Greeno notes, at one time researchers made a distinction between "problem solving" and "productive thinking," with the former referring disparagingly to a situation in which one's behavior was based on prior knowledge, and the latter referring to a situation in which one went beyond one's experience and knowledge, to produce something truly new. (This issue was discussed in the section on insight in Chapter 2.) However, at least partly as a result of research on expertise, there has recently been a blurring of this distinction, as it has been realized that all problem solving is based on knowledge. Furthermore, because solutions to novel problems require creative thinking, then creative thinking in other domains, such as the arts, may also depend on extensive knowledge in those domains, as we will see in Chapter 7.

Soar: A Computer Model of Problem Solving

Allen Newell, one of the leaders in the analysis of problem solving as search in problem spaces, as discussed at the beginning of the chapter, has recently proposed a computer model of human cognition, called Soar, which is based on the notion that the crucial element in solving problems is, in addition to searching a problem space, switching from one problem space to another when the initial choice is not fruitful. The model is a computer program able to solve several types of well-defined problems by first searching its memory to find a problem space that can be applied to the problem. It then searches the space until it finds a solution to the problem, or until it reaches an impasse. Soar then attempts to resolve the impasse by searching memory to find another problem space that can be applied to the problem.

This process also produces learning, or the development of domain-specific expertise, which works by "chunking." The model also shows transfer. Assume that the elements A, B, and C in some problem space lead to an impasse that must be resolved, and that Soar is successful in finding operators in a new space that resolve the impasse. These elements are then stored in memory along with the operators that were successful. When any new situation is encountered which contains elements A, B, and C, the same operators will be carried out, so that no impasse will occur. This mechanism of transfer is similar to the "identical elements" notion proposed by E. L. Thorndike many years ago. Thorndike believed that in order for transfer to occur, a new situation had to have elements in common with the old.

The analysis of problem solving embodied in Soar seems to be relevant at a general level to many of the problem-solving situations discussed in this chapter. In the candle problem, subjects begin by "searching the attaching space," and feedback can then lead to switching to a new space. In the Charlie problem, the "human murder space" is searched initially, and feedback results in a switch to a new space. The research on expert X-ray diagnosis also follows this pattern: presentation of an X-ray results in the radiologist considering one possible diagnosis (searching one particular space), and further examination may then add more evidence for this diagnosis or trigger a switch to another possible diagnosis (switching to another space). In this connection, Soar explains discontinuity in thinking through the mechanism of switching problem spaces.

However, on a more specific level, there are a number of questions concerning how well the processes in Soar describe human functioning. The first issue is: how does presentation of a problem result in selection of an initial problem space? The evidence from the problem-solving literature has pointed to analogy as the basis for this selection, and at this point Soar simply has the problem spaces made available in its memory by the programmer, rather than through the model in some way selecting the problem space.

The second issue is: What if transfer does not occur in our thinking the way it does in Soar? In the candle problem, we saw that attaching solutions come about because of the partial overlap between the problem and previous attaching experience; that is, the *candle* can be attached to the wall because the subject has previous experience attaching *things* to walls. In Newell's terms, if the candle problem is schematized as containing elements A, B, and C, then retrieving an attaching solution is based in elements A + B, while attempting to use wax as glue might be based on A + C. That is, human thought may be more flexible than Soar postulates, in that humans are able to use as the basis for transfer a subset of the original elements, while Soar may be dependent on the presence of all of the original elements.

Related to this issue is the possibility that Soar would — without difficulty — exhibit remote analogical transfer across contexts, which we have seen is difficult for humans to do. Because Soar transfers on the basis of identical elements in the problem situation, if these elements are present, remote transfer across contexts will be found, even though that does not occur with humans. This raises a problem for the Soar model, since it has been proposed as a theory of human cognition. Therefore, it seems that Soar's performance may be at once both too narrow and too broad, although these specific issues have not yet been examined in research, and these conclusions are therefore speculative.

Another interesting issue raised by the Soar model centers on the idea that switching problem spaces is the basic mechanism whereby discontinuity in thought occurs. We have seen evidence in this chapter that problem solvers construct new spaces as they work through a problem. For example, when a subject working on the Charlie problem determines that Charlie is not human, he or she may then have to rethink the problem in a way not done by Soar, which has the problem spaces set in memory before it begins to work on a problem. Similarly, when Calder discovered Mondrian's abstractly decorated studio (see Chapter 1), it opened for him a whole new "problem space," that of abstraction, which may not have existed for him before that. That is, Calder may not have contemplated the production of abstract work until he visited Mondrian's studio. If so, then there was no "space" to be searched: Calder had to construct one.

Domain-specific Expertise and the Teaching of Problem Solving

The above discussion has emphasized domain-specific expertise, and this represents a movement away from the view discussed at the beginning of the chapter that problem solving depends on domain-independent heuristics. As we have seen, one difficulty for the general heuristics view came from studies of problem solving in informationally-rich domains — chess, physics, and medical diagnosis — in which problem solving is directed by large amounts of domain-specific expertise. Even "creative" domains, many theorists believe, require expertise, which raises questions about the role of general heuristic search methods in creative thinking.

These conclusions have important educational implications. There has recently been much interest among educators and psychologists in teaching "critical thinking" as part of the school curriculum, and one of the components of critical thinking is problem solving. Peter Polson and Robin Jeffries reviewed several training programs, including one developed by deBono, and concluded that the programs run aground on the issue of domain-specific expertise versus generalized transfer. These programs often take for granted — as the basis for improvement in thinking — the occurrence of spontaneous, remote, analogical transfer. In these programs, general rules or methods of solving problems are presented using one or a few example problems, and it is assumed that presentation of a novel target problem that is a remote analogue of one of the training problems will result in spontaneous transfer and retrieval of the appropriate method.

Based on the studies reviewed earlier in this chapter, which have found no evidence for remote analogical transfer to the radiation problem without overlap of surface information, it would be expected that little or no transfer will occur unless many specific examples are presented during training to increase the possibility that one of them has at least some surface elements in common with the target problem. If this lack of remote transfer can be extrapolated to genuine experts in any domain, it may mean that expertise, rather than being based on development of general rules, is based on the accumulation of knowledge about a large number of specific problems. Thus, the expert would have a data base large enough to almost always have available in memory a base analogue to retrieve because it has surface similarities to the target.

It is interesting to contemplate whether a radiologist who has examined tens of thousands of chest films even has to go beyond his or her data base to analyze a new film. The data base in question may be so large that every "new" chest film turns out to be related to some old one. This may mean that when one accumulates extremely large amoungs of expertise in a domain that is relatively circumscribed (i.e., chest films), one may not need to go beyond what one knows. The experienced radiologists studied by Lesgold and associates may be the paradigm case of subjects solving problems by switching among problem spaces as postulated by Newell in Soar. The generality of this finding is an important question, and the answer will become more clear as the case studies are examined.

Douglas Hintzman has presented a model of memory which assumes that information is stored only as specific experiences. He has shown that such a model can deal with the acquisition and use of "abstract" concepts, even though abstract information is not stored in memory from the experiences. This perspective might also be relevant to the acquisition of expertise within the problem-solving domains studied by cognitive psychologists. The experts may have acquired a broad data base of potentially useful base analogues, rather than a set of general rules that describe the domain. This conclusion has important implications for teaching, because it means that one should not try to teach general rules alone, but should rather provide within the domain as wide a data base as possible. Providing the general rules as well may provide additional assistance, but the specific base analogues must be the basis on which any rules are built.

In an analysis of several difficulties that arise in the teaching of thinking skills, John Hayes has also raised questions about the advisability of teaching general problem solving skills. The first difficulty pointed out by Hayes is that general thinking skills may be based on large bodies of knowledge, which would take very long to learn. That is, if general skills are to be truly general, then they must encompass many examples, which the thinker could only encounter over long periods of time. Second, even if general skills can be taught, there may be a very large number of such skills to teach. Hayes teaches a course on increasing skills in learning, reasoning, and problem solving; he analyzed his course materials and found that he covers at least fifty different thinking strategies. Furthermore, when one considers that other individuals teaching the course would include at least some different strategies, there may be a very large number of thinking skills to be taught.

Finally, even after students are taught a useful thinking skill, there still is the problem of transfer. Hayes teaches at Carnegie-Mellon University, where the students are of high caliber, and even there one finds problems with lack of transfer. A statistics teacher reported to Hayes that a statistics principle taught using distance as a measure did not transfer to a test problem involving time, for example. Hayes suggests that to increase transfer we should be aware of the potential difficulties students will face. When a teacher wishes to get transfer across domains, one should be prepared to give an example of the principle in each domain, that is, one should not expect spontaneous remote transfer. This, then, may mean that general skills are not actually being taught.

These conclusions do not provide much encouragement for those who would teach general thinking skills. It is interesting to compare this view with that underlying the programs that attempt to increase creative thinking (see Chapter 2), where strategies are sometimes very general, such as "question your assumptions," "try to break set," and "try to think of a useful analogy."

Conclusions

Problem solving begins with continuity, a match between the problem and the individual's knowledge, which can result in the retrieval of a possible solution. Effective problem solving requires detailed knowledge in the domain in question, and there is little evidence for spontaneous transfer based on remote analogies. Surface elements play an important role in determining what information from memory is retrieved as potentially relevant to the target problem and how this information is used to construct a possible solution. Any possible solution is then adapted to the problem, which can result in failure and feedback that initiates a new memory search that produces a new solution, and so on. Discontinuities are produced when the new information triggers a switch in solution mode.

These conclusions will serve as reference points in the analyses of the case studies presented in the next several chapters, which raise the question of how generally the notion of problem solving can be applied to creative-thinking situations. Many situations in which humans exhibit creative thinking can be considered problems, although they are not always problems in the formal sense of having been set for the thinker by some other individual, although that sometimes does occur. This is clearly seen in invention, when one talks of the Wright brothers solving the problem of designing a heavier-than-air machine that would fly. In science too, a number of well-known discoveries can be considered solutions to problems. One example is Watson and Crick's development of the double helix of DNA — a solution to the problem of specifying the structure of DNA. A second is Darwin's developing the theory of evolution through natural selection, or his solving the problem of explaining the evolution of species. Again, in both these cases, the problems had been formulated by earlier generations of thinkers.

In the arts as well, one can talk of an artist carrying out the task of solving a problem, as when one says that Coleridge solved the problem of writing a poem about Kubla Khan. However, in this case there is not the formal aspect of a problem being presented by an agent outside the thinker, since Coleridge's "problem" came out of himself.

This issue will be examined more closely as we consider the case studies in the chapters to follow. One question in those chapters will be, how much of the thinking in each domain can be explained by assuming that the individuals were solving problems?

CHAPTER 5

Invention: Case Studies

Watt's separate condenser and his double-acting rotative steam engine, which proved so versatile in application, were undoubtedly the greatest advance in mechanical engineering of the late eighteenth century. The new engine was hailed by a world that had forgotten Newcomen as a giant's stride forward on the road to a scientific Utopia and its inventor was lauded as a universal benefactor. So originated the still current popular fallacy that James Watt "invented" the steam engine.

(Rolt & Allen 1977, 12)

This chapter presents the development of three seminal inventions: James Watt's steam engine, Eli Whitney's cotton gin, and the Wright brothers' flying machine. The study of invention is an ideal domain in which to begin analysis of "ordinary" thought processes in "real" creative thinking, since an inventor is usually working to produce a novel device to carry out a specific task. Creative thinking in invention is therefore problem solving, and the conclusions from the last chapter should be easily generalizable here. There should first of all be evidence for continuity of thought: these seminal inventions should be based on work that came before, and the use of earlier work should be the result of "near" transfer. Also, any discontinuities of thought should be traceable to new information arising as the individual works on the invention or to external triggers.

The case studies in this chapter were chosen to provide information of several sorts concerning the relationship of the new product to what was already available. James Watt's steam engine is an example of modification of an already existing engine in order to remedy problems with it. Eli Whitney's cotton gin is an example of invention based on analogical thinking, and will provide evidence whether "real" creative thinking uses more remote analogies than can ordinary thinking. The Wright brothers' invention of the airplane is informative in two different ways. Because there were at that time no already existing airplanes (although there was more information about flight available to the Wright brothers than is generally realized), the Wrights had to work out many specifics, so analysis of this case will provide evidence concerning how creative thinking works when there are no direct antecedents available. The Wrights also provide a graphic example of the role of strong motivation in creative genius.

A Chain of Continuity: The Invention of the Steam Engine

James Watt (1736–1819) is often given credit for inventing the steam engine, and because of its importance in the development of the industrial revolution, he has been according hero's status. A myth has grown from a cousin's story that the young Watt once sat intently watching as steam escaping from the spout of a boiling tea-kettle condensed on a spoon that he held above the spout. This observation supposedly was the trigger for the invention of the steam engine. In actually, Watt's engine was but one in a long line of machines, stretching back many years.

Watt was a scientific-instrument maker by trade, and was appointed instrument maker at the University of Glasgow in 1757. In 1763, he was assigned to repair a model for a lecture demonstration, and thus began the sequence of events that culminated in his seminal invention, not of *the* steam engine, but of the *separate-condenser* steam engine. Watt could not have invented the steam engine in 1763, because steam engines had been in use in England for over sixty years. Watt's assignment was to repair a working model of an engine that had been designed by Thomas Newcomen over forty years earlier to

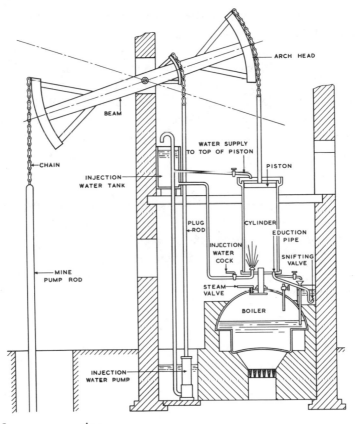

The Newcomen engine.

pump water from coal mines. The Newcomen engine was already well known when Watt was repairing the model, with several hundred in operation in the British Isles.

Newcomen's engine was designed on the principle that steam contracts when it condenses. Its basic operating principle was different from the more modern use of high-pressure steam as a source of power, as in steam locomotives. If steam filling a sealed compartment is condensed by cooling the compartment, a partial vacuum is created. If a piston forms one of the walls of that compartment, and on the other side of the piston is normal atmospheric pressure, the piston will be pushed by the atmospheric pressure toward the side of the partial vacuum, and the movement of the piston can be harnessed to do work. Newcomen's engine is thus technically an "atmospheric" engine rather than a particular type of steam engine, since atmospheric pressure is the motive force. It was not practical at that time to harness high-pressure steam as a source of power, because of difficulties in constructing chambers strong enough to withstand the pressures involved, although its potential had been noted.

Because the parts were poorly constructed, Watt had difficulty getting the model Newcomen engine to work. When he finally had it running, he was surprised at its efficiency: it was constantly running out of coal. He concluded that this was because the constant heating and cooling of the cylinder resulted in a large waste of energy, and he devised a system whereby the cylinder and the condenser were separate.

In Watt's design, the steam was condensed in a separate condensing cylinder, which eliminated the need to constantly cool and reheat the main cylinder, so that it could be insulated to stay hot, thereby saving energy. Watt also made several other improvements to Newcomen's engine, increasing its efficiency and making it practical for use in factories. Thus, Watt's great advance—and great it was, in its long-term economic significance—was an improvement to an already-existing engine.

Watt's engine was not without complications of its own. In order to provide greater efficiency, the parts of Watt's engine had to be made more exactly, by skilled machinists. Thus, its overall construction became very complicated and expensive. Newcomen's engine

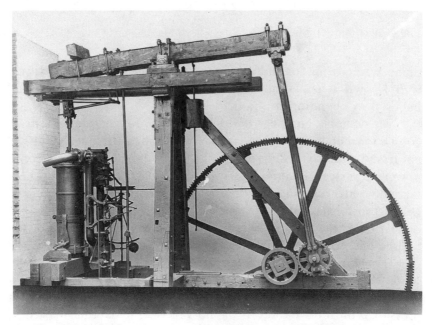

Watt's engine.

could be made without such exacting equipment and tools, which meant that nonprofessionals could make it. Nevertheless, without Watt's great advance, the Newcomen engine was not useful except in very limited circumstances.

If we then consider whether Newcomen invented the steam engine, we are faced with exactly the same issue one generation earlier, and the answer is the same: Newcomen also had antecedents, and those antecedents themselves had antecedents, and so forth. George Basalla notes that historian Joseph Needham, on following the "long chain of direct genetic connections" involved in the development of the steam engine, concluded that no single person, or single culture, was the inventor of the steam engine. Watt's invention is thus a case of continuity of development: he moved beyond what was already available, improving on it but, nonetheless, not developing something from whole cloth.

Watt's engine and the history of its replacement of Newcomen engines in England raise an important point for the understanding of the concept of genius. Because of its higher efficiency, Watt's engine replaced Newcomen's in many areas, except in those coal-mining areas where there was a plentiful supply of cheap coal, where Newcomen's engine was used long after Watt's was available. Designation of Watt as a genius, which was based on his engine's becoming dominant in English industry, thus depended on the relative lack of coal. If coal had been abundant and cheap throughout England, then it might not have been economically advantageous to replace Newcomen engines with Watt engines, and Watt's engine might not have become dominant. If it had become dominant, it would have done so much more slowly, which would have changed the course of history and might have left Watt relegated to a footnote in histories of technology.

As we discussed in Chapter 3, the concept of genius is much more complicated than it first appears. Attributing the label of genius to an individual is not based simply on the characteristics of the individual or of the product he or she produces, but also on the role of the product in the culture, which for the most part is independent of the creator.

Watt's invention in several ways corresponds to the problem-solving situations discussed in Chapter 4. First, the overall situation can reasonably be described as Watt's attempt to solve the problem of getting the model Newcomen engine to work, which then led him to the problem of improving its efficiency. Also, in a parallel to an undergraduate solving a problem posed a psychologist in a laboratory, Watt's original problem was imposed from without. ("Please repair this engine.") Watt's actions in the initial attempt at repairing the Newcomen engine parallel the situation of a subject working on a laboratory problem, producing a solution, and finding that it did not work. This difficulty served as the basis for a reanalysis of the situation and production of a modification of the original solution. One difference between Watt's invention and subjects working on a laboratory problem, however, is that Watt had not proposed the initial solution — the Newcomen engine — but rather was given that engine as a starting point.

Watt's modification of the Newcomen engine to increase its efficiency is an example of what has been called "problem finding," since the inefficiency of that engine and the problem of reducing it had not been directly pointed out to Watt, but rather had been discovered by him in the course of repairing the model. However, it did not take a special sensitivity to note the lack of efficiency in the Newcomen engine, since it was fairly obvious: Watt kept feeding it coal, but it would not run for more than a few strokes before needing more. Watt, furthermore, was by no means the first to be impressed by the inefficiency of Newcomen's engine, nor the first to try to increase its efficiency.

Thus, in this case, problem solving and problem finding do not appear to be based on different processes; the difference is that in one case the problem is imposed from without and in the other it comes out of the problem-solving activities themselves. The critical judgment that Watt used in assessing the inefficiency of the Newcomen engine appears to be the same as he would have used in evaluating a product of his own; nothing new is thus required to understand what happened when he started up the engine and it ran for a few strokes and stopped.

Transfer Based on a Near Analogy: The Cotton Gin

Eli Whitney's invention of the cotton gin in 1793 has an importance in the economic history of the antebellum South comparable to that of Watt's engine in the history of industrial development in England. Because of this, Whitney is afforded a position of eminence like that often given to Watt, although this too is a great oversimplification of the true course of events.

Whitney was born in 1759 in Massachusetts, the son of a farmer. During his childhood he had exhibited mechanical aptitude, and as a boy during the Revolution he had his own business, making nails. After working his way through college by teaching, Whitney arrived in Georgia after graduating in 1792, expecting to fill a teaching position and to study law, but found the position filled. He stayed to study, and became aware of difficulties besetting plantation owners because of the difficulty in profitably growing cotton, largely due to the time required to clean the seeds from the bolls. This task was carried out by slaves, but the work was very slow and uneconomical. In a short time, Whitney had developed a cotton gin that could mechanically remove the seeds from cotton at a rate fifty times faster than by hand. (The name "gin" is a short form of "engine.") The cotton gin worked by having the cotton drawn by a toothed roller through a fine comb-like piece. By cranking the roller, the cotton fibers were drawn through the comb, while the seeds were trapped and left behind. This invention served to make cotton production highly profitable in the South, with wide-ranging economic and social repercussions.

When Whitney arrived in the South there were already cotton gins in use, although they were limited to cleaning long-staple or Sea Island cotton. This is the finest type of cotton, but it is very slow-growing and therefore not economical. For this reason, the plantation owners wanted to grow short-staple cotton, which grew well in the region. Whitney's invention was thus based on an easily available antecedent, and again a change in description is warranted: Whitney did not invent *the* cotton gin, but rather, a gin to clean short-staple cotton.

If we examine the history of the already-extant long-staple gin, we see the same pattern repeated again: it had a long series of antecedents, going back through Italy to ancient India, where cotton had been produced for more than two millennia. For example, an Indian gin or *charka* has several similarities to Whitney's, although they are separated by many years and half the world. The charka uses rollers turned by a crank to squeeze the cotton bolls and to separate fiber from seed, which was not possible with short-fiber cotton. Furthermore, as might be expected, the charka can be traced further back, to Indian sugar-cane presses.

Whitney's cotton gin is thus an example of "near" analogical transfer, as he used the cleaning of long staple cotton as a base analogue in his construction of a machine to clean short-staple cotton. As with Watt, the problem was not formulated by Whitney; it was well-known to anyone connected with the cotton-growing industry.

As in Watt's case in England, Whitney rightly holds a firm place in American industrial history, given the great economic and social importance of his invention. The development of his invention does however raise questions about the cognitive processes usually attributed to inventors when antecedents and continuity are not taken into account. In a further parallel with the case of Watt, if the South had been an area in which it had been possible to grow linen, say, or if it had been easier to remove by hand the seeds from short-stapled cotton, Whitney's invention would not have had wide-ranging effects; it would not have led to a whole stream of new inventions, and Whitney would be a footnote rather than a genius.

> Thus, the significance of an invention cannot be determined
> solely by its technological parameters — it cannot be evaluated
> as if it were a thing unto itself. An invention is classified as
> "great" only if a culture chooses to place a high value upon it.
> Likewise, the reputation of its inventor is tied to cultural
> values. In either of the alternative worlds just described [i.e.,
> linen rather than cotton or very cheap labor], Whitney would
> not be honored as a heroic inventor; he would be ignored or at
> best be looked upon as the eccentric builder of a trivial device.
> (Basalla, 1988, 34)

Creativity with No Antecedents? The Invention of the Airplane

There were no flying machines in existence when the Wright brothers invented theirs, which leads to the question of whether a human can, like God, create something without antecedents. Examination of historical sources indicates that, although there indeed were no successful human-made flying machines, there were a number of relevant sources that the Wrights drew upon.

Interest in the possibility of powered human flight extends back at least to the Greeks, and is seen in the legend of Icarus, who is said to have flown too close to the sun, melting the wax holding feathers to his flapping wings, and sending him crashing into the sea. A distinction should be made here between gliding, in which the apparatus is not able to sustain itself in the air, and powered flight, in which the apparatus itself generates the power to stay airborne; Icarus was thus flying, according to legend, when he had his accident.

By the time of the Renaissance, several people had written about the possibilities of human flight, and there is evidence that more than one person built a glider and attempted to use it. The most famous early example of interest in flight is of course Leonardo da Vinci, who drew some possible flying machines, based on the flapping wings of birds, although there seems to have been no attempt on anyone's part to build and fly them.

By the mideighteenth century, a number of individuals had made attempts at gliding; among them was Sir George Cayley, who has been called "the father of the airplane," although that seems to be an exaggeration. Cayley spent about fifty years involved in various ways with the possibilities of flight, although the sum total of his actual "flying" seems to have been two piloted glides, and Cayley was the pilot for neither.

Interest in the problem of human flight had become relatively intense by the 1890s, with research being carried out on both sides of the Atlantic. The Wright brothers read, in the September 1894 issue of *McClure's Magazine*, "The Flying Man," an article about the experiments of Otto Lilienthal, illustrated with photographs of him gliding while suspended from a pair of batlike wings. Lilienthal, born in 1848, was a German mechanical engineer and businessman who, like most of his predecessors, belived that success would come from imitating the flight of birds. For six years, starting in 1889, he built gliders with wings of various shapes, and tested them himself in over 2,000 glides, the longest of which lasted 12 to 15 seconds.

Lilienthal also published, in the 1897 *Aeronautical Annual*, the last of three annual publications, a table which presented pressures on wings of various sizes under various wind conditions. This could be used to calculate how much wing area was needed to lift a given weight in winds of a given velocity; to determine, for example, what sized wings would be needed to keep aloft a 200-lb. man and a 25-lb. glider in winds averaging 20 m.p.h.

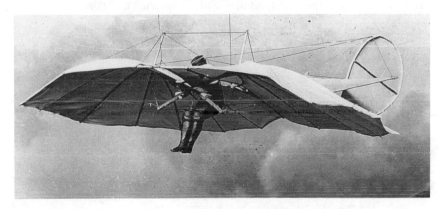

Otto Lilienthal experiments with a glider in 1891.

The Wright Brothers — A Brief Chronology

1867	Wilbur Wright was born in Dayton, Ohio.
1871	Orville Wright was born.
1878	Father gave them toy helicopter.
1880s	Worked with grandfather's tools, built lathe, printing press, etc. Experimentation and making things encouraged.
1887	S. P. Langley began to build and test model airplanes.
1889	Otto Lilienthal built glider and attempted glides.
1890s	Brothers added front and side porches to house, turned posts, built fireplace.
1891	*October.* Octave Chanute began a series of printed articles on attempts to fly.
1892	Wrights opened bicycle shop where they repaired, rented, and sold bikes.
1893	International Conference on Aerial Navigation held in Chicago, chaired by Chanute. Paper presented by Langley.
1894	Chanute's articles printed as *Progress in Flying Machines*.
1895	Wrights began to manufacture bikes from parts made by manufacturers.
	First *Aeronautical Annual* published.
1896	*May 6.* One of Langley's steam-powered pilotless models flew. Further success that day and with another model in November.
	August 10. Lilienthal killed as result of crash of one of his gliders.
	June 22–September 17. Chanute constructed person-carrying glider.
	Second *Aeronautical Annual* published.
1897	*September.* Chanute's assistant, A. M. Herring, made successful glides.
	October 20. Chanute reported on 1896–1897 experiments to meeting of Western Society of Engineers. Detailed accounts of Chanute's experiments appeared in last *Aeronautical Annual*, as did Lilienthal's "Table of normal and tangential pressures."
1899	*May 30.* Wilbur wrote Smithsonian for materials on flight.
	July. Wrights constructed kite-glider; made plans to try out next summer their control system on pilot-carrying glider.
	November 24. Wilbur wrote weather bureau about wind velocities.
1900	*May 13.* Wilbur wrote Chanute about possible locations.
	October 8–9. First flights of glider at Kitty Hawk.
	October 20. A good day of free glides with pilot.
	November 16. Wilbur from Dayton wrote Chanute about results.
1901	*June 26–27.* Chanute visited Dayton.
	July 12. The Wrights arrived at Kill Devil Hills.
	July 27. The first testing of new glider.
	August 4–11. Chanut visited the Wrights.

The Wright Brothers — A Brief Chronology

	September. The Wright brothers returned home.
	September 18. Wilbur — at Chanute's invitation — addressed Western Society of Engineers.
	October. Wind-tunnel experiments.
1902	*August 28.* Wright brothers arrived at Kill Devil Hills.
	September 10. They began flying new glider.
	October, first week. "Well-digging" occurs.
	Autumn. Brothers began planning flyer at Dayton.
1903	*February.* Wrights, in Dayton, began construction on flyer.
	September 23. They left Dayton for Kitty Hawk.
	October 9. News of Langley's failed attempt is received.
	November 5. Wrights tested motor first time; parts broke; month for repairs.
	December 14. First attempts at flight.
	December 17. Success.

Lilienthal controlled his glider by shifting the position of his body, which did not provide much in the way of positive control. On Sunday, August 9, 1896, in the midst of a glide, the wind tipped up the wings of the glider, making it impossible to control. Lilienthal crashed, breaking his spine, and died the next day. His death was reported in newspapers around the world, and the Wright brothers read about it. Lilienthal was not the only person to die gliding; in 1899, Percy Pilcher, a British experimenter, was killed when his glider flipped over while it was being towed to get it airborne.

In the United States at about the same time, at least two series of flight experiments, very different in their orientation and their success, were carried out. One was by Samuel Pierpont Langley, secretary of the Smithsonian Institution, the other by engineer and businessman Octave Chanute, who was to have a significant interaction with the Wright brothers.

Langley had investigated powered flight for about ten years when in 1887 he began to have built and tested more than thirty rubber-powered pilotless light model airplanes, in order to determine the best arrangement of wings. He then had built several different airplanes with a miniature steam engine and propellers in between two sets of wings, to be used in tests to determine the best design for powered flight.

Langley attempted to fly these models from a platform built atop a workshop on a barge in the Potomac River, near Washington, D.C. He had no success until May 6, 1896, when one model, after being catapulted from the platform, rose to a height of approximately 100 feet. When it ran out of steam, it landed on the river. A second successful flight was carried out with the same model, and more success followed later in the year. Langley then announced his retirement from aviation, but he seems to have continued his research in secret, in order to develop a military airplane capable of carrying a person.

Chanute was an engineer, whose major professional accomplishments had been the design of the Chicago stockyards and completion of the first bridge across the Missouri River, in 1870. He had been interested from his youth in the problem of human flight, but he was not able to pursue this interest until 1889, when he was almost sixty years old and had been successful in business. He read and studied everything that was available concerning attempts of humans to fly and over several years he wrote a series of articles, collected in *Progress in Flying Machines*, published in 1894.

The basic direction of Chanute's research was different from Langley's, who had been experimenting with engines in planes which he could not control. Because Chanute was interested in first developing a control system, he began — as had Lilienthal — with a hang-glider, but with a different mechanism of control. The wings on Chanute's glider were attached by a hinged mechanism, so that when they were hit with a sudden gust of wind, they could tip back and then return to their original position.

In the summer and early fall of 1896, Chanute and his assistants carried out many successful glides with multiwinged gliders, on the Indiana dunes on the shores of Lake Michigan near Chicago. The best glider was two-winged, a biplane, that had been made by removing the lowest wing of a triplane, because that wing dragged on the ground, and was used in glides that lasted more than ten seconds and travelled over 250 feet. These experiments and others were discussed in an article Chanute published in the *Aeronautical Annual* for 1897 and one he published in *McClure's Magazine* in 1900.

The Wright brothers were thus not operating in a vacuum when they developed an interest in powered human flight. Although there was nothing like a voluminous literature in the area, and though much of what was written was incorrect, there were still some concrete accomplishments to start with.

Wilbur Wright was born in 1867; Orville, in 1871. They were raised in Dayton, Ohio, in a family in which there was encouragement of mechanical activities. In 1878, the boys received a toy helicopter of a sort that had been available for many years, made of cork, bamboo, and paper, with two propellers powered by a rubber band. The Wrights themselves built some toy helicopters with only limited success, because they tried to make them larger and found that larger models were more difficult to fly.

The Wrights' grandfather owned a farm, which gave them much opportunity to work with tools and to build machines. During the 1890s, they added front and side porches to their house, turning the posts on a neighbor's lathe, and they built a fireplace in the parlor. In 1892, they opened a bicycle shop, in which they had a good business selling, renting, and repairing bikes. They soon began to manufacture bicycles from parts made by manufacturers. For this task, they designed a brazier — a pan for holding hot coals to provide heat for soldering with brass.

When one reads that the Wrights were two bicycle-mechanics, the impression is of teenagers who spend summers tinkering with bikes, but these two were much more sophisticated. They had invented new machines; they knew algebra and trigonometry for calculations; and they were experienced mechanics capable of constructing wood and metal parts. In addition, working at the bicycle shop was a mechanic-machinist who was able to supply needed expertise in several other areas.

Invention of the Airplane: A Chronology

Although one thinks of the flight of December 17, 1903 when the invention of the airplane is mentioned, the Wrights' work on the airplane actually began in 1899, some five years earlier. "Inventing the airplane" was not one single act, but was the result of the combining of solutions of many different sorts of problems. There were problems, such as where the pilot of the plane should be located, that were dealt with through logical analysis of the situation. Other problems, such as the size of the wings, were solved on the basis of continuities with earlier work. The antecedents were information provided by earlier investigators, such as Lilienthal's mathematical tables, and the designs and experiences of others. Finally there were problems, such as the method of control of the plane, that were solved through "near" analogical transfer combined with logical reasoning.

1899: The Kite Glider

On May 30, 1899, Wilbur wrote to Samuel P. Langley of the Smithsonian, asking for any materials that they had published or knew of in
English on human flight. They soon received four pamphlets, including reports on Langley's power-model flights of 1896 and Lilienthal's
description of some of his gliding experiments. There was also a list
of books, including those by Langley and Chanute and the three *Aeronautical Annuals*. They read the pamphlets and ordered and read the
books, which gave them familiarity with summaries of almost everything that had been said about flight.

What most impressed the Wrights was the waste in attempting to
mount heavy machinery on a flying machine that no one would have
known how to control even if they had managed to get it into the air.
Gliding had not produced much more impressive results, as shown by
the tragedies of Lilienthal and Pilcher. Chanute had made wings or tail
vanes slightly movable, but this still was a long way from a positive
control system.

Control during flight requires first that the machine be kept in
equilibrium both longitudinally (from front to back, so that the plane
does not nose-dive into the ground) and laterally (from side to side, so
that the plane does not roll uncontrollably). However, maneuvering
requires that this equilibrium be upset, as when one makes a turn on a
bicycle: one leans into the turn, thereby upsetting the vertical position
one takes when riding straight. In the same way, a plane in a turn is in a
controlled roll. The Wrights' experience with bicycles may have
played a role in their analysis of control problems in flight.

The Wrights focused their initial activities on gliding, so that
complications caused by power could be ignored. In July, 1899, a
month after receiving the material from the Smithsonian, they built
their first glider, the so-called kite glider. It was a biplane with a five-
foot wingspan, and was to be flown as a kite. The design can be described as a box-kite lying on its side. The camber or cross-section of
the wings was in the shape of an arc of a circle, which had been taken
from Lilienthal. The upright pieces that connected the two wings
were hinged so that the upper wing could be moved forward or backward relative to the lower, by the kite-flyer pulling on two pairs of
cords, which can be seen in the figure. This system was designed to
keep the glider level from front to rear and was related to ideas used in
simpler form by others, including Chanute.

The second component of the control system involved lateral
control, or making turns. In modern aircraft, turns are carried out

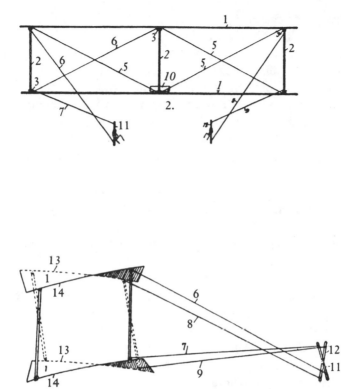

Sketches of the Wright brothers' 1899 kite, built to explore the effectiveness of wing warping. Top: front view; bottom: side view. Numbers 11 and 12 are the sticks used to control the wings through strings 6, 7, 8, and 9.

through ailerons, or separate flaps on the rear edges of the wings, which are moved in opposite directions. This control system is analogous to that used by birds. According to Wilbur, he discovered the birds' method while bird-watching, observing one bird making an erratic flight, and noting that the positions of the wings were shifting, with first one wing high and the other low, and then the reverse. He reasoned that the bird might be controlling its flight by changing the positions of its wings. Lilienthal and Chanute also spent time studying birds, who do achieve lateral control by altering the angle of their wings to the direction of flight.

Wilbur's report of his bird-watching is contained in a letter written to Chanute soon after they began working on flight, which gives it some credibility. (This was one of many letters that passed between them over the years; they also met several times.) Orville many years later said that they learned little specific from watching birds, however, so that there is some question as to exactly where the method of control came from. (This is not the only example of discrepancies in the reports of the brothers.) John Walsh spent time observing birds in flight, in order to try to replicate the Wrights' experiences, and he concluded that it is not possible to actually see the wing tips being used for lateral control. He therefore speculates that Wilbur's observations of bird flight might have been supplemented by material in two books that he is known to have read: one book discussed in some detail the variations in position that bird wings can assume during flight, and the other presented a series of photos of pigeons in flight, which showed the wing tips in various orientations. These sources may have combined with the observations of birds to provide a starting point for the control system.

Given the need to control the wing tips, the Wrights designed a system of wires to raise or lower the outer rear tips of the wings, so that the left-hand rear tips of the two wings would move together either up or down, and the right tips would at the same time move in the opposite direction. In this way, the two wings form an integrated unit, which is twisted, or warped, up at one end and down at the other. There had been discussion between the brothers as to how the tips could be moved up and down as needed, and mechanical movement through gears had been considered and rejected because of excessive weight.

It has been reported that Wilbur discovered the wing-warping solution in the bike shop while selling an inner tube. After removing the tube from its long narrow box, he was twisting the empty box absent-mindedly when he realized that the same could be done with the wings of a glider. Since the reports of the twisted-box incident are not very detailed and occurred significantly after the fact, one cannot determine, for example, whether Wilbur was twisting the box while thinking of the problem of wing-tip control. In addition, Orville reported at a later time that the twisted box merely served to make more clear a mechanical embodiment of a principle they already knew.

The box-twisting discovery occurred near the end of July 1899, and Wilbur made a bamboo model to examine the feasibility of warping on a small scale. Satisfied that things were promising, the five-foot kite glider was then quickly made. The model was flown once that summer, controlled by two sets of cords attached to sticks, and the system worked.

Based on this very limited success, they began to plan work for the summer of 1900, using the same control system with a larger glider, capable of carrying a pilot. They had a rough idea of the dimensions of the larger glider, and from Lilienthal's table in the 1897 *Aeronautical Annual*, they determined that they would need winds of about 15 miles per hour. Because Dayton was not windy enough, in November 1899, Wilbur wrote to the U.S. Weather Bureau and obtained information on wind velocities for the entire United States.

1900: The Glider — Kitty Hawk

On May 13, 1900, Wilbur wrote Chanute, describing their work, and asked advice concerning locations for testing. Chanute suggested that in addition to steady wind, soft sand was needed for practicing. He suggested California, Florida, or the Atlantic coast of South Carolina or Georgia. Because these were all too far from Dayton, Wilbur examined the Weather Bureau data and found a closer site — Kitty Hawk, a fishing village on North Carolina's Outer Banks, a sand bar less than a mile wide that runs the length of the state's coast. They worked there for two or three months per year for the next four years, depending on how easily they got away from the bicycle shop.

The Wrights' success, of course, made the name Kitty Hawk synonymous with the development of aviation, and North Carolina's license plates now read, "First in Flight." Given the reason for the choice of Kitty Hawk, perhaps the license plates should read, "Steady, strong winds; soft sand; and reasonably close to Dayton, Ohio."

The 1900 glider was an expanded and elaborated version of the 1899 kite glider. The camber was in the shape of a parabola and was flatter than recommended by Lilienthal, because Wilbur had read that a shallow camber made a wing more stable, although no exact calculations were available. The wings were designed in a V-shape for lateral control, as had been recommended by several earlier works.

An addition to the design was an elevator, or "front rudder," which could be raised and lowered by hand to control fore-and-aft position. There was no tail, since the experience of others seemed to indicate that it served no purpose. The wings were trussed together with wire, in a variant of a technique used by Chanute, except for the rear tips, which were free for warping. The operator was to lie prone on the lower wing, to reduce wind resistance.

When they flew the glider on the beach at Kitty Hawk in the fall of 1900, they found that side gusts of wind were making it unstable. For this reason, they straightened the angle of the wings. That year, almost all the flying was done with the glider used as a kite, with no operator on board. Their glider was less resistant to the wind than Chanute's biplane had been, which was gratifying, but it did not produce as much lift as Lilienthal's tables predicted, which was not encouraging.

The best day of gliding was October 20, a Saturday, with winds of 12 – 14 m.p.h. The pilot was one of the brothers, and the other brother and a helper each held a wing tip and ran into the wind to get the glider going, and stayed with the glider to keep it from rising too high and getting out of control. At first they used only the rudder for control, to keep things simpler for the pilot. They made about a dozen glides, which totaled more than two minutes in the air. The longest glides lasted approximately twenty seconds and covered 400 feet. They then tried to use the warping mechanism together with the rudder, but they could not control the glider. That was the end of the work for 1900.

1901: Kill Devil Hills

In 1901, the Wrights camped and worked at the Kill Devil Hills — a few miles south of Kitty Hawk — which gave them easy access to launching places for the glider. The procedure was to have two men run to the top of the hill and throw the glider over the crest, with the pilot on board. Because of the lift problems with the 1900 glider, they had at home in Dayton carried out some small-scale experiments with model wings of wood, had concluded that Lilienthal's tables might have been wrong; therefore they needed more wing surface area than they had had in 1900. They then doubled the surface area of the new glider, making a total lift area of over 320 square feet, although it weighed only 100 pounds. They also made the camber deeper than in 1900. This glider was much bigger than those of other experimenters: Lilienthal's, for example, had only 151 square feet of lift area.

When they carried out their first tests, they immediately found that the glider was much slower than they had expected and also more sluggish in response to the rudder. Their work on redesign had not been very effective. They reduced the size of the rudder but that made no difference. They tried a different cloth covering for the wings, but that too made no difference. They then flattened the wings by adding new pieces, which brought the camber closer to that of 1900, and they also made the front edges of the wings smoother, to decrease resistance. These changes increased performance to their expectations.

They then discovered another unexpected problem. They had not yet attempted a turn during a glide (no one had ever made a controlled turn in a glider), and when they were attempting to turn, and had warped the wings to produce a roll, the glider turned around the higher wing, which was opposite to what they expected and indicated that their control system was not working correctly. This so befuddled them that they left early for home, having learned about the importance of camber and that their control system still had some kinks in it.

Wilbur was invited by Chanute to give an address presenting the results of their work at the September meeting of the Western Society of Engineers. In preparing the address, he raised questions about the inaccurate data from Lilienthal's tables. Because Orville was of the opinion that Wilbur should say nothing about others' data until they had results of their own, they decided to test Lilienthal's calculations in a more formal way. They made miniature metal wings of various cross-sections and tested them in a wind tunnel they had made out of a box, using a fan to supply a controlled breeze.

1902: Well-digging

The 1902 glider was constructed from the results of their wind-tunnel experiments. The wings were longer and narrower, and overall much less curved in cross-section, and the camber varied at different points in the wings, rather than remaining the same from wing tip to wing tip. The shape of the front rudder was changed from rectangular to elliptical. They also added two vertical fins six feet high as a tail, as a result of an analysis of what might have been causing the problem of turning around the higher wing in 1901.

The new glider flew well, and they made some record glides, covering more than 500 feet and lasting more than twenty seconds; the new tail seemed to be controlling the turning problem. Now, however, still another problem arose when they tried to warp the wings to raise one wing to bring the wings level. Instead of the low wing coming up, the glider would sometimes slide down toward the low wing, which would then strike the sand. The glider would then swing around that wing, driving it deeper into the sand, "digging a well." This new problem was another indication that their control system was not yet complete. Wilbur, on thinking through the problem, decided that the tail should be made movable, so that it could counteract the tendency to slide toward the low wing. He also concluded that they could do this by using the same wires that warped the wings. Thus ended their 1902 flights.

1903 — The First Flyer

Chanute had visited Kitty Hawk in 1902, and suggested that it was time to power their glider. In February 1903, after several months' planning, they started to build a new machine. All the parts of the frame were reinforced for strength, because of the increased size, weight, and speed of the flyer. The wingspan was now over forty feet, with tips that drooped, and the total area of the wings alone was more than 500 square feet.

Because no motor manufacturer would make a motor to fit their needs, they designed one, based on an automobile engine. Their mechanic built it. Propellers were more of a problem, since there was no information on propeller design, not even marine propellers. They finally designed blades, using their lift tables from the wind tunnel (because a propeller can be considered a rotating wing), as well as much trial and error.

They returned to North Carolina in October. To launch the flyer, they set up a sixty-foot-long track, along which the flyer would ride on a small wheeled truck until it had enough speed to take off. On October 9, they received news that Langley had failed in an attempt to launch a piloted, powered plane over the Potomac River. Although Langley's work was not nearly as advanced as theirs, they could not know this, and the news quickened their pace.

On Monday, December 13, after over a month of delays, they decided to launch the flyer from the side of one of the hills in weak winds to get a gravity-assisted start. Given the possible historical significance of the occasion, they sent a prearranged signal to the Kitty Hawk lifesaving station, and several men came to assist and to serve as witnesses.

The brothers tossed a coin for the honor of piloting, and Wilbur won. Orville ran alongside to help balance the plane on the track, holding a stopwatch to time the flight. The plane reacted more sensitively to the controls than Wilbur anticipated, and when he turned the front rudder up, the plane quickly took off at a too-sharp angle, losing speed as it climbed, so that it started to fall backward, with its nose in the air, before the excited pilot could turn the rudder down to try to level off. The flight ended with a minor crash, breaking several parts. The length of the flight was more than 100 feet, and it had flown for more than three seconds, but they did not consider it a flight because of the lack of control.

Four days later, on Thursday, December 17, they tried again. Since Wilbur had piloted the first day, Orville took his turn, with Wilbur balancing the wing and holding the stopwatch. The wind against the plane was so strong that its speed through the air was slow enough for one of the men to photograph it.

Orville had the same difficulty Wilbur had with the sensitive rudder, so that the flight was a roller coaster of ups and downs until the flyer landed in a minor crash after about 120 feet. Since Wilbur in his excitement forgot to stop the watch he held, they estimated a duration of 12 seconds for their flight:

> the first in the history of the world in which a machine
> carrying a man had raised itself by its own power into the air
> in full flight, had sailed forward without reduction of speed,
> and had finally landed at a point as high as that from which it
> started. (Orville Wright 1913; quoted in Howard 1987, 137)

They were able quickly to repair the crash damage, and Wilbur made a second roller-coaster flight of about the same duration but covering 175 feet. Two other flights soon followed, with the last covering 852 feet in fifty-nine seconds.

They sent a telegram to their father, who had ready for the press a release that they had earlier prepared; a third brother had been appointed press agent. Although the transmission of the telegram was not completely accurate, the message was clear.

> Success four flights thursday morning all against twenty one
> mile wind started from Level with engine power alone average
> speed through air thirty one miles longest 57 [sic] seconds
> inform Press home #### Christmas.
>
> Orvelle [sic] Wright

Much work still remained to be carried out by the Wright brothers, since their first attempts were relatively primitive, even by their own standards. For example, they had not yet made a turn in powered flight. Work in 1904 and 1905 resulted in true control and impressive flights.

What Do We Learn from the Wrights?

The Wright brothers' development of the airplane is the result of a combination of factors working over many years. Examining their history in some detail makes clear the numerous difficulties and dangers that had to be dealt with, one at a time, before even their limited success could be achieved. We see a long history of slow, careful work, with each step being planned in advance to the degree possible, although much that occurred was not anticipated.

The initial idea for the control system may have developed from an already existing system, that of birds. When difficulties arose with the various components of their gliders and the flyer, these difficulties were dealt with through reasoning and problem solving. This development is summarized in the table on the facing page.

The case of the Wright brothers provides a graphic example of the importance of a high degree of motivation in the production of important works. In actuality, this case study demonstrates that there may be motivation of several kinds—perhaps interrelated—underlying creative work.

The Wrights had to work for five years to invent the airplane, because the task was of extreme difficulty. Many separate problems had to be solved, and several of those required significant amounts of time. When all these separate tasks are joined together, the resulting project required an extraordinary time commitment and motivation in terms of energy to keep focussed on one topic.

Even more than a time commitment was required, however, because in working out each of those problems almost nothing went smoothly. In many cases, solution of one problem was followed quickly by another, so that the Wrights in many cases were faced with cascading difficulties. As an example, the wing-warping control system took several years to develop, but the path of development was anything but straight, as the examples of "well-digging" and related phenomena make clear. The same was true concerning problems of size and shape of wings and other surfaces, and also design of the engine and propellers and related parts. Motivation in the sense of not being discouraged in the face of newly discovered subproblems was thus crucial in enabling them to overcome one intermediate hurdle after another in working out these major issues.

There were also several cases when a season's work at Kitty Hawk resulted in some advances but left them wondering about some newly discovered difficulty that they did not understand, with no guarantee that they could resolve the difficulty before they returned

Some Components of the Wright Brothers' Design, and How They Were Brought About.

Component	How Derived?
	1899
biplane	Chanute? Langley?
hinged wing	Chanute
wing warping	bird wing tips? (near analogy)
	1900
dihedral angle	precedents
flat rudder	precedents
operator prone	inference: to reduce wind resistance
	1901
increased wing area	inference: wanted more lift than in 1900
skids for landing	inference; to protect glider and pilot on landing
changed cloth covering	inference: to increase speed and lift (worse than 1900)
changed camber to 1900	inference: return to 1900 configuration, when speed and lift were greater
	1902
vertical nonmovable tail	inference: to eliminate turning around high wing from 1901
changed wing proportions	from wind tunnel experiments
varied camber	from wind tunnel experiments
shape of rudder	from wind tunnel experiments
movable tail	inference: to eliminate "well-digging"
	1903
new motor	adapted automobile engine
propellers	reasoning; wind-tunnel tables; trial and error

the next year. There thus had to be a strong underlying belief that they could work things out, motivation in the sense of confidence that they could successfully deal with the new problem as they had with earlier ones, even though right then there was no evidence that they could.

When one reads a thumbnail sketch of an incident of creative work, as in the brief histories given in this chapter of Watt's steam engine and Whitney's cotton gin, one can lose sight of the multiple complexities entailed in the invention of a complex machine (or scientific theory or work of art), and therefore be led to believe that things ran smoothly over a relatively short period of time. This detailed presentation of the Wrights provides a more realistic picture of the long distances traveled by those individuals who achieve recognition for important works, and makes graphic the need for extraordinary motivation in anyone who would stay the course.

Conclusions

Creative thinking in invention begins with what is already known, when a possible invention is retrieved from memory, based on a near analogy to the situation the inventor is dealing with. It also goes beyond the already known, as new problems arise which demand solution before the desired invention can be produced. Watt's steam engine was built on Newcomen's, Whitney's cotton gin on an already-existing gin, and Edison's kinetoscope on his phonograph (see Chapter 1). When there are no antecedents in human artifacts, then the natural world is used as a source, as when the Wrights used bird flight as the basis for wing-warping.

Because the cases discussed in this chapter seem relatively straightforward and reasonable, perhaps even overly simple, people sometimes raise the question of whether these examples *really* qualify as being creative. Perhaps invention is a domain where one does not really need creative thinking to produce something new, all one has to do is stumble around until success occurs through some chance occurrence. However, the examples we have discussed clearly embody creative thinking, since these inventions were novel and of value. Also, all of these products had important technological and economic implications, and important social and cultural influences, so that even under an interpretation of creativity that takes into account the social significance of a novel product, there seems little doubt that these examples qualify.

The skeptic then raises another question: How can these inventions be creative if there were easily specified antecedents for each of them? This is, of course, based on the assumption that in areas that require "real" creativity, in art and perhaps in science, we will find radically new products developing without antecedents; in the next two chapters — on creativity in science and the arts — we will see that this assumption is incorrect.

CHAPTER 6

Scientific Discovery: Case Studies

From my first day in the lab I knew I would not leave Cambridge for a long time. Departing would be idiocy, for I had immediately discovered the fun of talking to Francis Crick. Finding someone who knew that DNA was more important than proteins was real luck. Moreover, it was a great relief for me not to spend full time learning x-ray analysis of proteins. Our lunch conversations quickly centered on how genes were put together. Within a few days of my arrival, we knew what to do: imitate Linus Pauling and beat him at his own game.

(Watson 1968/1980, 31–32)

Scientific thinking might not at first glance seem to require creativity if the scientific enterprise is conceived of as the collection of objective facts, there for the observation. However, as discussed in Chapter 3, and as any working scientist knows, science goes far beyond the mere collection of facts in several important ways.

The "facts" that scientists collect are less objective than they appear and often their "collection" depends on the development of very sophisticated methods, which itself can be seen as requiring creativity. An example of this — the X-ray diffraction technique — played an important role in the discovery of the structure of DNA. Also, turning the measurements made by scientists into the "facts" that become part of science often requires a complicated thinking process. The use of X-ray diffraction produced photos that gave scientists clues about the structure of DNA, but the information was not just sitting there waiting to be plucked by the scientists. Much interpretation was necessary before the scientists could understand the facts in those pictures.

Even more important than the collection of facts is their interpretation, or the development of scientific theories. Once a set of facts is available, they must be interpreted through the construction of a theory that can explain them; some philosophers of science believe that one's theoretical beliefs also play a role even in the collection of facts.

Creativity in the development of two scientific theories will be the focus of the case studies in this chapter: James Watson and Francis Crick's discovery of the structure of DNA and Charles Darwin's development of the theory of evolution through natural selection. Watson and Crick's accomplishment was more circumscribed than Darwin's, since they were dealing with the problem of the structure of a specific molecule, whereas Darwin was attempting to synthesize an explanation for evolution of all living things. However, Watson and Crick's discovery, arguably the most important in biology of the twentieth century, and Darwin's, arguably the most important of the nineteenth, both qualify as "revolutionary," and therefore provide evidence whether "ordinary" thinking processes play a role in revolutionary outcomes.

Discovery of the Double Helix

DNA was discovered in the 1860s, and by the turn of the century had been shown to be in all cells. It is composed of four different kinds of nitrogen-rich compounds, or bases (adenine, cytosine, guanine, and thymine); a five-carbon sugar; and phosphoric acid. The building block of DNA is the *nucleotide*: one sugar molecule, one phosphoric acid molecule, and one base. Nucleic acid is thus a *polynucleotide*, built up from many nucleotides linked together. The DNA molecule looks something like a spiral staircase. There are two helical strands, or backbones, held together by pairs of bases that form the "stairs."

The belief that DNA is the hereditary material is relatively recent: until the 1950s, there were strong reasons for believing that other

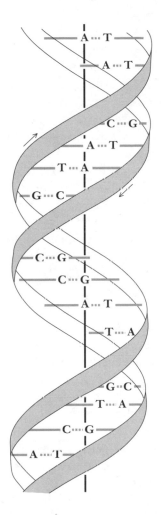

The double helix.

material — the proteins in the cell nucleus — formed the gene. It was thought that since genes directed the synthesis of proteins they should also be proteins.

In the late 1940s, an important experimental finding pointed toward DNA as the material making up genes. Albert Hershey and Martha Chase showed that when a virus infects a host, only viral DNA enters the host; the protein remains outside. This led to the hypothesis that the shell of the virus is a protein "hypodermic," which serves to inject DNA into host.

In the 1930s and 1940s, a number of physicists, including Francis Crick, moved into biology, bringing with them a new way of looking at questions. One of the stimuli to this move was the book *What Is Life?* written by Erwin Schroedinger, the Nobel-prizewinning physicist. Schroedinger discussed the transmission of genetic information, and speculated that, whatever its composition, the gene was made up of a small number of units, with the exact combination of these units determining the specific genetic message.

The initial stimulus for Schroedinger's book was the work of Max Delbrück, one of the first physicists to become interested in biological questions. Delbrück, with Salvador Luria (a geneticist who was the Ph.D. advisor of Watson at Indiana University), and Hershey (of the Hershey and Chase experiments on DNA), founded an informal network of scientists, whose goal was to determine the physical nature of the gene. As a result, Watson and Crick had intellectual influences in common, from Delbrück through Schroedinger to Crick, and from Delbrück through Luria to Watson.

In the spring of 1951, Watson was a recent Ph.D. in genetics on a postdoctoral fellowship in Europe to study the chemistry of nucleic acids. At a scientific conference, Watson saw an X-ray photograph of crystalline DNA presented by Maurice Wilkins, a researcher at King's College, London (and, as it turned out, a friend of Crick). In order to take an X-ray photograph, one first forms a crystal of the substance one wishes to examine, such as a salt crystal. The researcher then places the crystal in the path of a beam of X-rays, which are diffracted by the crystal or reflected in a pattern that can be captured on film, since X-rays expose film.

Watson was excited by the fact that the DNA crystal produced a regular pattern of X-ray diffraction, because that meant that DNA had a regular structure, and thus might be analyzable in a relatively straightforward manner. This stimulated in him a desire to relocate his fellowship at a facility where X-ray techniques were used to study large molecules. This in turn led him to an interest in the Cavendish Laboratory at Cambridge University, which had for a long time been using X-ray crystallography to analyze the structures of molecules. When Watson moved to the Cavendish in the fall of 1951, he met Crick, who was a Ph.D. student there.

The molecular-modeling orientation which attracted Watson and Crick had as its most well-known practitioner Linus Pauling, the world-famous chemist at California Institute of Technology, who had recently scored a great triumph with a helical model that he proposed for the structure of the protein alpha-keratin, which forms many structures, including hair, horn, and fingernails. Pauling's success was at the expense of the Cavendish group, who had also been intently pursuing this structure.

By the 1950s, the most advanced work on the structure of DNA was being carried out by Wilkins and his colleagues at King's College. The X-ray pictures produced by Wilkins's group provided information about the diameter of the molecule, the distance between consecutive bases, and the fact that the pattern repeated itself in some way as one went along the molecule. The pictures did not provide information about the specific shape of the molecule, however, or how it was constructed: on examining this X-ray picture, it can be seen immediately that the "helical X-ray pattern" does not look like a helix; there is

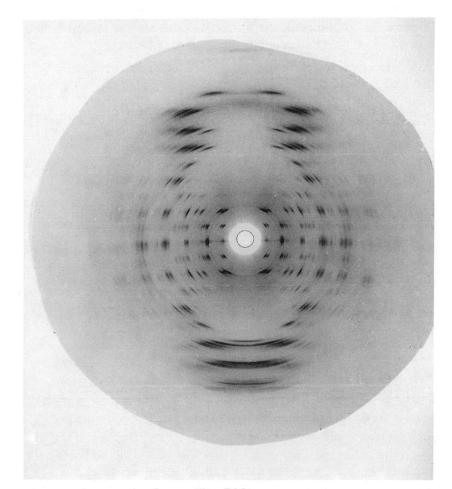

An x-ray photograph of crystalline DNA.

no visible evidence that can be directly interpreted by anyone who does not understand X-ray crystallography. Thus the scientists involved in the discovery of DNA were not simply observing facts that were directly presented to them; they were drawing conclusions based on indirect evidence. Much more than simple observation was involved.

Wilkins went on to investigate the properties of the fibers of DNA by doing what others had done with other large molecules: he tried, among other things, stretching them and changing the relative humidity and seeing the effects that resulted. He hoped to connect the normal and stretched states with two kinds of diffraction patterns. By the summer of 1951, at a conference held at Cambridge, Wilkins had come to the conclusion that the DNA molecule might be helical in shape. In October 1951, after Watson had arrived at the Cavendish, Crick invited Wilkins for the weekend; Watson was present when they talked about DNA, and all agreed it was helical.

In addition to Wilkins's work, Rosalind Franklin, another member of the King's College group, made important contributions to the discovery of the structure of DNA. Franklin was an expert crystallographer who joined the King's group in January 1951, although by her own admission she at that time knew little about biology. She had been told that when she joined the staff, the DNA work would be hers. This led to some friction and a lack of communication between Franklin and Wilkins, who had been working on DNA before she arrived. In the fall of 1951, Franklin and her assistant R. C. Gosling took many X-ray photographs of DNA, and discovered that by increasing the relative humidity it was possible to produce a second structure (called the B or "wet" form), with a diffraction pattern different from that already found from Wilkins's fibers (the A or "dry" or crystalline form). Franklin and Gosling were able to obtain additional information about the structure of the molecule from the B pattern.

Watson and Crick's Collaboration

When Watson came to the Cavendish he and Crick agreed on the importance of building a model of the structure of DNA. Data obtained from X-ray crystallography would provide one of the bases for their work. The second base for their work would be the methods of Pauling; their approach would be to try to build a helical model of DNA, analogous to Pauling's helical model of protein.

A Brief Chronology of the Discovery of the Double Helix

1950–1951		Pauling's alpha-helix
1951	May	Wilkins DNA talk attended by Watson
	Fall	Watson joins staff at Cavendish Laboratory
	October	Wilkins, Crick, and Watson discuss DNA: agree that it is helical
	November 21	Franklin's colloquium
	December	Watson and Crick's triple helix, with bases outside
		King's group visits and critiques model
		Watson and Crick barred from working on DNA
1952		Crick works on dissertation
		Watson learns to read X-rays
		Other desultory thinking about DNA
	July	Chargaff's visit
1953	January 30	Watson visits King's with Pauling's paper; sees Franklin's new "B" photo; also learns that the "A" to "B" transformation results in 20% increase in length; Watson deduces two strands
	January 31	2 and 3 strands to be considered
	February 1–2	Watson works on bases outside model, repeated failures result in rejection.
	2nd week	King's report—shape of unit cell. Crick deduces anti-parallel chains, which allows deduction of pitch of helix
	February 27	Base pairings: like-with-like "torn to shreds"
	February 28	Watson works out complementary pairings

Pauling's working methods were of particular interest to Watson and Crick because proteins are in many ways analogous to DNA: they are also long chain molecules, composed of building blocks (amino acids), each one joined to the next through chemical bonds (peptide bonds); analogous to the polynucleotide structure of DNA, proteins are polypeptides. Based on near analogical transfer, this leads to the possibility, utilized by Watson and Crick, that Pauling's methods might be applicable to analysis of DNA.

In November 1951, there was a colloquium at King's College attended by Watson, at which Wilkins and Franklin described their recent work. Watson had been at the Cavendish for only two months, and had not learned enough to be able to extract all of the information from this talk. Furthermore, as was his habit, he took no notes, relying on his memory.

According to Franklin's notes for her talk, she presented the following description of the DNA molecule: it was hexagonal in cross-section (therefore cylindrical in structure); there was a spiral within that cylinder; and there was a repetition of the spiral pattern at specified distances. She concluded in her notes that either the structure was a big helix or a smaller helix containing several chains. The phosphates (the backbones of the helix) were on the outside of the molecule. This is obviously a solid foundation for the description of the double helix.

In his account of Franklin's talk in *The Double Helix*, Watson says nothing about her saying that the molecule was helical, although one would expect that he would have been struck by her conclusions. Robert Olby suggests that Franklin's presentation of her results did not really provide Watson with any new information. Watson already knew from Wilkins and from earlier work that there was a repeat in the molecule and he knew the distance between the bases; Wilkins had told Watson and Crick that he favored a three-chain helical model. Thus, according to Olby, when Franklin repeated these points, they were not new to Watson.

There is another possibility, not considered by Olby, for Watson's lack of interest in Franklin's talk: perhaps Franklin did not discuss the possibility of a helical structure of DNA. She might have been waiting until she felt more secure, and perhaps she did not want anyone to use her then-tentative conclusions to produce a complete model before she did. This is conjecture, but given the difficult relations among Franklin and some of the individuals who were in attendance at her talk, the suggestion of reluctance on her part to make public her ideas may not be totally out of the question.

The Triple Helix

Soon after Franklin's colloquium, Watson and Crick built their first model of DNA. Two specific problems arose in constructing it: How many helical strands should it contain, and where should the bases be located? Neither the chemical nor the crystallographic information made clear the numbers or locations of the parts of the molecule, although it was known that the molecule was wider than a single-

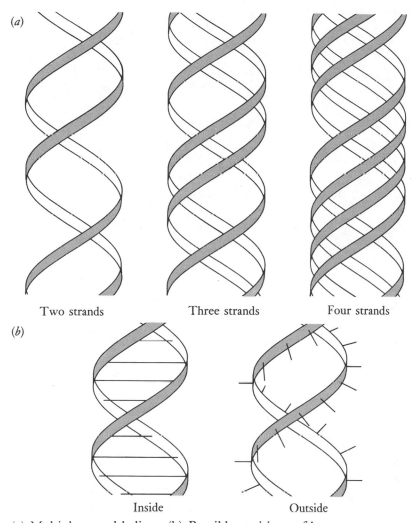

(a) Multiple-strand helices. (b) Possible positions of bases.

stranded helix. In Watson and Crick's initial model there were three strands, rather than the correct two, and the bases projected outward from the backbones, rather than being between them.

Watson and Crick chose a three-strand structure for their initial model because evidence reported by Franklin at her talk concerning the density and water content of the DNA molecule pointed to three strands. Also, Wilkins had indicated that he thought the molecule contained three strands. A related question involved how the three strands were held together: the twisted backbones had to form a rigid rod with a constant diameter. Watson and Crick built their model on the assumption that the three strands were held together by magnesium atoms at the center, although there was no evidence that there was magnesium in DNA.

Watson and Crick put the bases on the outside of the triple helix because at that time they could not see a way to put them between the backbones. Since the bases are of different sizes, it seemed impossible to make regularly-sized rungs of the staircase out of them. Putting the bases on the outside did away with this problem, and it also made the bases more accessible for chemical reactions, which seemed to be potentially important, since the genetic information would have to play a large role in many reactions.

The structures of the bases also raised problems for the model. Some molecules can exist in nature in more than one form, called tautomeric forms, and Crick believed that was true of the bases in DNA.

Continuity and Discontinuity in the Discovery of the Double Helix

Continuity	*Source*
Triple helix	Analogical transfer: Helix from Pauling; three strands based on experimental results (X-rays, density, etc.); Wilkin's opinion
Rigidity — Mag. ions	Analogical transfer: Similar mechanisms in other structures
Bases outside	Problems with base size and tautomeric forms; makes bases more accessible for chemical reactions
Discontinuity	*Trigger*
3 → 2 Strands	X-ray data; new density and water-content data; reasoning
Backbone position	X-ray data; reasoning
Anti-parallel chains	Unit cell
Mag. ions to H bonds	No magnesium present; evidence for H bonds in DNA
Base pairing	Like-with-like "torn to shreds"; complementary pairs: trial and error

If so, it made the number of combinations of bases much larger and much more difficult to understand. This problem too was eliminated if the bases were on the outside. These aspects of Watson and Crick's thinking are outlined at the top of the accompanying table.

Very soon after Watson and Crick produced the triple helix, they invited the King's College group to see it, and the King's group told them in strong terms that their model surely was incorrect, based on the King's data concerning the amount of water DNA contained, among other things. It turned out that Watson had misrecalled by half Franklin's results concerning the amount of water, which threw off all the calculations, and made parts of their structure very unlikely. Franklin also presented some of her reasons for believing that the backbones were on the outside of the molecule, not, as Watson and Crick proposed, on the inside.

The scientific reasoning being carried out by Watson and Crick was by no means of a trivial nature. About a year after Watson and Crick discarded their triple helix, Pauling (a Nobel prizewinner) and his associate Robert Corey published a very similar incorrect model, also with three strands and the bases outside. There is also evidence that a three-strand model was considered at about this time at King's, as well. Thus, there were many factors to be considered in developing models of DNA, and many as-yet-unknown factors that turned out to be important, and it was very difficult at the beginning to get everything correct.

The disastrous meeting with the King's group had two effects on Watson and Crick. First, the director of the Cavendish Laboratory forbade them to work on DNA, because of the embarrassment they had brought to the lab. Second, Watson and Crick, trying to quietly continue thinking about DNA despite this restriction, went back to the drawing board. They retained the helical structure, but changed it in response to new information that became available, although more than a year passed before they built another model. During this time, Crick worked on his dissertation, which was not on DNA, and Watson learned to carry out crystallography and read X-ray photos. They also did some work on DNA when they could. They were finally able to return to building models of DNA when Pauling published his. Although Pauling's model was incorrect, his being in the hunt for the structure enabled Watson and Crick to convince their superiors that nothing in the way of model building was being done at King's, so that if nothing were done at the Cavendish, Pauling would be first to arrive at the correct structure.

From Triple Helix to Double Helix

There were two sorts of information that led to the discontinuity from the incorrect triple helix to the correct double helix: the sort that made it clear that aspects of the triple helix were incorrect, and the sort that made clear various aspects of the correct structure. As one example of rejection of the old, Watson still wanted to use magnesium ions to hold the structure together. Franklin had argued against such ions having a role when she criticized the triple helix, but Watson had not been convinced. In autumn of 1952, he tested a sample of DNA for the presence of magnesium and found none, so that idea was rejected.

In July, 1952, Erwin Chargaff visited Cambridge. He had done important research which showed that, in any sample of DNA, the amount of adenine was equal to the amount of thymine, and the amount of guanine was equal to the amount of cytosine. These "Chargaff ratios" would seem to directly lead to the conclusion that just those base pairings should be used in any model, but Watson and Crick at that time did not use them. Questions had been raised about the reliability of Chargaff's data, and Watson and Crick were still concerned about the tautomeric (changeable) forms of the bases, and thus could not assume that the bases were simply paired in the center of the molecule.

At the end of January, 1953, Watson and Crick were able to see a copy of the paper that contained Pauling and Corey's DNA model. To their amazement, they found that it was three-stranded, with bases on the outside, just like theirs of 1951 had been. This initially led Watson to feel distressed that he and Crick had been on the right track over a year earlier, but a close examination of Pauling's model indicated that its chemical structure was incorrect.

On Friday, January 30, 1953, Watson visited King's College to show that group Pauling's paper. Wilkins showed him an X-ray photograph which Watson had never seen before, made by Franklin of the B form of DNA. (Franklin had discussed the B form in her notes for the colloquium of November 1951, and may have shown a much less precise and less detailed photo at that time, but if she did, Watson missed the significance of it.) Much additional information was available in this photo, and Watson, with his new expertise in reading X-ray photographs, was able to remember enough to help in the new model building, specifically the number of chains.

Fewer than two chains or more than three were ruled out by measurements of the density of the molecules used in crystallographic studies. At the time of Watson's visit with the Pauling paper, Wilkins also gave Watson information about some of Franklin's recent results showing an increase of 20 percent in the length of the DNA fibers when they went from the A to B forms. This information, in conjunction with the data from Franklin's new B photo, allowed Watson to deduce that two strands were involved, not three.

The day after Watson's visit to King's, he and Crick agreed that they should now consider two- and three-strand models, although Watson by that time was ready to deal only with two strands. He therefore spent two days building two-strand models with the backbones in the center, because he still believed that the bases had to be on the outside. However, two-strand backbones-inside models could not be built without the distances between atoms violating important rules of structural chemistry, which led a reluctant Watson to abandon the backbone-inside orientation. This put him face to face with the problem of fitting the bases between the backbones and determining how they were connected.

During the second week of February, Max Perutz, a senior scientist at the Cavendish, gave to Crick his copy of a report concerning the current status of work on DNA at King's, including — most importantly — Franklin's work. One new piece of information in this report concerned the shape of the basic building-block unit of the crystal of DNA (the "unit cell"). This information enabled Crick to deduce that the backbone chains of the DNA molecule ran in opposite directions (were "anti-parallel"), which then allowed him to deduce the pitch of the helix (the angle of the screw turn of the molecule). There has been some controversy about Watson and Crick's possessing this report; it has been implied that they stole data from others, but the report was a public document. Crick used it as the basis for a series of deductions about the structure, since nothing was explicitly laid out.

Thus, in the middle of February, Watson and Crick had built a model of one backbone chain, a model that was the result of the work of several individuals. Watson had produced the argument for a double helix, Franklin for the backbone outside, and Crick for the anti-parallel chains and the pitch of the helix. Wilkins had influenced the general orientation of the work.

There were still two problems with base pairings. First, as already mentioned, was the different sizes of the bases. Second, the structure had to be held together. Watson now considered the idea that hydrogen bonding between bases was possible, and searched the literature for any clues on how hydrogen bonding between bases might occur.

He found a diagram of hydrogen bonding between a pair of adenine bases and another diagram of hydrogen bonding between a pair of guanine bases. This "like-with-like" pattern of bonding impressed Watson greatly, although he was still concerned about the size problem with such pairings. There were precedents in Watson's background for his interest in like-with-like pairing. As a student at Indiana, he had taken genetics courses with Felix Haurowitz, who was a strong advocate of like-with-like pairings in other contexts; and the best-known geneticist at Indiana at that time, I. H. Muller, was an advocate of a like-with-like scheme for gene replication.

Watson's like-with-like scheme was soon "torn to shreds" by Jerry Donohue, a postdoctoral fellow who shared the office with them. Donohue argued that the diagram in the literature contained the wrong tautomeric forms for the bases, forms which would not be found in nature. Donohue had already published a paper in which he made these arguments, and he had received his Ph.D. under Pauling and had published with him, so that his opinion was to be taken very seriously.

Similarly, Crick pointed out to Watson that his like-with-like scheme was not compatible with the shape of the crystal found by Franklin or with Chargaff's ratios. Crick reports that after the like-with-like scheme was rejected, it was agreed that they would try to pair the bases in accordance with Chargaff's ratios (that is, they would try to pair adenine with thymine and glycine with cytosine), but Watson does not remember such a specific plan.

The next morning Watson came in early and worked on the base pairings using cardboard molecules in the tautomeric forms suggested by Donohue, and he discovered the correct pairing.

> When I got to our still empty office the following morning, I quickly cleared away the papers from my desk top so that I would have a large, flat surface on which to form pairs of bases held together by hydrogen bonds. Though I initially went back to my like-like prejudices, I saw all too well that they led nowhere. When Jerry [Donohue] came in I looked up, saw that it was not Francis, and began shifting the bases in and out of various other pairing possibilities. Suddenly I became aware that an adenine-thymine pair held together by two hydrogen bonds was identical in shape to a guanine-cytosine pair held together by at least two hydrogen bonds. All the hydrogen bonds seemed to form naturally; no fudging was required to make the two types of base pairs identical in shape. . . . Upon

his arrival Francis did not get more than halfway through the door before I let loose that the answer to everything was in our hands.

The last part of the puzzle, and by now it almost literally was a puzzle, was resolved in a very quiet way. Watson and Crick had narrowed down the problem so that all that was left was the fitting in of the bases, which could be accomplished by moving cardboard models of the bases around on the top of a desk, that is, by searching the base-pairing problem space.

The simplicity of the end of the discovery should not obscure the complexities of what came before. A host of decisions had already been made, including the positions of the backbones and that the bases were connected through hydrogen bonds. Sometimes discussions of the discovery of the double helix focus on Watson's trial-and-error base pairings, and thereby overlook the earlier hard scientific work that was carried out over years by several people, much of which involved more than trial and error.

Continuity and Discontinuity in DNA Discovery

There were many examples in this discovery of the use of analogies as the basis for development of new ideas. Wilkins's early experimental exploration of the characteristics of DNA was based on analogous work by earlier investigators with other complex molecules, as was Franklin's early work. Also, Wilkins's early theorizing about DNA was based on structures of other large molecules. Analogical thinking was also used by Watson and Crick, most dramatically in their adoption of Pauling's method and his helical structure. These were "near" analogies, drawn from earlier work in the analysis of complex molecules. In the use of Pauling's work as the base for attacking DNA, the similarity in structure between protein (a polypeptide) and DNA (a polynucleotide) is particularly close.

There were also several discontinuities in Watson and Crick's discovery, outlined in the table on page 160. The most obvious is the change from three to two strands, but other changes are the change in position of the backbones; from parallel to anti-parallel backbone chains; and from like-with-like to complementary pairings. These discontinuities came about in different ways. The change from three to two strands was a function of difficulties with three-strand models as well as new data pointing to two strands. Moving the backbones outside was based on Franklin's data and analyses. Like-with-like to complementary base pairings was due to difficulties with like-with-like (sizes and tautomeric forms) as well as reasons for complementary forms (Watson's trial-and-error as well as Chargaff's rules).

In all of these discontinuities, both alternatives existed as possibilities throughout the work; when the first idea was rejected, an alternative did not have to be formulated, it simply had to be chosen. As one example, the issue of the number of strands was down to two or three, it was not two strands or an unknown number. This is different from what will be seen in the case of Darwin's development of the theory of evolution, because various options were not available to him; Darwin had to construct them. This issue will be returned to later in the chapter.

This conclusion leads to a further question concerning the problem of the structure of DNA: was it well- or ill-defined? The goal was not specified, that is, no one knew the structure of DNA; thus, it was ill-defined. On the other hand, once Watson and Crick decided that they would use Pauling's methods, the problem became specified enough so that something like search took place, although here, too, it was based on pieces of data and reasoning rather than on general heuristic methods of search.

Why Didn't Wilkins, Franklin, or Pauling discover DNA First?

There were several groups of expert researchers working on the structure of DNA; yet only Watson and Crick formulated the double helix — a fact that can lead to a search for the mysterious "something" they had that the other otherwise equal groups did not. However, the information we have considered indicates that the groups were in fact unequal: there were differences among them in their basic orientation to the question of molecular structure and how to analyze it, and also differences in the information each group had available. Watson and Crick were, from the beginning, pursuing model building as their basic strategy, while Wilkins came relatively late to model building, and Franklin joined even later. Pauling was, of course, directed toward model building from the beginning.

Franklin was probably the first to conclude that there were two strands, followed later by Wilkins and Watson and Crick. Pauling had proposed a triple helix. The backbones at the outside of the molecule was proposed first by Franklin, and accepted by Wilkins and

Components and Chronology of the DNA Model

Research Group	Use Models	Two Strands	Strands Outside	Helix Pitch	Base Pairings	Chains Anti-Parallel
Watson/Crick	1	2	3	1	1	1
Wilkins	2	2	2	?	?	2
Franklin	?	1	1	?	?	1
Pauling	1	?	?	?	?	?

Note: Entries in each column refer to relative time that a given component was developed by a given researcher. For example, in "Use Models," Watson and Crick and Pauling were using them first, Wilkins had decided to use them at the time of Watson and Crick's formulation of the DNA model, but had not yet begun to work on them. and Franklin had not yet concentrated on models.

then by Watson and Crick. The pitch of the helix had been deduced by Watson; and the anti-parallel structure by Crick. The complementary base pairings had been worked out by Watson.

In order to see the complexities underlying each of these decisions, let us consider in a bit more detail the anti-parallel structure of the backbone pair, deduced only by Crick. According to Robert Olby, of all those working on DNA, only Crick was able to grasp this crucial fact. First of all, he and not Watson was familiar with the particular unit-cell shape discovered by Franklin and what it meant. Franklin did not consider her own results, because she was not in favor of a helix for the crystal form until after Watson's January 30 visit carrying Pauling's paper. Wilkins did not think of anti-parallel chains in response to Franklin's result because he was not thinking at that time of a double helix, but of four chains.

This discussion is summarized in the accompanying table, and it is clear that Watson and Crick formulated the structure of DNA first because they had available everything necessary, and none of the others did. This is not to say that none of the others would have formulated the correct structure had Watson and Crick not done so. Crick has stated that he believes that if he and Watson had not formulated the structure, it would have come out in bits and pieces over the next few years. Crick also believes, however, that if the structure had appeared in that manner there would have been much less impact on biological research. The relatively sudden appearance of the complete structure, with easily seen genetic implications, created a sense of excitement that caught people in its implications.

If Crick is correct that the same discovery can have different effects on a discipline, depending on how it is made public, then attributions of genius in science depend on factors independent of the actual discovery, a possibility that points to social factors in scientific genius. A scientific discovery in and of itself is not a work of genius: it only becomes so when others have carried it far beyond where it began.

Darwin and Evolution Through Natural Selection

Acceptance of Darwinism resulted in a permanent change in the place of humans in the universe. However, Darwin's work has sometimes been accorded relatively little significance from a psychological perspective, as in the following.

The facts needed for the formulation of this theory had been available for some time. What eluded investigators was a way of combining these facts into a coherent theory of evolution.

Janet Davidson and Robert Sternberg thus argue that Darwin carried out his task through the use of *selective combination*. If they are correct, he was little more than a sifter or juggler, although perhaps a very good one. It therefore becomes of particular interest to examine just what was known when Darwin started to work, and what conclusions of significance were actually developed by Darwin himself.

Darwin's own writings present contradictory interpretations of how his theory developed. His *Autobiography*, written in his later years for the edification of his children, supports the view that the theory came about in a leap of insight, especially in a well-known passage in which he discusses how Thomas Malthus's *Essay on Population* influenced his thought. Malthus presented the view that any population grows faster than its food supply, resulting in many members of the population being unable to find food. Darwin reports that he contemplated Malthus's argument and realized that it meant that those animals which were "more fit" would survive in this competition for food. This, in turn, would result in those animals passing on their characteristics to their offspring, and thus the population would evolve.

> In October 1838, that is, fifteen months after I had begun my systematic enquiry, I happened to read for amusement Malthus on *Population*, and being well prepared to appreciate the struggle for existence which everywhere goes on from long and continued observation of the habits of animals and plants, it at once struck me that under these circumstances favorable variations would tend to be preserved and unfavorable ones to be destroyed. The result of this would be the formation of a new species. Here, then I had at last got a theory by which to work.

Soon after reading Malthus, Darwin wrote the following in his notebook.

> Three principles will account for all 1. grandchildren like grandfathers, 2. tendency to small change especially with

physical change, and 3. great fertility in proportion to support of parents.

This is an encapsulation of most of the theory of evolution by natural selection. First, each generation passes its characteristics to the following generations. Second, organisms within a given generation vary in many different small ways. (There is in this second point one strange phrase, "especially with physical change." This is a vestige from Darwin's earlier theorizing, to be discussed in more detail later, of the idea that changes in the physical characteristics of the environment, such as in climate, stimulated change in organisms.) Third, because of parental fertility, there are many more offspring than parents. This means that offspring must compete for limited resources, and that any variation that helps a given organism compete and survive will be passed on to the next generation.

One interpretation of the passage concerning Malthus is that Darwin had done no theorizing before that, and had just considered facts. Reading Malthus allowed him to formulate in essentially complete form the theory of evolution through natural selection. However, other evidence indicates that the incident was not the leap it appears to be, since Darwin had already formulated and rejected a theory of evolution before reading Malthus, and had already moved toward natural selection.

As occurred with the discovery of the double helix, Darwin did not make steady progress toward his final theory — his early views had to be partly abandoned and partly modified before progress could be made. As with Watson and Crick, Darwin was influenced greatly by the thinking of others, regarding both his general interest in biology and the question of evolution, and his more specific views concerning how evolution came about.

The beginning of the eighteenth century to the middle of the nineteenth century was a time of controversy in scientific circles, first in geology and then in biology, concerning questions of the development of the earth and the creatures on it. The orthodox religious view was that the earth had been created in six days, that all the species were created at that time and had not changed since, and that there had been one universal catastrophic flood which had wiped out all life except the animals aboard the ark. Based on a count of generations in the Bible, it was estimated that creation had occurred some 6,000 years earlier.

It was also held that species could not change; although some variability within species was seen, it was thought that this variability was around some ideal created by God, and that this ideal would always remain the center of the species. Any discussion of evolution was thus blasphemous as well as unnecessary.

However, this period was also one of great scientific activity, and facts were discovered which raised problems for the orthodox view. Explorers had found in new lands species of animals and plants that were nothing like those existing in Europe, raising questions about how this dispersion and change could have occurred after the flood. Fossils also came under increasing study, and records were found of organisms that were different than those then existing, raising questions about extinction and change of species. Geological explorations also indicated that the earth was much older than the orthodox view allowed. These findings led to modifications in the orthodox view, one of which was to postulate several floods, with Noah's being only the most recent, enabling the orthodox view to deal with the age of the earth and the evidence that species had been extinguished. The view that the earth was subject to periodic upheavals such as multiple floods was called "catastrophism."

Despite the dominance of the orthodox religious view, for several centuries, scientists and philosophers in Europe had been contemplating questions of how species originated and changed over time. As one example of pre-Darwinian evolutionary theorizing, the work of the Comte de Buffon (1707 – 1788) is particularly interesting because it mentions probably every significant ingredient in Darwin's theory. (This may have been what Davidson and Sternberg had in mind when they stated that all the facts were available before Darwin started to think about evolution.)

Buffon's *Histoire Naturelle*, published in 1749, discusses the following important factors. First, life sometimes multiplies faster than the food supply, thus producing a struggle for existence. Second, there are variations in form within a single species. These variations are often inheritable and can be taken advantage of by carefully breeding stock. This contrasts with the orthodox view that any variability is simply variability about the God-created ideal. *Artificial* selection, the human control of animal and plant development through selective breeding, was well-known in Europe long before Darwin. Third, there is an underlying similarity of structure among animals that are very different, hinting at evolution from a common ancestor. Fourth, long stretches of time are necessary to explain how life on earth developed. Fifth, some animal life has become extinct.

Buffon is only one example, though perhaps the most striking, of interest in the questions that were to concern Darwin. Furthermore, the tentative answers he proposed were similar to those ultimately proposed by Darwin. One thing that Buffon did not propose, however, was a mechanism to produce change. He did not mention selection as a positive factor, and only talked in very general terms of the climate's effect on the structure of species. Development of the theory of evolution was thus more than the selective combination of facts; it was also the development of a mechanism to *explain* the facts.

The reaction to Buffon's theorizing is also important. The *Histoire Naturelle* was seen by the Faculty of Theology at the Sorbonne as contradictory to the Bible, and to save his career, Buffon was required to affirm in print that he believed in the literal truth of the Bible and that he abandoned everything in his book that was contradictory to the biblical story of creation.

Darwin also had a strong personal reason for interest in evolution, due to his grandfather, Erasmus Darwin, who developed a theory of evolution based on the inheritance of acquired characteristics. The elder Darwin, who died before his grandson was born, proposed that during their struggle for survival some animals developed characteristics that enabled them to adapt better to the environment. These characteristics were handed down to the next generation and evolution thereby occurred. A very similar view was proposed independently by Jean Baptiste Lamarck, and this general viewpoint is called Lamarckian evolution. Lamarck emphasized that organs that are extensively used tend to increase in size, and he assumed that such changes could sometimes be inherited, which would result in evolution of species. To support this, he pointed to the changes in domestic animals brought about by selective breeding.

The difference between Lamarckian evolution and Charles Darwin's theory is that Lamarck believed that changes in organisms were in some way provoked by their struggle to adapt to the environment. In Darwin's final view, changes in organisms simply occur all the time, and some of these random changes result in some organisms being better able to compete in the struggle for existence. But in Darwin's early thinking, he assumed that changes in organisms can be stimulated by environmental conditions, which is close to the view of his grandfather and Lamarck.

The problem of evolution was familiar and important to young Darwin, since not only had his grandfather written about it, but the members of his family probably discussed it. Alfred Russell Wallace's independent and parallel development of the theory adds evidence for the broad-ranging interest in the problem of evolution. In addition, in a little-known book published in 1831, Patrick Matthew, a Scottish botanical writer, presented a theory of evolution by natural selection that was the same as Darwin's and Wallace's, so much so that Darwin acknowledged in a letter to Wallace that "He gives *most clearly* but very briefly . . . our view of natural selection. It is a most complete case of anticipation." Matthew's work went unnoticed partly because of his obscure position and partly because it appeared at the end of a book on trees.

Darwin did not go beyond undergraduate training, a fact that has been interpreted by some as a positive influence in his success, because extensive training in any discipline results in one's adopting the accepted wisdom and thereby being trapped inside it. This concept is made clear by Edward deBono, whose views about creativity and methods for increasing creative thinking were discussed in Chapter 2.

> Many great discoverers like Faraday had no formal education at
> all, and others, like Darwin or Clerk Maxwell, had insufficient
> to curb their originality. It is tempting to suppose that a
> capable mind that is unaware of the old approach has a good
> chance of evolving a new one.

On the one hand, deBono's claim is obviously correct: since Darwin produced a great scientific theory, it must be true that nothing curbed his originality (the claim is also circular). DeBono is also claiming that Darwin's education did nothing of a positive nature to facilitate his creative work, but examination of Darwin's education and its effects shows that deBono's claim is untrue.

Darwin entered Edinburgh University in 1825 — at his father's urging — to study medicine, but gave up that career and left the university in 1827. He then attended Cambridge University from 1827 to 1831, ostensibly to study for the ministry, but became a scientist. During his studies at Edinburgh and Cambridge, Darwin met many leading scientific thinkers, some who did not accept the orthodox explanation of the development of the earth and its inhabitants, and some who did.

While at Edinburgh, Darwin became close friends with Dr. Robert Grant, a zoologist who believed in Lamarckian evolution. Darwin notes in his autobiography that he was very surprised when, during one of their walks, Grant suddenly confessed his agreement with Lamarck. In 1826, there had appeared in a journal an anonymous article supporting Lamarck's theory, actually written by Grant. At some point, Darwin must have learned of this, and he would have been struck by Grant's fear of having his name associated with the article.

Darwin — A Brief Chronology

1809	Born
1825 – 1827	Edinburgh University — pre-med, but dropped out 3/27/1827 — presented papers to Plinian Society (student society) Interaction with Professor Robert Grant, believer in Lamarck
1827 – 1831	Attended University of Cambridge — originally as divinity student Summer 1829 — entomological tour of north Wales with professor F. W. Hope August 1831 — geological tour of north Wales with Professor A. Sedgwick
1831 – 1836	Voyage of H.M.S. Beagle 12/27/31 — sailed from England 9/23/32 — first important fossil find: various extinct mammals September 1835 — studied geology, fauna, and flora of Galápagos Islands. 10/2/36 — returned to England
July 1837	First notebook on transmutation of species; Monad theory of evolution
9/28/1838	Reread Malthus, grasped evolution through natural evolution
Nov. – Dec, 1838	Restated theory as three principles.
6/18/1858	Received letter from Alfred Russell Wallace, presenting theory of evolution through natural selection
7/1/1858	Papers by Darwin and Wallace read before Linnaean Society, London
7/20/1858	Began writing *Origin*
10/1/1859	Proofing finished
11/25/1859	*Origin* published
1882	Died.

At Cambridge University, too, Darwin met and was influenced by many important scientists. One of these, John Stevens Henslow, professor of botany and geology, welcomed him to the weekly open house he held for students and professors. Darwin became known as "the man who walks with Henslow." In the summer of 1829, he went on an entomological tour of north Wales with Professor F. W. Hope.

Professor Adam Sedgwick invited Darwin on a geologic expedition to north Wales in August, 1831. The scientific techniques of observation and data collection that Darwin learned on this latter trip were important for the rest of his scientific life.

Thus, Darwin seems to have pursued an active undergraduate career and received a full education. By the time he left Cambridge, Darwin was no longer a young man ignorant of modern science. He was able to embark on the next great adventure of his life — the voyage of the *Beagle* — as a scientist sophisticated both in methods of data collection and in modern scientific theory, including modern evolutionary views.

In addition, Darwin's education, like that of all scholars, did not cease when his formal training ended. During the *Beagle* voyage, Darwin came under the influence of Charles Lyell, who, while not strictly a teacher, played an important role in the development of Darwin's theory. Lyell in 1830 had published the first edition of the *Principles of Geology*, which was to become the most important book in its field. Darwin read Lyell's book while on the voyage, and became a strong admirer of Lyell. On Darwin's return to England, they became friends. In the *Principles of Geology*, Lyell discussed the origin and development of both the earth and its inhabitants, and he expressed many ideas that became important in Darwin's theorizing. Lyell opposed catastrophism and instead advocated *uniformitarianism*, the view originally proposed by James Hutton that there had been uniformity of natural processes throughout history, with no catastrophes.

Lyell also considered natural selection, but only as a negative process, when unhealthy organisms are displaced by healthier ones in the struggle for existence (called "nature's broom"). It remained for Darwin to propose that natural selection also worked in a positive manner, since any change that gave an animal an advantage in the struggle for existence would be passed along and thereby result in the evolution of the species.

One reason Lyell failed to see that natural selection could work in a positive manner may have been that he was unaware of the tremendous variation within a species. Darwin became aware of this potential during the voyage of the *Beagle* and therefore was in a position to expand upon Lyell's views. During the *Beagle* voyage, Darwin was in the perfect position to gather data concerning phenomena discussed by Lyell. Lorin Eiseley proposes that Lyell could be looked upon as composing and presenting the problem that Darwin and Wallace solved.

Darwin's education was much broader and deeper than he indicates in his autobiography and, contrary to deBono's claim, it played a crucial role in his scientific work. It is difficult to imagine how an uneducated or self-taught individual could have done what Darwin did. He needed to learn the scientific techniques of data gathering and cataloguing crucial to accumulating the data that formed the foundations of his beliefs. In addition, in order to go beyond what had been done on a theoretical level, he needed first to be immersed in theory, and this immersion was provided by his teachers. Furthermore, many of the ideas in Darwin's final theory can be traced to ideas of his teachers. Contrary to deBono, Darwin's was a capable mind that was *aware* of and *used* the old approach in evolving a new one.

The Voyage of the *Beagle*

On August 29, 1831, Darwin was offered the post of naturalist on HMS *Beagle*, which was scheduled to carry out a five-year journey around the world, paying particular attention to exploring the shores of South America. The post of naturalist involved collecting and cataloging specimens of animal and plant life. During the voyage, Darwin acquired information that convinced him that evolution was a fact, and that set the stage for his attempt to solve the problem of how evolution occurred, which are two very different things.

There were two sorts of influences on Darwin during the voyage. The first, already discussed, came from his reading of Lyell's *Principles of Geology*, and the second came from some of his observations, most particularly those of the animals inhabiting the Galápagos Islands. As his diary and notebooks show, Darwin was already leaning toward a belief in evolution when he left on the voyage. This belief was strengthened by his observations. As the *Beagle* traveled south along the coast of South America, for example, Darwin noted that a series of similar animal groups occurred, with the replacement of one group by another of very similar form. Such a series of similar groups suggested that a single species had differentiated into several highly similar forms. In addition, while exploring the pampas of Argentina, he discovered fossils of huge animals anatomically very similar to the armadillos existing at that time in the region. This supported the notion that the modern species gradually evolved out of the ancient species.

These similarities—the first based on the distribution of organisms in space; the second based on distribution in time—were somewhat surprising if one believed the literal orthodox view that all species were created at once. Why then had the creator made these various species so similar? If one believed that these species were related to one another, then these similarities made sense.

When the *Beagle* reached the Galápagos Islands, a group of approximately twenty islands off the west coast of South America, in September, 1835, Darwin found even more remarkable similarities and differences among species of animals. He collected animals from the various islands and found that the local inhabitants could tell from which island each specimen had come. Thus, the species of animals on these islands differed from each other; they were not stable. Darwin was particularly impressed by the various species of finches on the islands, especially the variations among their beaks. Some species had small beaks, while others had large thick beaks — differences which pointed to great variability within groups of animals, even when the physical environment and the climate were essentially identical, as they were on those islands. Thus, Darwin was faced with the question of how, by what mechanism, all this variation came about.

Continuity — The Monad Theory

After his return to England in October 1836, Darwin began to think systematically about evolutionary theory. In July, 1837, he began his first of four notebooks on transmutation of species (evolution) and, contrary to the statement in his autobiography, he formulated his first theory of evolution, based on the idea of the "monad."

The monad theory is based on the concept that simple living particles, or monads, are constantly springing into life. They originate in inanimate matter and are produced by natural forces, so that one does not have to assume that there is a separate supernatural creation for each monad. A monad has a fixed life span, during which it differentiates, matures, and reproduces, becoming a whole group of related species. These organisms respond to changes in the environment with adaptive changes, which produce evolution. When a monad dies, all the species it has become, at all levels of complexity, die at that same moment. Darwin was working under the assumption that the total number of species on earth at any given time was constant, a vestige of the orthodox view, which his theory could accommodate since when a monad and all its related species die, new species will develop to replace them.

This theory has components that seem very primitive today, but that were accepted at the time. The idea of the spontaneous generation of life from nonliving matter, for example, was not disproved until Louis Pasteur's experiments in 1861. Lamarck also argued that spontaneous generation occurred continuously, while Lyell claimed that species were created in succession and endured for a fixed period. Nor was the monad concept new with Darwin. The sources for Darwin's theorizing are summarized at the top of the following table.

There were at that time several reasons for believing that extinction occurred through the simultaneous deaths of all the products of a single monad. Fossil evidence indicated that whole groups of species disappeared suddenly, although this "evidence" was actually a mistaken conclusion drawn from imperfections in the geologic record, which in reality is very fragmentary. Second, in order for extinction to come about through *environmental* change, which would make the belief in monads unnecessary, a relatively large-scale change in the environment was required. Basically, this would be a version of catastrophism, which already had been rejected by Darwin, through the influence of Lyell, among others. Also, if environmental change rather

Continuity and Discontinuity in Darwin's Theory

Continuity	*Source*
Monads	Common philosophical concept
Spontaneous generation	Commonly accepted concept
Adaptation in response to environment	Lamarckian evolution
Simultaneous deaths of monad offspring	Fossil "evidence"; uniformitarianism
Discontinuity	*Basis for Change*
Rejection of monads	Discoveries of unicellular fossils — some organisms stay simple
Variation is assumed	Beagle voyage — saw great deal of variation without environmental stimulation
	Logical questions about assuming that environment causes variation in monads
Emphasis on superfecundity	New data in literature

than monad death produced extinction, any change in a species could be erased by a change in the environment. This would mean that there would be no overall evolution. Darwin, therefore, looked for a non-environmental cause for extinction.

Thus, Darwin's monad theory dealt with the facts of species change as he knew them, and was a synthesis of accepted ideas. Over the next fifteen months or so, great changes occurred in Darwin's thinking that resulted in rejection of the monad theory and development of the theory of natural selection. These changes came about as a result of his logical analysis of his theory and its implications, his consideration of new pieces of evidence, and a change in emphasis concerning what his theory should account for.

From Monads to Natural Selection

The monad theory attempted to account for the origin of life through the development of monads. However, Darwin's interest shifted to the possibility of life as an ongoing system rather than a system involving the constant creation of new forms. One important factor in this change was the discovery of fossils of unicellular organisms, which meant that some organisms remained simple. One did not have to assume that all simple organisms alive at present had just been created.

In Darwin's early thinking, variation among the members of a species was a conclusion drawn from the assumptions first that changes in the environment produce changes in organisms and second that monads develop into complex organisms. In Darwin's final theory, variation is accepted as a premise ("tendency to small change . . ."), indicating a basic shift in viewpoint. A theory of evolution that assumes an inherent tendency for organisms to become more complex and to adapt to changes in the environment may not explain how evolution actually comes about. Also, Darwin became increasingly impressed by the extent of variation in nature. His experiences on the *Beagle*, especially in the Galápagos, showed him that animals in the same environments can differ, indicating that variations are not in response to environmental changes. Variation is, therefore, a fact of organic life.

One factor that became increasingly important in Darwin's thinking is the great fertility (fecundity) in nature, the fact that organisms reproduce at a very high rate. This *super*fecundity was emphasized by Malthus in his *Essay on Population*, as well as by others. The German biologist C. G. Ehrenberg, who was becoming well known in British scientific circles at the time, provided evidence that micro-organisms reproduced at nearly unbelievable rates. As an example, Darwin wrote in his notebook shortly before reading Malthus that a single micro-organism could produce enough offspring in four days to form a stone of considerable size.

As already mentioned, the idea of natural selection did not originate with Darwin. It was generally acknowledged that deviant organisms tended to be less fit and therefore had less chance of survival. Darwin was also familiar with the phenomenon of artificial selection, in which humans breed plants and animals for special characteristics. Though an analogy can be made between the human role in artificial selection and the struggle for survival in natural selection, when Darwin began theorizing about evolution this analogy was not clear to him. Others had also noted that artificial selection could produce changes in species, but it was thought that the absolute amount of those changes was limited by the species boundaries set by God's creation. Only when a belief in evolution was accepted could artificial selection be seen as a basis for understanding evolution in nature.

Given these changes in his thought since the formulation of the monad theory, Darwin's reading of Malthus, rather than producing a great leap of insight, was simply the final step in a long process. These changes in thinking, summarized in the second half of the table presented earlier, were made up of modifications based on pressure from new data, or logical problems which became apparent to Darwin. Furthermore, the Malthusian insight itself did not originate from nothing, that is, Darwin's views had to change before Malthus could have just the right effect on him.

There is also evidence that Darwin did not originally perceive his response to Malthus to be a great leap of insight or a profound unveiling of something completely hidden. In the passage from Darwin's autobiography presented earlier, Darwin wrote "it at once struck me. . . ," which leads one to believe that everything fell into place at once. That passage, however, was written many years after the event actually occurred. The entries made in his notebooks fail to indicate that anything particularly momentous occurred. The entry that refers to his reading of Malthus *looks* no different from other entries, and other entries in the notebook made about that time continue to refer to other topics, indicating that Malthus's essay had not produced an illumination that had eclipsed all his other interests.

Perhaps most important, more than a month elapsed before Darwin wrote the "Three principles will account for all" passage cited earlier, in which he succinctly summarized his theory. There still seemed to be a lot of working out to be done after he read Malthus, which was just another source of information and ideas which Darwin used as the basis for his thinking.

Analysis of the changes in Darwin's thought in the time between his return from the *Beagle* voyage and his construction of the theory indicates that, contrary to Davidson and Sternberg, he did much more than combine facts. Darwin initially developed the monad theory, so that the issue was not simply one of "facts," but rather of their interpretation. Then, the monad theory had to be rejected before the correct theory could develop. Some of the changes that occurred in Darwin's thought between the two theories, such as the change in his views toward variation, were changes in emphasis and orientation. They involved more than combining facts. Many (although not nearly all) of the "facts" that Darwin dealt with in his theory were available to others, but the most important aspects of Darwin's theorizing centered on the interpretation of facts. Darwin was able to develop the theory of natural selection not because he was a better shuffler of facts than was anyone before him, but because he had different facts than had others, due in part to his unique experiences — particularly the *Beagle* voyage — and because his way of thinking about the facts had developed into something different from anyone before him.

Scientific Discovery and Computer Models

Researchers have recently attempted to demonstrate that scientific discoveries such as Darwin's and Watson and Crick's can be understood as heuristically guided searches through problem spaces. Pat Langley, Herbert Simon, Gary Bradshaw, and Jan Zytkow have developed a set of related computer models of scientific discovery in several domains. Each model possesses heuristics that enable it to search a particular type of problem space. When these programs have been presented with data taken from the history of science, a number of important scientific laws have been "discovered" by the programs. These results have led Langley and colleagues to conclude first, that heuristic search through problem spaces may be the mechanism whereby much — and perhaps all — scientific discovery is brought about, and second, that scientific discovery uses the same ordinary processes of problem solving employed in situations such as Missionaries and Cannibals (see Chapter 4).

As of now, Langley and colleagues are not concerned whether their models carry out discoveries in exactly the same way as historically occurred in individual cases. Rather, they are interested in demonstrating that heuristic search is plausible as a mechanism whereby scientific discovery is brought about. However, simulating individual examples of scientific discovery appears to be a long-term goal of the program.

The simplest of these computer models is called Bacon, in honor of Sir Francis Bacon, the prime mover behind the induction method used by this model to determine quantitative laws in such diverse areas as planetary motion, electricity, and gases. The Bacon program derived Kepler's third law of planetary motion, which states that if one measures the distance of any planet from the sun and the time it takes the planet to travel one circuit around the sun (its period), then the cube of the distance is proportional to the square of the period ($D^3/P^2 = C$, where D is distance, P is the period, and C is a constant). This was an important early law in physics that played a role in Newton's development of his laws of planetary motion.

The model is provided with three heuristics by the programmer.

(1) If the values of a term are constant, then infer that the term always has that value.
(2) If the values of two numerical terms increase together, then consider their ratio.
(3) If the values of one term increase as those of another decrease, then consider their product.

These heuristics are not related to physics, which is important, because if one programmed heuristics directly related to the subject matter, one might be hiding the derivation of laws within the program, which would make the exercise of little value. These heuristics are also of the sorts that were available to Kepler.

The data from three planets as presented to Bacon, including the distance from the sun (D), and the period (P), are shown in the first three columns of the table on the facing page. On examining these data, Bacon would conclude that the second heuristic can be used, since D and P increase together for all the planets. Thus, Bacon computes the ratio of D and P (Term 1 in the table), with the results shown in the fourth column. The three values of Term 1 are not equal, and there is now a new relation to be considered: Term 1 decreases as D increases, so that the third heuristic is now used, and the product of D and Term 1, which is (D/P) (D) or D²/P (Term 2), is calculated, with the results shown in the next column. Since the three values of Term 2 are not equal, Bacon determines that Term 2 increases while Term 1 decreases. The third heuristic is now used, which results in the calculation of the product of Terms 1 and 2 (Term 3), which results in the value of 1 for all the planets. The first heuristic is then used, to infer that Term 3 is always equal to one. Thus, Bacon has determined that for the three planets in the table, the cube of the distance and the square of the period are equal.

The Bacon program is structured so that the heuristics are carried out so long as the available data fit one of them. When there are no further steps to be carried out, the program stops. The program's heuristics are very general in nature, and comparable to what was available to the scientists of the time. In some cases, these heuristics were made explicit by the scientists of the time as laws or rules for carrying out the scientific enterprise.

Langley and associates developed several versions of the Bacon program, which differed in the heuristics and the sorts of data that they could work with, and the more complicated versions were able to invent new terms, such as "density" and "specific heat," to describe properties of objects on the basis of data concerning their behavior in certain situations. As an example, Bacon defined a new term, which we can call "volume," to refer to the volume of an object, determined from the amount of liquid displaced by the object, which was given to the program. It then used volume and weight to calculate density, another new term. In neither case was the new term in any way written into the heuristics. Rather, the heuristics were of the form "If you have a series of numerical values that has no label, then define a new property of the object in question and give that property those values." Thus, when Bacon determined that there was a series of

Bacon Program's Determination of Kepler's Third Law of Planetary Motion

Planet	D	P	Term 1 (D/P)	Term 2 (D²/P)	Term 3 (D³/P²)
A	1	1	1	1	1
B	4	8	0.5	2	1
C	9	27	0.33	3	1

numbers corresponding to the amount of liquid displaced by a series of objects, it defined the volumes of the objects and gave each object the value of the amount of liquid displaced, which is how Archimedes used the term.

Although the several versions of the Bacon program have achieved a broad range of remarkable success with a relatively simple set of heuristics, there are aspects of scientific discovery beyond its capabilities. One limitation is in the analysis of components of objects based on their "behavior," such as when chemists became capable of explaining chemical reactions by developing concepts like acids, bases, and salts. Another example is explanation based on theory, as when one explains the results of some experiment through a theoretical analysis of the objects, such as explaining the formation of water from oxygen and hydrogen on the basis of atomic theory.

To deal with such situations, Langley and associates developed a number of additional programs. One program, called Glauber in honor of an early chemist, uses qualitative data of the form "HC1 has a sour taste"; "A reaction of HC1 and NaOH forms NaCl"; and "NaCl tastes salty." Based on statements such as these, which describe the "behavior" of different substances under different circumstances, the program's heuristics attempt to form classes of substances that behave in the same ways. When Glauber learns other things about HCl and also about HNO_3, it determines that these two substances can be classed together. In this way, it developed categories corresponding to acids, bases, and salts, parallel to the classes developed early in the history of chemistry on the basis of qualitative analysis.

Finally, the Dalton program, named after one of the developers of atomic theory, uses knowledge of the theory to analyze chemical reactions and to analyze the structures of the participating substances.

In contrast with Bacon, which basically works with quantitative laws and stays relatively close to the input data, the Glauber and Dalton programs exhibit a degree of theoretical analysis that impresses one as more like "real" scientific thinking. In addition, Langley and associates discuss the possibility that several of these models might be combined, so that the output of Bacon, say, could be made available to Glauber. Then, much more complicated analysis could be carried out.

Langley and associates believe that these programs and their heuristic structure represent the beginning of an enterprise that will result in the entire range of scientific discovery being modeled by computer programs using heuristically-guided problem solving, based on search.

Are Computer Models Creative?

Langley and associates believe that the programs exhibit creativity, since the programs have discovered scientific laws important in the development of science, and have done it in a wide range of areas. Furthermore, the heuristics in the programs are of a general nature, which makes it unlikely that the discoveries are hidden in them. If one objects that these heuristics are simply written by the programmer, and therefore represent the programmer's knowledge of the domain, these very heuristics were — in some cases — explicitly used by the scientists initially working in these areas.

Mihalyi Csikszentmihalyi, on the other hand, has argued that these models cannot be called creative. As discussed in Chapter 3, Csikszentmihalyi argues that for a work to be considered creative, it must be accepted by the members of the field, and thus become part of the domain in question, to be handed down to the next generation. Creativity is the result of the interaction of all these factors, and the computer programs cannot be creative, since they did not participate in the entire process.

Csikszentmihalyi makes a comparison between a computer model's production of some product called creative in historical context and a very good copy of a painting. Even though the copy might be indistinguishable from a work which we might revere as great, it is not creative, because the creativity of the original work is in part a result of the historical, social, and cultural factors that brought it about. Since the computer programs do not partake of these factors, their output — even though it is the same as that of a scientist now revered as creative — cannot be called creative.

However, in my opinion, the most important question is whether the ways of processing information built into these programs can produce output like that produced by humans. It may not matter whether we agree that the program is creative, because the issue is more narrow: given a motivated individual, if he or she were using these methods alone, could that person produce the same output as produced by these famous scientists? Given this slant on the problem, then, whether or not we agree that they are creative, the programs are intrinsically interesting and have produced promising results.

These computer models are based on the assumption that all scientific creativity can be described as heuristically guided search through a problem space. Let us reconsider Watson and Crick's discovery, which, as mentioned earlier, can at first glance be described as search through a "helix problem space." Watson and Crick were attempting to specify the parameters of a helix, such as two or three strands, and so on, and were examining results that were potentially relevant to distinguishing among these various alternatives.

It now becomes interesting to ask where the search space came from. Watson and Crick's expertise in the area led them to retrieve Pauling's methods as a possible basis for their work, but a comparable move could not be carried out by any of the models designed by Langley and associates, since they do not possess expertise in the domains that would make available to them possible base analogues on which to build. From the results from studies of analogical transfer in human problem solving, it might not be easy to elaborate these models to enable transfer to occur in some circumstances but not others.

The possibility of computer simulation of creative thinking is of great potential importance, on practical as well as theoretical grounds. However, a number of difficult issues remain to be worked out before it can be concluded that heuristically-based computer models explain creative thinking in science.

Is All Scientific Thinking Problem Solving?

From Thomas Kuhn's perspective, revolutionary science changes the way in which science is carried out, which in turn redefines the types of problems that are to be examined. A scientific revolution can thus be looked upon as "problem finding," rather than problem solving (see also the discussion of problem finding in invention in Chapter 5). In the opinion of some, problem finding is more important than problem solving, since without problem finding there would be no problem solving. In science, this view is expressed by the statement that the really creative act in science is asking a good question, rather than answering it. The classic case of problem finding in science is Einstein's original formulation of the theory of special relativity, which only developed after Einstein discovered problems with already existing formulations. Therefore, the revolution brought about by the development of relativity theory was the result of Einstein's initial finding of the difficulty.

However, scientific revolutions are not always the result of problem finding rather than problem solving. The two cases in this chapter are examples of revolutionary discoveries, and both were problem solving. Ordinary thinking about a scientific problem can have a revolutionary outcome. Also, in both cases in this chapter, the break with the past was not as sharp as the notion of revolution leads one to expect. Many evolutionary ideas were around in various forms before Darwin came on the scene. The same was true with Watson and Crick. In response to Kuhn's theorizing, there has developed a view that argues that scientific change is smoother than the notion of revolution leads one to believe, and the case studies in this chapter support that view.

The Social Nature of Scientific Research

Scientists are sometimes described as working in splendid isolation in an "ivory tower," spending all their time away from the petty issues of the outside world, thinking solely about their research problems as they objectively seek the truth. This view of science and scientists focuses on the individual scientist and thereby overlooks the cooperative nature of scientific research. In addition, scientists are often involved in more than the disinterested pursuit of truth.

The two discoveries discussed in this chapter came about in very different ways. Watson and Crick engaged in a collaboration, while Darwin worked alone; Watson and Crick were part of one of the most well-known scientific laboratories in one of the most well-known universities in the world, while Darwin worked in his home. These differences raise questions about the role of collaboration and more generally about the social nature of scientific creativity.

There are a number of important ways in which the social aspect of science played a role in the discovery of the double helix. The most obvious is the collaboration of Watson, a geneticist, and Crick, a physicist. Since they approached the problem from different backgrounds, each was able to provide unique facts and ways of looking at things. Watson and Crick incorporated into their work the experimental results and theoretical ideas produced by others, and critiques from other researchers were particularly important in directing their work at several places. Finally, the teachers of these two scientists also played a role in their interest in the problem of DNA and how they approached it. Vera John-Steiner has documented the important role of mentors in the development of individuals who make creative contributions.

Darwin's work was done outside the scientific establishment, since he did not hold a position at a university, but his thought was influenced at many points by other individuals — both during and after his formal education — indicating that he, too, was part of a social network. A number of Darwin's teachers (later, colleagues) played important supportive roles during the *Beagle* voyage and during the development, publication, and dissemination of Darwin's theory. Henslow was the recipient of many letters from Darwin, and he read many of these to the Cambridge Philosophical Society before Darwin returned, alerting others to the importance of his work.

Joseph Hooker, a well-known botanist, was a lifelong friend of Darwin, who in letters presented many ideas to him for discussion. T. H. Huxley, a well-known biologist, was a strong supporter of Darwin's theory, urged him to publish, and defended the theory in public debate against the orthodox view. Darwin thus had many individuals available to serve as constructive critics as well as to provide moral support. We have also seen that Darwin was aware of developments in the scientific literature, and these influenced his theory development.

Thus, even though Darwin's work was not collaborative, the image of the isolated thinker out in the country poring over his notes and specimens is misrepresentative of Darwin's involvement in the scientific community.

Conclusions

In at least two well-known cases, revolutionary scientific creativity came about through the same sort of thought processes ordinary people use to solve ordinary problems. Both Watson and Crick and Darwin showed continuity of thinking in their initial formulations of their theories, and these theories underwent sometimes radical changes, in specifiable and understandable ways, in response to inadequacies that became apparent. These inadequacies were addressed by modifying various parts of the old theory, in a series of accommodations which resulted in a new theory. These modifications were based sometimes on logical analysis of the structure of the original theory; sometimes on new facts; sometimes on new interpretations from others. There seemed in neither discovery to be one point at which everything suddenly fell into place in a large-scale reorganization, but rather there was a gradual closing in on the final theory as bits and pieces were fit together.

In the next chapter, we will see similar processes occurring in the creation of art. As in invention and science, creative thinking in the arts begins in continuity with the past, and goes beyond it on the basis of feedback from the situation as well as from outside events that serve as triggers for discontinuity.

CHAPTER 7

Case Studies in Artistic Creativity

There is a popular and absurd conception of the "inspired" artist who works in a kind of hypnotic frenzy. His creations gush forth from some hidden reservoir of emotion without any effort on his part, although sometimes with considerable physical agitation followed by dramatic exhaustion. This simply does not happen. Or if it does happen, what gushes forth is formless and chaotic and hence not art.

(Canaday 1980, p. 23)

[W]e are told that Picasso changes his style so frequently and so rapidly that no one would realize that works of different periods were by the same artist. But what art historian—if he did not know the intervening stages—could guess that early and late works by Titian, Rembrandt, Poussin, or Cézanne were by the same hand? And if, with Picasso, one carries out the process of following through the intervening stages, it becomes apparent that, although the first and last productions of his imagination are widely separated—even fundamentally different—the change was brought about by a series of steps, each of which is intelligible and can be seen as following logically on the earlier

> moves, and each of which was arrived at by a
> process of experiment and thought.
>
> (Blunt 1969, p. 2)

In this chapter, I will consider creativity in the arts — painting, poetry, music, literature, film — a set of domains in which one might expect to find processes different from those in problem solving, invention, and science. A belief in the uniqueness of artistic creativity is supported by reports from many artists that works come to them whole, in a creative outburst. In Chapter 2, a number of these reports were found to be of questionable accuracy. The present chapter presents data from case studies showing how artistic creativity actually comes about. The results will show great similarities between the creative process in the arts and what we have already seen in problem solving, invention, and science. As in those other domains, creative thinking in the arts begins with continuity and goes beyond it in rational ways.

In the domain of painting, I will examine the development of two of Picasso's great paintings, *Les Demoiselles d'Avignon* and *Guernica*, as well as the development of Jackson Pollock's "allover" poured paintings. *Les Demoiselles* was a radically new work, and will serve as the basis for an investigation of discontinuity in art. Picasso's *Guernica* was the work of a mature artist, and was created very quickly. Examining its development will illuminate creative thinking in the mature artist, and comparing the development of the two paintings will show how creative thinking — in one case at least — changed as an artist developed.

Pollock's "allover" poured paintings seem to be totally "free" and independent of influences, the result of some upwelling of creative energy from deep inside the artist. Works so radically different from traditional works of art pose a particularly difficult problem for any explanation based on continuity.

In poetry, there is a long tradition of reports of works suddenly springing whole into consciousness, especially among the English romantic poets. We have already critically examined Coleridge's report concerning his production of *Kubla Khan*. The genesis of this work has been given extensive analysis by J. L. Lowes, providing valuable information concerning the operation of the artistic imagination.

In music, there is as well a full literature claiming that compositions appear complete to the composer, who then just writes them down (e.g., Mozart's "letter" discussed in Chapter 1). In this chapter, I shall examine more objective evidence that sheds light on the process of musical composition.

Fiction writing has also produced its share of self-reports claiming that plans for works, if not whole works, came complete. One strong advocate of this view was Fyodor Dostoyevsky, and I will present analyses of his notebooks for his novel *The Idiot*. I will also examine the role of personal experiences in writing fiction.

Charlie Chaplin's highly productive eighteen months making a series of two-reel silent comedies for the Mutual Film Corporation provide a marvelous opportunity to observe him at work, because he did not work with scripts, and thus did his thinking on the set, on film. One can compare the initial form of a film with the final version, examine the changes that occurred, and consider how they were brought about.

Picasso as The Young Revolutionary: Les Demoiselles d'Avignon

Les Demoiselles d'Avignon (see Chapter 1) was painted in 1907, when Picasso was 25, and contains stylistic developments different from anything that had been seen before in the work of any artist. This painting has been called by art historians the most important painting of this century, because it was the foremost example of work that severed the link between painting and the objects represented. The women in *Les Demoiselles* are portrayed as they are to suit the artist's purpose, with his *conception* taking precedence over *perception*; their grotesque appearance and poses are there to repel the viewer.

Les Demoiselles is a painting of a scene of sexual license: the women are prostitutes and the setting is the parlor of a brothel. The title comes from Avignon Street in the red-light district in Barcelona, Spain, which Picasso may have frequented as a young man. The leftmost woman is drawing back the curtain to expose the scene to the viewer, and therefore only her hand and part of her forearm are visible behind her head. Her masklike face seems separate from the rest of her body, which is partly covered by a robelike garment. The second woman from the left has her right arm thrown behind her head in a sexually inviting gesture, while her left hand grasps a cloth. Her face has staring lozenge-shaped eyes, a flat nose, and large scrolled ears. The third woman, in the center, is similar.

The woman opening the curtain and entering at the upper right is similar to the woman on the far left. The woman seated at the right has a severely distorted masklike face, with a curved flat nose with striations, and she does not have a neck. Her face seems to be looking in the general direction of the viewer, but we seem to get a back view of her body, which means that her head must be severely twisted.

The painting contains as well a still-life of fruit set on a table that sharply protrudes into the bottom of the painting from the viewer's space; this serves to bring the viewer into the painting — we are visiting the brothel.

The Origin and Development of a Creative Work

A finished painting in several ways hides its development from the naive observer. A painter may carry out preliminary work in sketchbooks that never appears in the final painting. Once paint is put on canvas, it can be removed, modified, or covered over, which can sometimes be seen in the final painting; X-ray analysis can also reveal earlier stages of a work. A painter can also carry out solely mental work on a painting, which leaves no direct physical trace of any sort, although there is sometimes indirect evidence, such as the artist's comments or changes in a work from one time to another.

Examination of Picasso's voluminous preliminary work for *Les Demoiselles* shows changes in his conception before he started to work on the painting itself. As shown in several sketches, there were originally seven figures — five women and two men — and the still life was near the center of the painting. The women are hardly distorted in the early sketches.

The man in the center of the scene has been identified, based on other preliminary sketches and on Picasso's own report, as a sailor, a customer of the brothel. He and the five women are looking to their right as a second man draws back the curtain and enters. The intruder has been identified by Picasso as a medical student. In the final version of the painting, the two men are gone. All attention centers on the five women, who face the viewer, now the intruder into their domain. The still life moves from the center of the painting to the foreground; in some of the sketches there are two still-lifes, one in the center and one at the bottom of the painting.

The earliest version of *Les Demoiselles* seems to have been an attempt to tell a story: the sailor, who may be having his first sexual experience in the brothel, is risking his life through the possible con-

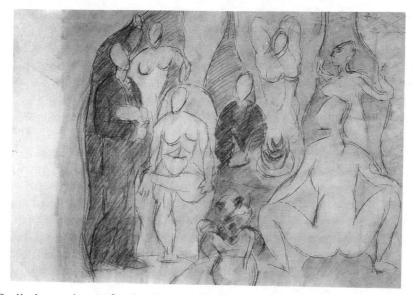

Preliminary sketch for *Les Demoiselles d'Avignon* by Pablo Picasso.

Final composition study for *Les Demoiselles d'Avignon* showing five women.

traction of venereal disease, a possibility emphasized by the presence of the medical student. There is evidence that at this time Picasso frequented brothels and had strong fears about contracting venereal disease. He had spent time visiting a hospital in Paris observing prostitutes who were suffering dreadfully from advanced stages of venereal disease, which produced on their faces large tumorous growths and festering open sores and led to dementia and death. Venereal disease was at that time looked on with great fear, much as AIDS is today. The final version of the painting presents these sentiments in a less direct way; we react in a strongly negative manner to the women as Picasso has portrayed them.

Antecedents of Les Demoiselles: Picasso's "Iberian" Period

Although *Les Demoiselles* looks like nothing anyone had painted before, there are nonetheless strong links to it from works of Picasso and of his contemporaries, as well as of artists of earlier generations. There are as well several discontinuities in this painting, and each can be traced to significant external events.

Based on X-ray analyses of *Les Demoiselles*, it has been determined that Picasso carried out two cycles of painting. The painting was initially very similar to the final compositional study, in which all the women have faces like those of the two central *demoiselles*: oval-shaped, with large lozenge-shaped eyes, large scrolled ears, and flat noses. Examination of the development of these two faces can shed light on the painting as a whole.

The source for these faces was an exhibition of antique Iberian reliefs at the Louvre museum in Paris in the spring of 1906. An example of a piece from this exhibit shows the particular shape of the face and the form of the eyes and nose which spread to much of his work at that time, resulting in his "Iberian" style.

Another striking characteristic of the two central demoiselles is their large scrolled ears. These are a discontinuity from Picasso's Iberian period. Such ears can be seen on two other antique statues, not part of the Louvre exhibit, which were briefly acquired by Picasso in 1907. Large scrolled ears can be seen in other paintings and sculpture by Picasso at about this time.

The noses of the two central demoiselles are also different from Picasso's "classical" Iberian noses in their extreme flat shape. The source of these noses, according to a report by Picasso, was a painting by Henri Matisse — one of the leaders of the "modern" artists in Paris

Iberian relief.

at the turn of the century — acquired by Picasso from Matisse in early 1907, in exchange for one of his own paintings.

The "Second Campaign" of Painting

After completing the Iberian phase of the painting, Picasso changed everything in the painting but the two "Iberian" demoiselles in the center. These modifications were stimulated by a visit to an ethnographic museum, and his "discovery" there of primitive art. This visit was stimulated by a suggestion by André Derain, another important modern artist in Paris. Picasso relates how he was struck by the strong emotional quality of works from various non-European cultures, including Africa and the South Pacific. Primitive art was seen by Picasso as a vehicle for releasing the strong emotions involved in the subject matter of *Les Demoiselles*, and this produced the distortions. Spain's highly emotion-laden artistic tradition might have made Picasso particularly sensitive to what he saw as the emotionality of primitive art.

It has been proposed by some art historians that these changes were based directly on specific primitive masks that Picasso had seen. Contrary to such a "direct influence" hypothesis, however, records of importation of art into France indicate that these particular masks were not available in Paris until years after the painting was carried out. Therefore, the exposure to primitive art may have served to make the emotional content of *Les Demoiselles* more intense, but it did so indirectly. Other faces with flat noses and striations were painted by Picasso during his Iberian stage, and this effect may have been made more extreme as a result of the exposure to primitive art.

Continuities with the Works of Other Artists

There is a long tradition in Western art of painting women of sexual license, although usually they were placed in exotic settings in order to reduce the emotional intensity of the subject. Examples of this are J. A. D. Ingre's *Turkish Bath* and Eugène Delacroix's *Women of Algiers*, both of which were well-known to Picasso. Another antecedent of *Les Demoiselles* is paintings of women of sexual license in nonexotic settings: works depicting prostitutes and courtesans, such as Francisco de Goya's *Nude Maja* and Eduard Manet's *Olympia*. The overt sexuality of the latter caused a great scandal when it was first shown in 1863. Picasso was familiar with both of these paintings.

The work of Paul Cézanne had great influence on the entire generation of "modern" artists who followed him, and this can be seen in *Les Demoiselles*. A print of Cézanne's *Three Bathers* was owned by Matisse, and therefore probably seen by Picasso. The influence of Cézanne is most directly seen in the original form of the squatting figure at the lower right, who originally had a tress of hair falling down her back and an arm that was not twisted.

The same influences and interests in subject matter can be seen in Picasso's peers, the modern artists whose studios he visited and whom he met frequently in cafés for many long discussions of artists' issues. One such example is André Derain, who, like Picasso, was strongly

The Three Bathers by Paul Cézanne.

influenced by primitive art. A painting of bathers by Derain shows many of the same influences seen in Picasso's work at about the same time.

A more important contemporary of Picasso was Matisse, whose influence on Picasso's work has already been briefly discussed. A number of other works by Matisse were related to *Les Demoiselles*, perhaps the most important of which was the *Le Bonheur de Vivre* (*The Joy of Life*), painted by Matisse in 1906. This painting, although very different in emotional tone from *Les Demoiselles*, was similar in its subject matter, as well as in the presence of distortions in the bodies and faces of the women. It has been speculated by some art historians that *Les Demoiselles* was painted in response to the *Le Bonheur de Vivre*, and that the strong negative tone of Picasso's painting may have been a reaction to the idyllic scene by Matisse.

The Joy of Life by Henri Matisse.

Multiple Pathways in Artistic Development

Les Demoiselles d'Avignon developed out of the coalition of several streams: Picasso's Iberian period; a subject matter common among artists of the day; Picasso's fear of venereal disease and conflicted feelings toward women; and the influence of earlier generations of artists, as well as of his contemporaries. In addition, there were several discontinuities: the movement away from the Iberian style (triggered by Matisse's painting and the antique head) and the "primitive" distortions (triggered by Picasso's exposure to primitive art).

There are several different ways in which antecedents were used by Picasso. There was the relatively direct incorporation of something from someone else into his own work, such as use of the flat nose from Matisse's *Portrait of Marquerite*. One can also find some element, from Picasso's own work or that of others, carried to a more extreme degree, so that the element becomes very different in significance and/or emotional tone. For example, the angularity and distortion of human bodies and faces in works of Cézanne, Matisse, and others are in *Les Demoiselles* used in such a way as to contribute to a much different and much stronger emotional tone. A second example is the use of striation and crosshatching, which in *Les Demoiselles* are seen as cuts in the faces. The development of *Les Demoiselles* is summarized in the following table.

Summary of Development of Two of Picasso's Paintings

Element	Source(s)
Continuity and Discontinuity in Les Demoiselles	
Continuity	
Overall theme and scene	Cézanne, Matisse, Derain
Style of preliminary work Curtain raiser	Picasso's "Iberian" period; Delacroix
Seated at right	Cézanne
Two at center	Manet's *Olympia*; Goya's *Naked Maja*
Discontinuity	
Change in orientation and number of characters; removal of men	Picasso's evaluation of painting
Non-Iberian flat noses	Matisse's *Portrait of Marguerite*
Non-Iberian scrolled ears	Sculpture
Distortions; second campaign	Exposure to primitive art
Continuity and Discontinuity in Guernia	
Continuity	
Initial conception: studio	Picasso's earlier work
Overall composition	*Minotauromachy*
Upraised arms in final sketch	Communist posters
Discontinuity	
Studio to Guernica	Bombing
Upraised arms removed	Picasso's political judgment
Warrior's head	Work on display in pavilion

Creativity in the Mature Artist: Guernica

If one compares the development of *Les Demoiselles* with that of *Guernica*, another Picasso masterpiece but one painted many years later, one finds significant changes in artistic creativity (in one case, at least) as an artist develops in his career or, put another way, as the artist gains expertise. One still sees continuity with works of others, but in the mature artist there is another source of continuity: the artist's own work. In *Guernica*, there are many traces of Picasso's own works, although the earlier work can be significantly transformed in form and emotional tone as it is used anew.

On April 26, 1937, during the Spanish Civil War, the Nazi air force, allied with Francisco Franco, the leader of the Spanish fascists, attacked and almost completely destroyed the Spanish town of Guernica. The town itself seems not to have been important militarily, but it had played an important role in the history of Spain for over 600 years, especially in the history of the Basque people. Thus, the destruction of the town and the massacre of civilians were highly symbolic, making the brutality of Franco and his Nazi allies vividly clear.

The bombing of Guernica served as the stimulus for Picasso's most well-known work. In January, 1937, the Spanish government had commissioned him to paint a mural for its building at the Paris World's Fair, to be held in June of that year. Picasso, then 55 years old and world-famous, deeply hated the Spanish fascists who were winning the civil war. Although he began with other plans, he carried out

Guernica by Pablo Picasso. Padro, Madrid. Copyright SPADEM/VAGA, New York, 1986).

his commission by painting a mural stimulated by the bombing of Guernica.

Guernica has become a universal statement on the horrors of war, as well as a symbol for the Spanish people of their liberation from oppression under Franco. After Franco's victory, the painting was loaned by Picasso to the Museum of Modern Art in New York, with the stipulation that if democracy were returned to Spain, the painting would go there permanently. The emotional response to the painting was so strong that during World War II it was displayed at several fund-raising events for Spanish refugee relief. With the change in government in Spain following Franco's death, it became possible to fulfill Picasso's request. In 1981, more than forty years after its creation and eight years after the death of its creator, the painting was returned to Spain. On the 100th anniversary of Picasso's birth, it was put on permanent display in Madrid; this was an occasion for great celebration, and the painting was treated like a hero returning from exile.

Guernica is painted on a grand scale: it measures over 25 feet long by 11 feet high. There is no color: the painting is in shades of gray, ranging from white to almost black. Although it was a response to the aerial bombing of a city, the characters are animals, several women, and a statue. On examining the picture and Picasso's history, one sees that Picasso chose the characters in order to express feelings about war through the responses of its victims.

The central figure is a horse with its head raised in a scream of agony. Above the horse's head is a light, which may be the sun with a light bulb superimposed on it, or a street lamp with a sunlike halo; a bird flies up toward this sun. On the left is a large bull, whose body faces the middle of the scene, but whose head is turned away. Beneath the head of the bull is a mother, her head tilted back and her mouth open in a scream, holding a dead baby whose head lolls backward. To the right of center, a woman holding a lamp leans out of a burning building. On the far upper right, a woman with burning clothes is falling out of a building, while below a woman rushes into the scene. Along the bottom left are the head and arms of a statue of a warrior, in whose hand is a broken sword.

There is some ambiguity about the location of the scene. The tile roof indicates an exterior, as does the lamp-bearing woman leaning out of the upper window, but the lines at the upper corners of the painting can be taken to indicate an interior setting. It has been claimed that the ambiguity of the location of the scene was done purposely by Picasso, in order to deepen the response of the viewer.

However, these lines might designate the courtyard in a Spanish house, meaning that the scene is outside, but surrounded by the interior walls of the house, in which case there is no ambiguity of location.

Picasso had originally planned to fulfill his commission by painting an artist's studio, a motif that he used throughout his career. When the news of the bombing of Guernica reached Paris, he quickly sketched out a new painting. As was the case with *Les Demoiselles*, Picasso carried out much preliminary work on *Guernica*, some forty works, although the time constraints were tight due to the scheduled opening of the Spanish pavilion in June, which gave him only six weeks. Seven of the preliminary works for *Guernica* are composition studies, in which something like the entire mural is presented in varying degrees of detail. Two of these compositional studies appear in this section.

It is clear from these sketches that Picasso originally had set the scene outdoors. The characters appear in various combinations and the overall composition is similar to the final form of the mural. However, there are relatively major changes that occur from one sketch to the next in the characters. The bull, for example, a most important character in the final mural, is not present in some of the sketches, and its position and attitude vary greatly from study to study when it is present. The same is true of the horse and the woman holding the lamp. Picasso seems to have had a general conception in mind when he began the sketches, and he tried several more or less independent variations on it before settling on a version with which to begin painting. The art historian Herschel Chipp comments on how quickly the overall structural basis of *Guernica* was developed; in the sketches of the first day it can already be seen.

In addition to the compositional studies, each main character was examined in several variations, in sketches and in the mural itself, before reaching its final form. A particularly important example is the bull, which was examined in various forms in these studies, and especially interesting are several in which the bull is made almost human, with a vulnerable expression.

Picasso had photographs taken of the mural in various stages of completion, which provide evidence concerning "hidden" aspects of the painting. The earliest painted version was dominated by a defiant upraised arm with clenched fist, present in one of the last preliminary sketches although in less dominating form. This arm, seen elsewhere in works by Picasso at about this time, is not present in the final version, which may have been due to its being too obviously a symbol of the Communists (because of its similarity to their clenched-fist salute)

Composition studies for *Guernica* by Pablo Picasso. Padro, Madrid. Copyright SPADEM/VAGA, New York, 1986).

and Picasso's not wanting to add excess political baggage to the painting.

The bull's orientation in the final version of the mural also differs from its orientation in the earliest painted version and in the compositional studies. The warrior, introduced in a compositional study as one of many fallen human beings at the bottom of the mural, changes position considerably throughout Picasso's working on the mural, until it becomes a broken statue in the final version. Picasso continued making revisions even after the mural was hung in the Spanish pavilion in the Paris exposition, and art historian Anthony Blunt believes that one late revision was stimulated by another work on display in that pavilion.

Continuity with Picasso's Career

Many of the characters in *Guernica* also appear frequently in Picasso's work before and after *Guernica*. Most importantly, a dominant bull and a suffering horse are portrayed together many times in Picasso's drawings and paintings of bullfights, going back at least to when he was 11 years old. However, the emotional tone of the bull in Picasso's bullfight work is often aggressive, as one would expect, and the bull is often being lanced by the picador mounted on the horse that the bull is attacking. In addition, the horse is often the victim of the bull's aggression.

In *Guernica*, however, the bull's emotional expression is one of calmness in the face of destruction all around, and he seems to be providing shelter for the mother holding the dead baby. This near-human emotional expression is seen in Picasso's many paintings of the minotaur, half-human and half-bull, in the 1920s and after. In addition, the horse's agony is brought about by a lance wound (one can see the lance coming down from above and the point protruding below), which is a reversal of what occurs in a bullfight, where the horse carries the picador but does not receive the lance. Furthermore, the lance is not a picador's lance, but is a classical soldier's lance, seen in Picasso's earlier work. Thus, Picasso has changed the scene from a bullfight, since a Spaniard would not consider a bullfight an evil event. Although the bull may die, it is not because he is evil. And if the fight is carried out well, both bull and matador are elevated to positions of high honor.

The light-bearing young woman or girl also appears frequently in Picasso's, work often in conjunction with a bull or minotaur. This symbol was described by Picasso as deriving from a Spanish children's story. A woman is startled one night by terrible noises from the street, and to investigate holds her candle out the window. Her light reveals the cruel king as a murderer, which results in his being driven from power. The light-bearer is thus a good person who illuminates human evil, again strengthening the message in *Guernica*.

It thus seems clear that the horse and, by extension, all the other victims, are being made to suffer through human military action, not through the ritualized action of the bullfight. In this way, Picasso subtly shifts the focus to use the symbols to express something greater than their ordinary meaning.

Another example of continuity within Picasso's career can be seen by comparing *Guernica* with Picasso's etching *Minotauromachy*, which contains many characters similar to those in *Guernica* in a similar physical organization, although the overall theme is very different. *Minotauromachy* contains a minotaur (a variation on a bull, again with a human emotional tone), a suffering horse with a raised head, a dead human figure clutching a sword, a female holding a light, a woman looking out of a window located at the corner of a building, birds, and a vertical human figure along the border.

The positioning of the characters in *Minotauromachy* is particularly intriguing when one considers how an etching is made. If we put

Minotauromachy by Pablo Picasso. From the Philadelphia Museum of Art: Given by Henry P. McIlhenney.

objects in locations A-B-C on a printing plate, the printed image on the paper will appear C-B-A. When Picasso drew *Minotauromachy* on the printing plate, therefore, the bull was drawn on the left and the building with its windows, the vertical person, the horse, and the dead human were all located in positions similar to those they hold in *Guernica*. Thus, Picasso may have been so rapid in developing the structure of *Guernica* because he had the whole structure available in his recent work.

Historical Antecedents of Guernica

The influence of the great Spanish artist Francisco de Goya (1746–1828) is reflected in *Guernica* by Goya's series of etchings, *The Disasters of War* (1816). A number of the characters and poses in *Guernica* can be seen as being adapted from Goya, although filtered through Picasso's style. Goya's being Spanish made his work important to Picasso. Anthony Blunt's provocative analysis of *Guernica's* place in art history points out many connections between Picasso's work and that of earlier artists.

The Disasters of War, no. 50, by Goya.

Discontinuity in *Guernica*

There were also several discontinuities in this painting, and these are in all cases comprehensible. One was the change in subject matter, from the studio to *Guernica*, triggered by the bombing. Another was the removal of the upraised arm in the early painted version, seemingly motivated by political concerns on Picasso's part.

Jackson Pollock — The Evolution of Spontaneity

In the late 1940s, there burst upon the American art scene a young artist, Jackson Pollock, who painted pictures like none ever seen before: large-scale pictures that were completely nonrepresentational (that is, their subject matter could not be traced to objects), in which endless lines and splashes of paint created a shimmering mass which seemed to breathe with life as one watched. The paintings produce strong and varied emotional experiences, although there are no objects in them to cue emotion in the traditional sense.

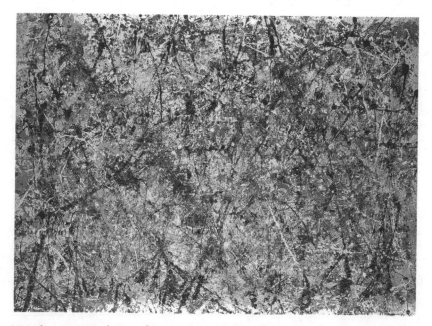

Number 1, 1950 (Lavender Mist) by Jackson Pollock.

These revolutionary works were painted using a revolutionary technique: rather than applying paint to canvas with brush strokes, Pollock poured paint on the canvas directly from a can or flung or streamed the paint onto the canvas using a stick, a hardened old brush, or even a turkey baster. In this way, the paint could be applied continuously, without the usual breaks needed to replenish the brush. In addition, the canvas was stretched out on the floor, so that Pollock could work around and over the painting.

Pollock became the most well-known of the Abstract Expressionists, a group of painters centered in New York who redefined the limits of painting by producing abstract works that made no attempt to produce figures of any kind. At present, it is generally acknowledged that Pollock was the first great American painter, because of the revolutionary techniques and style he developed, and because of the scale of his work, both physically and psychologically. He attempted to produce works of grandeur by recording his emotions directly, without any intervention by traditional objects and their related associations. Many of those who knew Pollock commented that his ambition was to surpass Picasso and the other masters of art in Europe, and to produce a uniquely American art that would last.

Although Pollock's family had no formal artistic tradition, there was a strong interest in art expressed by both parents, and especially by Pollock's mother, the dominant parent. All five boys in the family took up art as a career. Jackson, the youngest, in 1930 moved to New York at the encouragement of his brothers Charles and Sande, who were already there. Jackson had had exposure to art in high school, where he was influenced by an art teacher who encouraged him, although Pollock himself was dissatisfied with his own early efforts. This art teacher also introduced Pollock to Eastern religion and philosophy, which remained an important influence.

When Pollock joined his brothers in New York, he began to study art in classes conducted by Thomas Hart Benton, a well-known "regionalist" painter who strongly advocated the development of a unique American art, based on American themes. In his work, he portrayed American scenes in a dramatic manner, exaggerating the grandeur of the common person. Benton in the 1930s carried out many commissions, including a number of large murals for public spaces in New York City. Pollock posed for a number of these works, and attended one of Benton's classes in mural painting.

Pollock's early works look nothing like his mature paintings and show strong Benton influences in style and subject matter, although the influences of other artists can also be seen. In addition, Pollock was influenced by Benton's theories about how paintings should be structured. Benton had his students study works by classical masters such as El Greco, and analyze the paintings as a series of interrelated geometric forms, to finding their rhythmic structure and the way the shapes were interrelated to produce appearances of depth. Benton's system of analysis of the rhythmic structure of paintings had an effect on Pollock's work of many years later.

After leaving Benton's classes, Pollock came under two strong influences: the work of the Mexican painters and muralists Diego Rivera, David Alfaro Siqueiros, and José Orosco; and the teaching of John Graham, a Russian expatriate artist and art theorist living in New York. The Mexicans were using the art and legends of the Indians of Mexico in their work, in an attempt to produce on a grand scale a new art independent of that of Europe. Before coming to New York, Pollock had already read about their work, and had seen and had been impressed by a mural by Orosco in Los Angeles.

Siqueiros had a direct influence on the development of the allover poured technique of Pollock's later works. One of Siqueiros's interests was the use of nontraditional techniques and materials in painting, which led to experiments with industrial paints, surfaces other than canvas, and industrial techniques — such as air-brushes — for ap-

Going West, an early work by Jackson Pollock.

plying paint to surface. Siqueiros established a workshop in 1936 in New York, in which a number of young painters—including Pollock—worked with him on these experiments, which included flinging and dripping paint onto canvas and other surfaces, sometimes spread on the floor rather than framed in an easel.

John Graham was a charismatic and forceful individual who exerted an influence on many of the young artists in New York in the 1920s and 1930s (including Calder). He wrote a treatise on art, in which he stated his belief that true art came about through the "immediate and unadorned record of an authentic intellecto-emotional REACTION of the artist set in space . . . " This reaction could be seen in the variations in the strokes produced by the artist. Graham also advocated a role for the Freudian and Jungian unconscious in creation of art, and he extolled Picasso's use of primitive art as inspiration, as a way to tap into the unconscious.

Pollock's interests in emotional and "unconscious" expression as the path to "truth" in art also led him to an interest in surrealism, a movement established in France around 1920, with many advocates in New York in the 1930s. The surrealists attempted to tap into the unconscious and to use it to develop images which could be elaborated into works of art. One technique to accomplish this was "automatic drawing," in which the pencil was allowed to move without conscious control, in an attempt to have unconscious material come to the surface. This technique was adapted by the surrealists from Paul Klee, a Swiss artist of great influence who had developed it in Europe. Pollock and his artist friends and their spouses practiced automatic drawing. Under these influences, Pollock's work moved away from the realism of regionalism to more primitive forms, in which the influence of Picasso and primitive art can be seen.

In late 1943–early 1944, Pollock produced works in which one can see the development of components of his later style. *Composition with Pouring* of 1943 has poured and dripped paint, although they are not its main components. In late 1943 or early 1944, using a brush, Pollock painted a large mural which was totally abstract and strongly rhythmic; with an "allover" structure, meaning that the structure was uniform over the entire canvas, with no organization within the canvas into objects; and some use of the pouring technique. Other artists had already been working in nonfigural painting, several of whom, such as Klee, Joan Miro, and Piet Mondrian (the latter two had stimulated Calder in Paris in 1930, see Chapter 1), were very well known.

In 1944, Pollock studied in Stanley William Hayter's engraving studio in New York. Hayter was a well-known printmaker, artist, and teacher, who had moved his studio from Paris to New York during World War II. He was a advocate of Klee's automatic-drawing technique, which he had learned in Europe from Klee, and placed strong emphasis on the free and abstract use of line as an important element. Hayter taught that the artist should not approach the work from a static point of view, but should move around and "into" the work as expression required.

Thus, by the mid-1940s, the components of Pollock's mature style were in place: he had painted large nonrepresentational works, with allover structure, using the brush, but with occasional dripping and pouring; he was aware of and interested in expressing the unconscious as directly as possible through movement and was not limited to one position relative to the work-in-progress; he had experience

Combat by William Stanley Hayter.

with nontraditional materials and methods of applying paint to canvas.

In the late 1940s, Pollock made his first allover poured work. Other artists about this time were also using pouring and dripping in their work, as exemplified by Hans Hoffmann's 1940 painting *Spring*, which was overlain with drips. Pollock was not familiar with Hoffmann's work; these similarities merely show what was "in the air" in the New York art community around that time.

The surrealist painter Max Ernst had carried out experiments with "oscillation" paintings, exhibited in New York in 1942. For these paintings, Ernst used a can — with holes at the bottom — filled with paint and swung it over the canvas so that paint would drip through the holes and form patterns on canvas. This work was not as free as Pollock's, since it depended on the regular oscillation of the can, but it was based on a similar principle. In addition, Benton's analyses of the structure of paintings and of the works of the old masters provided Pollock with examples of allover rhythmic patterns which may have played a role in his pictures.

Although Pollock's painting was an activity that required the participation of his whole body, more like ballet or gymnastics than traditional easel painting, this did not occur without thought. During a painting session, Pollock would stop working and spend time study-

Summary of Development of Pollock's "Allover" Poured Style

Style	Source(s)
Regionalism	Benton
Primitivism	John Graham introduced Pollock to Picasso's work as example of use of primitivism to free emotion
Abstraction	Siqueiros workshop; John Graham introduced Pollock to surrealism and to automatic painting; Hayter introduced him to Klee's linear style; Benton's rhythmical stylistic analysis

Components of Pollock's mature paintings

Scale: muralistic	Benton; Mexican muralists
Abstract	Hayter; Klee; Siqueiros
Rhythmic structure	Benton; Hayter; surrealists

ing the work in progress; he also sometimes hung an unfinished painting on the wall of his studio for weeks or months, so that he could study it and determine what he wanted to do next. Through his years of extensive experimentation with different pouring techniques and with different materials, he had complete control of the direction and quality of his line, so that he was able to plan before he began to paint.

In conclusion, antecedents of Pollock's work can be clearly seen, even though that work did not seem to have any antecedents when it burst on the American public. The discontinuities in his style can also be traced to external triggers. Pollock's development is summarized in the accompanying table.

Creative Thinking in Poetry

I have written this poem from immediate Dictation, twelve or sometimes twenty or thirty lines at a time, without Premeditation and even against my Will; the Time it has taken in writing was thus rendered Non Existent, and an immense Poem Exists which seems to be the Labor of a long Life, all produced without Labour or Study. (William Blake)

William Blake's description of his compositional process is very similar to Coleridge's description of his writing *Kubla Khan*, and to the reports of other poets. There is available a variety of sources, such as on-line studies of composition and early drafts of poems, which provides more objective evidence concerning how poetry is actually written.

In an investigation of processes in the creation of poetry, David Perkins had poets write poems in the laboratory; they were asked to bring only an idea for a poem, and to think aloud as they wrote. One poet began with the idea that her day was like an air-raid drill, because that was how her crying children sounded. She then worked out the notion that her babies, like air-raid sirens, were warning her to preserve herself. This was to her a much more satisfactory basis for developing the poem than simply the children's noise.

Well, I was thinking, [reads] "and I am still fighting that cold war alone. The wailing babies" — what did they signal me to do? What is it [air-raid siren] a signal for me to do? And actually, (pause) why do you hide? It's because you're trying to preserve yourself, and that's what the babies are signaling me to do too, because basically I can't, I don't tolerate them very well, and it does me in so much that I have to leave them and go into silence, someplace that's silent so I can preserve myself.

The poet applied her critical judgment to the idea that had been retrieved by her babies' wailing. She used the air-raid drill as a base analogue, which resulted in her becoming able to fill in the information which led to elaboration of the poetic idea.

This study demonstrates that one source of poetic inspiration is external stimuli which can make the poet think of things that in his or her judgment present interesting possibilities for poems. This judgment is based on the expertise of the poet, acquired through formal and informal training, and through experience composing poems. In addition, when one has undertaken a career as a poet, one approaches events with a poet's sensibility: one is looking for things that will make good poems. A nonpoet might also be reminded of an air-raid siren by a wailing baby, but might not linger over that thought. A poet has a constant problem to solve: What can I write about now? External events are one source of answers to that problem.

Reconstruction of Coleridge's Poetic Imagination

In a fascinating example of detective work that would impress Sherlock Holmes, John Lowes attempted to trace the origins of *Kubla Khan*, by first using Coleridge's notebooks to determine possible sources in Coleridge's voluminous reading for lines in the poem. Lowes then used these sources as the basis for outlining how Coleridge's imagination worked to take the available material and convert it into poetry. Here are the first few lines of the poem.

In Xanadu did Kubla Khan
A stately pleasure-dome decree:
Where Alph, the sacred river, ran
Through caverns measureless to man
Down to a sunless sea.
So twice five miles of fertile ground
With walls and towers were girdled round:
And there were gardens bright with sinuous rills,

Where blossomed many an incense-bearing tree;
And here were forests ancient as the hills,
Enfolding sunny spots of greenery.

Coleridge reported that when he fell asleep he was reading a description of Khan's capital city from Samuel Purchas' *Pilgrimage*, a seventeenth-century book of descriptions of travel to exotic locales. That description was as follows.

In Xamdu did Cublai Can build a stately palace, encompassing sixteene miles of plaine ground with a wall, wherein are fertile Meddowes, pleasant springs, delightfull Streames, and all sorts of beasts of chase and game, and in the middest thereof a sumptuous house of pleasure, which may be removed from place to place.

There are obvious similarities between Purchas' description and Coleridge's poem, most particularly the structure of the first phrase and some of the elements described, but there are also significant differences in spellings, specific descriptions, and objects described. Lowes attempts to account for all the elements in the poem. The reference to the sacred river Alph running through measureless caverns is traced to various sources familiar to Coleridge, including several descriptions of the discovery of the origin of the Nile river, considered sacred; and the legend that the Nile was one of the four rivers emanating in the Garden of Eden. The Nile then supposedly traveled underground to its origin in Africa. This is the source of the sacred river and the caverns, measureless because according to legend it was impossible to measure the depth of the fountains from which the Nile sprang to life. The name Alph was taken by Coleridge from Alpheus, a legendary underground river which Coleridge knew from his reading of the classics.

Lowes assumes that the poem came to Coleridge as he reported, in a dream as a series of visual images accompanied by words, and Lowes analyzes the images that would have been produced originally by Coleridge's readings, and how these images might have fused during his dream to form new images serving as the basis for the poem. Lowes spends some time discussing the issue of how, if Coleridge conceived the poem in a dream, the meter and other aspects of the poetic structure were worked out. Coleridge had recently solidified his style after much work, so that it was now at least partly automatic, and he could have produced well-structured poems in dreams.

It is true that our dreams can contain well-formed novel conversations, so that it might be possible for a poet's dreams to contain novel poems. If, however, there was more than dreamwork involved in *Kubla Khan*, including conscious revision, then there may be less unconscious working-out of structure. Novel ideas might come about as Lowes hypothesizes, through associative links that are activated as the poet thinks about the topic, but these associations may produce only fragments that must then be worked on further before true poetry is produced. Lowes's analysis points out the importance of external sources as the basis for new ideas, even though the source may be disguised in the final poem.

Revision in Writing Poetry

The English Romantic poets (e.g., Coleridge, Blake, Lord Byron), at least partly in response to the prevailing neoclassical philosophy that creative thinking was the result of conscious logical reasoning, emphasized the spontaneous and nonlogical nature of thought processes in writing poetry. The notebooks of these poets, however, raise questions about their claims, and look much like the notebooks and sketchbooks already discussed. As can be seen in the illustration, even a short poem like Blake's *The Tyger* was subject to much revision, which makes it doubtful that he composed thirty lines at a time without pause or need of revision. The same is true of Byron, who told his publisher in a letter that rewriting was impossible for him, although his notebooks provide evidence that extensive reworking had already occurred in the very poem in question.

An exhibit at the New York Public Library presented early handwritten drafts of a number of famous poems. All had been extensively revised. The poems, which included work from the last 300 years, ranged from John Donne to Emily Dickinson to T. S. Eliot. An example of such critical revision can be found in the opening lines of the poem "Come, Said My Soul" by Walk Whitman. In one of three drafts, the opening line reads "Go, said his soul to a poet, write me such songs," Whitman then substituted "such verse write" for the last phrase, scratched it out and put "go write such songs" in its place, only to scratch it out also. then he wrote "such songs, such verses write," but this was still not the final version.

The author of a review of this exhibition in the *New York Times* comments, "These poems, encased like rare jewels under glass, make

WILLIAM BLAKE: The Tiger
[*First Draft*]

The Tyger

1   Tyger Tyger burning bright
In the forests of the night
What immortal hand or eye
~~Dare~~ ~~Could~~ frame thy fearful symmetry

      Burnt in
2   ~~In what~~ distant deep or skies
~~The cruel~~ ~~Burnt the~~ fire of thine eyes
On what wings dare he aspire
What the hand dare sieze the fire

3   And what shoulder & what art
Could twist the sinews of thy heart
And when thy heart began to beat
What dread hand & what dread feet

     ~~Could fetch it from the furnace deep~~
~~And in thy horrid ribs dare steep~~
~~In the well of sanguine woe~~
~~In what clay & in what mould~~
~~Were thy eyes of fury rolld~~

     Where   where
4   ~~What~~ the hammer ~~want~~ the chain
In what furnace was thy brain

                       dread grasp
     What the anvil what ~~the arm~~ ~~arm~~ ~~grasp~~ ~~clasp~~
Dare ~~Could~~ its deadly terrors ~~clasp~~ ~~grasp~~ clasp

6   Tyger Tyger burning bright
In the forests of the night
What immortal hand & eye

     frame
Dare ~~form~~ thy fearful symmetry

[*Trial Stanzas*]

Burnt in distant deeps or skies
The cruel fire of thine eye,
Could heart descend or wings aspire
What the hand dare sieze the fire

Drafts of "The Tyger" taken from William Blake's notebook.

(*continued*)

5 ∬　And ~~did he laugh~~ his work to see ^{dare he ~~smile laugh~~}

~~What the shoulder what the knee~~ ^{ankle}

4　~~Did~~ he who made the lamb make thee ^{Dare}
1　When the stars threw down their spears
2　And waterd heaven with their tears

[Second Full Draft]

Tyger Tyger burning bright
In the forests of the night
What Immortal hand & eye
Dare frame thy fearful symmetry

And what shoulder & what art
Could twist the sinews of thy heart
And when thy heart began to beat
What dread hand & what dread feet

When the stars threw down their spears
And waterd heaven with their tears
Did he smile his work to see
Did he who made the lamb make thee

Tyger Tyger burning bright
In the forests of the night
What immortal hand & eye
Dare frame they fearful symmetry

[Final Version, 1794]

Tyger! Tyger! burning bright
In the forests of the night,
What immortal hand or eye
Could frame thy fearful symmetry?

In what distant deeps or skies
Burnt the fire of thine eyes?
On what wings dare he aspire?
What the hand dare sieze the fire?

And what shoulder, & what art,
Could twist the sinews of thy heart?
And when thy heart began to beat,
What dread hand? & what dread feet?

Drafts of "The Tyger" taken from William Blake's notebook (continued).

What the hammer? what the chain?
In what furnace was thy brain?
What the anvil? what dread grasp
Dare its deadly terrors clasp?

When the stars threw down their spears,
And water'd heaven with their tears,
Did he smile his work to see?
Did he who made the Lamb make thee?

Tyger! Tyger! burning bright
In the forests of the night,
What immortal hand or eye,
Dare frame thy fearful symmetry?

a subliminal statement: that even for the greats, revision was recognized as a necessary element of the creative process." Whitman's poem was so revised as to be illegible to anyone but the poet.

The preceding analysis of the development of poetry supports the view that, contrary to the claims of a number of poets, poems only gradually take their final shape. An inspiration can be brought about by an external trigger, such as the wailing of a baby, or reading a description in a travel book, but that is only the first step in writing a poem. The poet must then shape initial ideas into final form, a task that takes much work and depends on experience.

Musical Composition

The composition of music has much in common with poetry, including reports of sudden spontaneous inspirations. Similar methods have been used to obtain information on the compositional process in music: observation of composers at work and examination of the notebooks and early sketches of composers.

Musical Composition as Problem Solving

An informative study of composition was reported by John Sloboda, a cognitive psychologist who is also a composer. Sloboda produced a protocol as he worked on completing a piece of sacred music that he had begun at an earlier time. The piece is a setting of the five versus of Psalm 92, to be used by a choir. Although the overall tone of the psalm is vigorous and triumphant, Sloboda felt that there should be some contrasting mood within it. For this reason, he began with the feeling that the middle verse should be serene in setting, which would make a three-part structure, with the first two verses and the last two strong in mood.

Sloboda Protocol

A. How am I to continue at bar 29? The next verse is going to be quieter and slower. A theme is needed for "From all eternity." The tentative one where composition broke down before didn't seem right, partly because it was over too quickly. This initial passage can be seen as a statement of the problem to be solved, and the setting of two immediate constraints. There was a general need to "wind down" from a rather extrovert and busy texture into something more easeful for the next verse; and a particular need to find a theme for the last line of verse 2. Lengthening the vocal phrases, which up till now had been short and separated, could be one way of introducing the required "easement." These constraints, however were not yet specific enough to suggest actual notes.

B. I decide to progress the accompaniment so that it slows down. It occurs to me that the word "eternity" can be represented by a repetitive circular motif. We already have a circular four-note fragment in bars 23–27. So I try to use it to slow down. The writing of bars 27–33 then becomes routine. A B-flat is added at bar 33 on the intuition that harmonic movement is needed by now. . . . The word "eternity" suggested the possibility of a repetitive cyclical motif, and the accompaniment happened to contain such a motif. . . . The task, then, was simply to repeat the falling motif over and over, at the same pitch, but with a spacing out and slowing. . . . Once the problem had been narrowed this far, I was able to compose fairly mechanically, thus the comment that this section is "routine."

One sees here a straightforward problem solving process, as for example Sloboda tries to work out how to slow the end of verse two so that he can generate a transition to his planned slow verse three. He decides to use the word "eternity" at the end of verse two as a focal point for deceleration into the next verse. The meaning of the word suggested itself as a point at which a slowdown could naturally occur. This is one of several examples in which something in the piece itself, either a word or some already written music, was noticed and used as the basis for further work.

Sloboda composes at the piano, and he comments at several places that he was working to find the right notes to serve at a particular point in the composition, such as a transition from one chord to another, or a chord to accompany the voices at a particular point. Here, too, one sees examples of the general musical constraints that he was working under, as when he notes that a particular combination of notes produced by the organ in combination with the voices was unsatisfactory because it was too dissonant.

Sloboda notes that when he made these various decisions he carried out no explicit reasoning based on some set of rules; he simply realized that something was unacceptable and set out to change it. This is parallel to the judgments made in many problem-solving situations presented in other chapters. One also sees much use of analogical thinking as Sloboda used what he had already written in this piece as the basis for constructing later parts. About half-way through composing, Sloboda felt that he had a good idea for the overall structure of the rest of the composition. This was not a sudden inspiration of the entire piece note-for-note, but rather was a feeling that he had gotten some momentum.

Mozart's Compositional Process

To modern audiences, Wolfgang Amadeus Mozart (1756–1791) has become the paradigm of the creator whose work borders on the miraculous. In the course of his short life, he demonstrated mastery of many musical forms and produced more than 600 compositions. With impetus from the notorious "letter" and the play and movie *Amadeus*, Mozart's compositional process has come to be looked upon as the outpouring of finished works with no preparation. There is, however, a research literature on Mozart that provides information on how he actually worked. Once again, the facts contradict the legend.

Mozart's father, Leopold, was a composer. Wolfgang and his sister Anna (1751–1829) both showed great musical precocity, and Leopold tutored them in music. Wolfgang's talent become evident when he was 4 years old and demanded to be taught to play the piano as his 9-year-old sister did, and showed an ability to play her exercises with barely any lessons. He also quickly acquired the ability to play the violin.

As was customary in the seventeenth and eighteenth centuries, Leopold traveled with the children to the cultural centers of Europe so that they could perform before the nobility, to earn money as well as to pave the way for a career in music for Wolfgang. Among the talents exhibited by the 7-year-old boy were the ability to play in an adult manner, to improvise in various styles, to play with a cloth covering the keyboard, and to name any note that was sounded (perfect pitch). Mozart was not unique in these gifts; a number of his contemporaries, including Leopold Gassman and Antonio Salieri, began composing early in life and were very productive. Their music was, at that time, as appreciated by the public as was Mozart's.

The earliest compositions attributed to Mozart are from the age of 6, but they survive only in his father's hand, which raises questions about the actual composer. Even if Wolfgang did the actual composing, the compositions are simple exercises for piano, similar to those prepared by Leopold for his children. Mozart's early compositions, while remarkable for a child, are not of the quality of his later work; his first great symphony has been ascribed by one scholar to Mozart's 16th year, when he had already been immersed in music for over ten years, and his first great piano concerto to his 20th year.

Compositions Without Sketches?

Mozart's almost effortless composing is evidenced by the many manuscripts which are without corrections, which look as if they had been copied, perhaps from a score already mentally worked out (as described in "Mozart's letter"). However, Erich Hertzmann suggests that perhaps these perfectly-written works were literally copied, from sketches that were then discarded. After Mozart's death, his widow kept his manuscripts, but in 1799 she noted in a letter that she discarded "unusable autographs," before selling the rest, which may have meant Mozart's working sketches which no one else could use. The few Mozart sketches that do exist indicate that he typically wrote the melody and bass lines as he composed, and filled in the other parts later, which contradicts the naive view that Mozart simply had the whole composition mentally available.

Some of Mozart's sketches also provide graphic evidence for difficulties in composition. In 1782–1785, he composed a set of six string quartets which he dedicated to Franz Joseph Haydn, at that time the greatest living composer, who had taken an interest in the younger man (see Chapter 3). In the dedication to Haydn, Mozart wrote that the quartets were the fruit of long and arduous toil, and at one time it was believed that Mozart must have been being modest, since he was believed to have composed everything without effort. Recent research, however, provides evidence that Mozart was being truthful.

In these "Haydn" quartets, Mozart wrote in a complex style, based on Haydn's recent quartets, in which the instruments engage in a complicated interplay. The sketches contain many corrections, false starts, and even rejected movements; some of the quartets were composed over long stretches of time, again indicating that they did not come without effort. Thus, as Mozart's style became more complex, his composing became more difficult. He was probably capable of writing a simple dance piece with little or no preliminary work, but even for Mozart, more complex pieces seem to have required some preliminary work.

There are times when our enthusiasm for an individual's work carries us away in our analysis of the creative process. An example of this involves the passage in "Mozart's letter" in which he describes hearing the "parts" of his compositions all at once and the "tout ensemble" all together (see Chapter 2). Ignoring the issue of the authenticity of the letter, it is interesting that — on at least two independent occasions — this passage has been interpreted as meaning that Mozart heard the beginning, middle, and end of his compositions all at once, using some kind of extraordinary musical imagination. However, the use of the term "parts" in the "letter" refers not to the parts of a composition, such as the movements of a symphony, but to the parts of the orchestra. This means that he hears in his imagination the whole orchestra playing together, which is not the extraordinary feat that has been inferred from the letter.

Continuity in Mozart's Creativity

Examination of Mozart's compositions over his career shows several sorts of influences from other composers, as well as his use of his own earlier works as the basis for new ones. The finale of Mozart's last symphony, the great *Jupiter*, contains five themes, and there is evidence that several, and perhaps all, came from other sources. Mozart also used the work of others as analogies on which to build his own works. His three E-flat concertos for French horn seem to have been modeled on horn concertos by Antoni Rosetti (1750–1792), who wrote a long series of concertos for wind instruments. Mozart's and Rosetti's concertos are very similar in overall structure, including the form of the slow movements and the rondo finales in six-eight time, as well as in melody.

Mozart also showed consistent patterns of composition within his own career. He had definite associations for different keys, which resulted in certain types of compositions being more frequent in certain keys. Music of a ceremonial character was often written in C major; music of strong emotional tone both in instrumental and operatic forms was often written in E flat; and operatic arias of vengeance were almost always written in D minor. This use of specific keys to express certain ideas was part of a tradition in which various keys acquired associations to extra-musical ideas.

Discontinuity in Mozart

There are several points at which Mozart's style changed, and these discontinuities can be traced to external triggers. Mozart's many trips across Europe as a child and young man exposed him to the most important musicians of the day, and as would be expected, these contacts influenced his music. His early symphonies written in London (1764 – 5) are in the style of Johann Christian Bach (1735 – 1782, son of Johann Sebastian Bach), whom he met there and who showed an interest in him. Of course, it is impressive that a 9-year-old can write symphonies at all, but it is still of some importance that they were nearly copies of Bach's. These symphonies, furthermore, are not the complex compositions of Mozart's mature years, and are made up of three movements of two to four minutes in length.

Symphonies written by the still-young Mozart after a visit to Vienna in 1767 – 8 show a different style, with a minuet movement and structural elements in the first movements (development and recapitulation) characteristic of the Viennese style. During a visit to Italy in 1770, Mozart wrote a number of symphonies in the Italian style, again different from the earlier ones. These influences and several others gradually were brought together into a unique style, in which traces of other styles can be seen, but now modified to become Mozart's own. There were also comparable shifts in other genres, as in Mozart's string quartets.

Although Mozart began his musical career extraordinarily early and he was extremely productive, his compositions were rooted in what had come before, both in his own works and those of others.

Those compositions may have been brought to life through processes of critical analysis and revision much like those of more ordinary individuals.

Beethoven's Notebooks: Development of a Symphony

In availability of preliminary material, Ludwig van Beethoven (1770–1827) is at the other extreme from Mozart, having left behind notebooks containing over 5,000 pages of preliminary material that make graphically clear the tremendous energy Beethoven expended in refining an idea over and over until he was either satisfied with it or cast it aside. The Ninth Symphony, completed in 1824, is a good example of the composer's extensive reworking of a piece. It is his final symphony, and is the first by any composer to include the human voice as an integral part. (The last movement includes a setting of Frederick Schiller's poem, "Ode to Joy.")

Like all such "revolutionary" advances, this work can be seen to have antecedents in earlier music and in Beethoven's earlier work. There was, of course, a long history of choral music, both of a religious and secular nature, with orchestral accompaniment, so that the general path had already been laid down. A clear antecedent for the Ninth Symphony in Beethoven's work was his "Choral Fantasy" of 1808, an orchestral piece with chorus that sounds like a practice attempt for the last movement of the Ninth Symphony, with similar melodies and an analogous structure.

Although based on clear antecedents in Beethoven's work, the development of the Ninth Symphony was very slow: Beethoven had had the "Ode to Joy" in mind as the basis for a composition even before he started the "Choral Fantasy." In 1817, and perhaps even as early as 1815, one finds the first sketches that can be directly related to the final version of the Ninth, though the elaboration of these sketches did not take place until 1822 or 1823. Beethoven originally contemplated two symphonies, which would have been his ninth and tenth. The choral movement was intended as the finale of the latter. He merged the two, and was concerned about whether the earlier movements and the finale would fit together. The notebooks are proof of the extensive work he did before he was satisfied.

Beethoven is known for the "organic" nature of his work, that is, the unity and cohesion of the various parts of even long pieces. The notebooks indicate that this cohesion is the result of his efforts to take separate ideas and unify them.

Beethoven's other eight symphonies also contain many examples or works started, put aside, and later returned to; of works in which parts were dropped after much elaboration; and of works in which a small phrase or idea was returned to again and again until it finally emerged as something very different. Nor is Beethoven's revisionist technique limited to his symphonic writing — his notebooks contain *thirteen* versions of one aria included in his opera *Fidelio*.

Sources of New Ideas in Music

Analyses of the compositional process of Mozart and Beethoven has shown that compositions develop relatively slowly into final form. This still leaves open the question of inspiration, or the source of the germinal ideas, themselves. Study of the works of the greatest composers has revealed many sources for ideas. We have already seen examples of this in the discussion of Mozart (use of melodies from others or from one's own works), but it is worth considering in more detail, due to its potential importance in understanding the issue of inspiration.

Learning Musical Structures

My discussion begins with the work of Johann Sebastian Bach (1685–1750), one of the most prolific composers, who produced over 1,000 works. He was born in central Germany into a family of musicians. Of his nine children who lived to adulthood, three became leading composers of the next generation, one of whom, Johann Christian, was, as we have already seen, an influence on the young Mozart.

Bach's professional life was spent in the direct service of others, and, as a requirement of his work, he composed and performed music. In 1723, he was appointed Cantor of St. Thomas's Church in Leipzig, one of the most important musical posts in Germany. He was the third choice for the post; there were at least two other musicians in the area with greater reputations.

Bach's duties as cantor were many and varied: he taught at the choir school and gave the choirboys lessons in Latin; in addition, he served as music director, composer, organist, and choirmaster of the church. Music was an integral part of the Lutheran Sunday service, and the cantor was expected to write much of it. Bach wrote many cantatas (musical settings for sacred texts) for the Sunday services at Leipzig. At least one cantata was needed for each week of the year and additional ones were needed for holidays, so that approximately sixty were needed for a yearly cycle. At Leipzig, Bach composed five cycles of cantatas, of which approximately 200 are now known.

The present-day interest of audiences in "old" music is a comparatively new phenomenon. Throughout the seventeenth and eighteenth centuries, audiences were interested only in new music and kept composers busy producing new pieces for their next performance. For Bach and the other composers of his era, there were several ways in which composition was made more manageable. The rules of composition, first of all, specified the musical structure of various sorts of compositions. The baroque fugue, for example, was written according to rules that specified how themes were to be used, what sorts of repetitions should occur, and so on. There were also guidelines for relating music to rhetoric, the ancient art of speaking whereby orators were instructed in the use of different figures of speech. In the seventeenth and eighteenth centuries, these rhetorical concepts were adapted to the art of writing music. Certain musical forms were customarily used to express various aspects of the meaning of the text the composer was setting to music. Mozart's use of certain keys to transmit specific emotions, just discussed, is a later example of this. Thus, the composer did not have to begin anew each time a new text was to be set to music.

Also, during the classical era, there were forms that served as structures on which to build compositions, such forms as the symphony, the concerto for solo instrument, and the string quartet. These were not rigid rules, and composers changed things as they saw fit, but the forms served as the basis for beginning a composition.

An additional device to ease the composer's burden was the practice of borrowing musical ideas, from oneself and from others. A composer such as Bach would often use an old melody as the basis for a new piece or perhaps adopt the compositions of another for personal use. Such borrowing was not considered plagiarism; using someone else's or one's own earlier work as the starting point for a new composition was accepted musical practice.

Norman Carrell has attempted to trace every instance of such borrowing by Bach, and has found that over 225 of Bach's nonvocal works contain borrowings from his own earlier works, and more than 80 contain borrowing from other composers, perhaps the most famous of which are the transcriptions for harpsichord of several of Antonio Vivaldi's violin concertos. Carrell believes that Bach owed

Vivaldi much in the way of inspiration in addition to the works which are based directly on Vivaldi's compositions.

Bach's vocal works, including the cycles of cantatas, also depended heavily on borrowing. Carrell estimates that approximately 65 percent of the presently known cantatas contain borrowings from Bach's own works. In addition, the cantatas also depend heavily on Lutheran hymns, and over 200 of them contain a hymn melody as the basis for a chorale — or choral setting of the hymn — in the last section of the cantata. Some cantatas use the hymn melody in several sections in addition to the chorale.

Another acknowledged master of the baroque era, George Frideric Handel, also is well known for his extensive reuse of his own works and his borrowing from others. In addition to explicit borrowing, Handel is also believed to have significantly changed his style of composition in response to the success of a rival composer, Giovanni Bononcini, making his own works simpler, more melodious, and more "singable" in imitation of the latter's style.

Many composers have written pieces that are variations on a theme by another composer, such as Brahms's *Variations on a Theme by Haydn,* and Beethoven's *Diabelli Variations.* Beethoven also used his own material several times, for example, the dance that serves as the basis for the finale of the *Eroica Symphony.* This piece also appears as one of a set of twelve dances and was also used as the basis for a set of variations. A theme by Carl Phillip Emanuel Bach (another of Bach's sons), which Beethoven knew well, may have been the source of this dance.

Folk melodies and folk dances also played an important role in classical composition; many works in the baroque and classical eras, such as baroque dance suites and the movements of many classical symphonies, were based directly on folk forms. In addition, the European folk melodies formed a tradition from which composers of the seventeenth and eighteenth centuries constantly drew inspiration. One musicologist estimates that 80 percent of Mozart's melodies also appeared in the compositions of his contemporaries, indicating a common use of sources. Many composers in different eras have taken folk melodies and used them as the basis for compositions, such as Dvorak's *Slavonic Dances* and Brahms's *Hungarian Dances.*

In conclusion, much musical composition is based on continuity with earlier ideas, either those of the composer in question or those of other composers. Though these traces may be more or less explicit, depending on the circumstances, they are almost invariably present.

Creativity in Literature

> If you wish — he [the author or poet] is not the creator; life
> is — the powerful essence of life, the living and essential God,
> putting his strength in many distinct creations at various places,
> and most of all in the great heart and in the strong poet, so
> that if the poet himself is not a creator — (and one must agree
> with this . . . because certainly a creative work comes
> suddenly, as a complete whole, finished and ready, out of the
> soul of a poet) . . .
>
>   (Fyodor Dostoyevsky, quoted in Miller 1981, 49)

Fyodor Dostoyevsky's description of his creative process is a precise
formulation of what has been called the messenger-of-God view of
creativity, in which creative work is done not by the author, but by an
outside agent (see Chapter 1). However, Dostoyevsky's notebooks
do not support his claims.

Extensive analysis has been carried out on the notebooks for
Dostoyevsky's novel *The Idiot*, which describes the influence of one
man on the members of several noble families in nineteenth-century
Russia. The character is called an idiot by his mother, who despises
him. The novel is divided into several parts, the first two of which
were especially difficult for Dostoyevsky to write. Dostoyevsky
worked on a total of *eight* plans for the first part of the novel as his
scheme for the book changed. Furthermore, each of these plans is full
of hesitations and alternate paths, indicating that at no point was he
very confident about where the correct direction of the novel lay.
After calling one passage in the first plan "the main point," he ends
with "or else." A passage in the fourth plan is called "the chief idea of
the novel," but the next entry is "Well, now there opens up a new
path. What is to come now?"

The second part of *The Idiot* involved Dostoyevsky's attempt to
portray what he called a wholly beautiful individual. He was aware
that other authors had attempted to portray such individuals, such as
Don Quixote and Pickwick, but felt that these attempts were only
partly successful. Both characters were comic characters and, according to Dostoyevsky, the emotion one feels toward them was not due to
their beauty, but because they were unaware of their own goodness.
Dostoyevsky was thus aware of precedents concerning such a charac-

ter and he used them, especially the flaw he saw in them, as part of the basis for his own attempt.

In Dostoyevsky's view, Christ was the only truly beautiful individual, and he set out to present such an individual in the second part of *The Idiot*. As the following passages from Dostoyevsky's notes show, the characteristics of Christ were used directly as a model for the prince. March 9, 1868: "The Prince forgives everything." March 10: "His way of looking at the world: he forgives everything, sees reasons for everything, does not recognize that any sin is unforgivable, and excuses everything." Finally, on April 10: "Prince Christ."

Dostoyevsky's original idea, to portray a wholly beautiful individual, led to retrieval of his knowledge of other literary examples of such individuals. This, in turn, led to his consideration of problems he saw in those characters. In attempting to remedy these problems, he used Christ, the paradigm case of such an individual, as a base analogy on which to build his character.

One important source is obviously life itself. A novelist's interest in certain general themes can arise from experiences in his or her life, or specific events from a novelist's life can be used more or less directly as part of a novel.

An example of the role that life experience can play in the development of a novelist's interest in general themes is seen in Dostoyevsky's *Crime and Punishment*, which revolves around Raskolnikov, a poverty-stricken former university student, who robs and kills a mean, dishonest, old woman, who is a pawnbroker. During the crime, Raskolnikov is discovered by the pawnbroker's sister, and he murders her also. The remainder of the novel involves Raskolnikov's reaction to the crime. He initially rationalizes his action because the old woman would not have lived long anyway, she was doing evil to others, and others would benefit from the money. However, guilt soon begins to torment him, as well as fear arising from the suspicions of a police inspector. Raskolnikov finally is driven to such desperate straits by his guilt and fear that he confesses, which brings him great relief, and he plans to start a new life after serving a prison term.

The theme of the criminal's desire to confess his crime appeared in several of Dostoyevsky's earlier works, mainly in notes for two stories. Dostoyevsky was arrested for reading in public a letter considered treasonous by the police. Originally sentenced to death, he was reprieved at the last moment and sentenced to four years of hard labor in Siberia. While suffering in prison, he spent much time considering a novel based on a criminal's need to confess.

A closely related theme in *Crime and Punishment* concerns Raskolnikov's initial justification of the crime on the grounds that certain extraordinary people are above the laws of society. Raskolnikov considers himself to be like Napoleon, one who shapes the law to his own will, rather than being forced to obey it. This theme also exists in other stories, Russian and otherwise, which Dostoyevsky knew and admired. While Dostoyevsky was writing *Crime and Punishment*, there was a report of a Russian aristocrat who had been imprisoned for killing a man in a duel, and who had claimed that he deserved to be above the law.

There were external sources, as well, for many of the characters in *Crime and Punishment*. Dostoyevsky was in constant financial trouble when writing the novel, and he borrowed a large sum of money from a senile elderly woman similar in many ways to the pawnbroker in the novel. Both women, for example, willed money to the church for prayers for their souls. Many lesser characters also seem to be drawn from people in Dostoyevsky's life. In an early draft of the novel, one character is given the name of one of Dostoyevsky's creditors. Writings by others also provided Dostoyevsky with sources for Raskolnikov.

Dostoyevsky is obviously not unique in using personal experiences in his writing. As one example, the novel, *Tender is the Night*, by F. Scott Fitzgerald, closely follows many events in the author's life. In other cases, the influence is less direct, though still traceable. The adventure stories of Robert Louis Stevenson are obviously not autobiographical: Stevenson never searched for Treasure Island, nor was he captured by pirates. In the Scottish Highlands where Stevenson grew up, however, stories were told of pirate adventures, and these stories served as raw material for his novels.

Creativity in Film

In February 1916, Charles Chaplin (1899–1977) signed a contract with the Mutual Film Corporation to make a series of silent comedies for then-astounding sum of $10,000 per week plus a $150,000 signing bonus. Chaplin, who was 26 years old, came from a family of entertainers and had been in show business for much of his life, singing, dancing, and doing comedy, first as part of the family act and then on his own. He had been working in films for a little more than two years, including a stint with Mack Sennett's Keystone comedies.

Chaplin did not work from scripts; he began with a vague idea for a story and/or some prop that had caught his interest, and began to work out a film in front of the camera. This meant multiple takes as scenes were developed, as well as much reshooting when an idea that developed late in filming resulted in major plot changes. The outtakes, or discarded material, from some of his early films are still available; although Chaplin wished them destroyed, his business manager did not do so. As one studies these outtakes, one sees that Chaplin's art was one of trial-and-error and revision, continuity and discontinuity.

One of Chaplin's classic Mutual comedies, *The Immigrant*, tells the story of a poor young couple who meet on a boat coming to America, he alone and she with her elderly sick mother. Charlie, as the tramp, is kind to the two women on the boat, and on arrival they part company with affection. Later, the young people meet by accident in a café; he buys food for her, since she is obviously alone, impoverished, and hungry. He is also impoverished, but they come across a bit of good fortune and can look forward to a better life, and he convinces her to marry him. One thus sees a film with a tight structure, in which each part leads nicely into the next, and where characters are developed over the course of the film.

The outtakes for *The Immigrant* reveal that this structure was constructed slowly as the film was shot. The film began as a comedy about a bohemian café, which allowed Chaplin to introduce many eccentric characters that could serve as the basis for gags of various sorts. The little tramp is one of the patrons, and his behavior makes it clear that he has never been in a café before. The impoverished young woman is introduced and Charlie buys a plate of beans for her.

Chaplin then decided that there would be a potential for comic action if the tramp saw that a patron who could not pay his bill was beaten by the staff. Charlie then checks on his own money and finds that it has slipped out of a hole in his pocket, and the waiter, mean and threatening, is standing on it. This provides the opportunity for panic and some further business until he is able to recover the money.

The early version of the film ended when one of the artists at the café decides that he would like to paint the young woman, which means that they will be more financially secure. However, there was not enough material filmed for a full two-reel film, so that Chaplin had to add something else to the story. He then concentrated on how the two young people met, which led him to the immigrant sequence. That is, the part that opens the film was added last, and only because what Chaplin had originally done was not long enough. Some of the seagoing material in *The Immigrant* had antecedents in *Shanghaied*, a film made by Chaplin about two years earlier.

After the shooting was completed, Chaplin had more than 40,000 feet of film. The finished length was supposed to be some 1800 feet. This discrepancy required over four days of almost continuous work editing the material down to the required length.

One sees in Chaplin's work continuity with the past, as certain situations and types of gags recur in his films. In addition, one sees the influence of external events, as when his observing a person falling on an escalator in New York served as the trigger for his deciding to build a film around an escalator, which he did in *The Floorwalker*. This film has a plot built around embezzlement in a department store, but the central feature of the store is an escalator, which plays a significant role in a chase scene that is the climax of the film.

Critical Analysis in Artistic Creativity

The case studies in this chapter point to the importance of critical analysis in the evolution of a work of art. This concept is further supported by a research study conducted by Jacob Getzels and Mihalyi Csikszentmihalyi, who asked thirty-one male fine-arts students at the School of the Chicago Art Institute to draw a still-life, while various aspects of their behavior were measured. (Parts of this study were discussed in Chapter 3.) The students were given many objects to use in the still-life, including a woman's felt hat, a bunch of grapes, a book, a manikin, and a lens. Different types of drawing materials were available, and choice of subject matter and medium were left to the student.

The investigators noted how many objects were manipulated, how unusual they were, and how carefully the student examined each one before beginning to draw. The investigators also measured the time from the beginning of a drawing to the emergence of its final structure, whether the student abandoned a drawing and started over, whether the arrangement of the objects was changed as the drawing progressed, and whether the final drawing simply copied the objects or represented them differently in some way.

Five art critics judged the drawings for quality, and those rated most highly were produced by students who manipulated a greater number of objects before starting to draw, and who examined them most carefully. The highly rated pictures also tended to contain more unusual objects, which were not simply copied. Getzels and Csikszentmihalyi also asked the students if they felt their final drawings were complete or if they could be improved in any way. The students who drew the highly rated pictures were more likely to report that further improvement was possible and that the drawing was not finished.

As was discussed in Chapter 3, Getzels and Csikszentmihalyi conducted a follow-up study with these students seven years later, when members of the group had achieved varying degrees of success. The most successful artists tended to be those who had carefully examined a relatively large number of objects before starting to draw, who had taken a relatively long time before arriving at the final structure of their drawings, and who tended to restart their drawings and/or change the arrangement of objects as they worked.

In conclusion, the tendency toward critical analysis before and during work was important in the success of the drawings produced in the original study and in the career success of these artists as well. The successful artist approaches all work with a high set of standards, both in determining what the work will contain and in judging how well the planned work is executed.

One cannot break this critical analysis down into neat stages of planning followed by execution, because, as was seen in the case studies in this chapter, the successful artist is ready to modify the structure of a work even when it is far along in its execution.

Learning to Create

In the case studies discussed in this chapter we have concentrated on the work of mature individuals, a fact that overlooks one crucial aspect of artistic creativity: it is a skill that must be learned. All artists undergo extended periods of formal or informal training before they are capable of producing something that others value. The great works of art that we revere were produced by individuals who studied and worked for years before they were able to express something of their own. To understand the processes involved in artistic creation, it is imperative that we have some idea of the arduous training involved.

Examination of biographies of composers reveals some common methods of study to which all student composers were, and still are, exposed. One of the most important methods is the immersion in the music of earlier composers, down to copying the works of others into notebooks, which was done even by Mozart. Several works that were at one time attributed to a very young Mozart are now known to be his copies of the works of others. Such works are studied and performed until they are known thoroughly, and the young composer practices by composing in the style of others. Again, we have seen evidence for this in Mozart's career.

A second important aspect of musical training involves learning certain rules of composition, some of which were discussed earlier. These rules changed somewhat as music evolved over the centuries, but certain central notions have been present for at least 300 years. Students are taught rules of harmony, which involve learning what sorts of sequences of chords are permissible and what sorts of notes go with which chords. Even relatively modern books on harmony refer to Bach for examples, indicating an underlying continuity despite the great changes that have occurred since Bach's time. These tools are just a foundation, of course, since each musical era has its own forms that go beyond the basics, but such building blocks enable composers to take the first steps of composing. It also goes without saying that each composer brings his or her individual capacities to the enterprise of making music, taking what he or she has learned and going further with it. However, in the beginning, even the greatest musical geniuses did little more than copy or imitate the great works of others.

A recent study by John Hayes provides strong evidence for the importance of experience in learning to create art. Hayes examined the time needed to become a "master" in the domains of musical composition, painting, and poetry. He first analyzed the compositions of Mozart, who as we have seen, began studying music at the age of 4 and produced his first symphony at the age of 8 — if any individual were exceptional enough to need little or no training or experience before producing great works, Mozart would be the one.

Hayes defined a "masterwork" as a composition for which five different recordings were available in recording catalogs (see Chapter 2). By that definition Mozart wrote his first masterwork in the twelfth year of his career. Hayes thus concluded that Mozart's early works were of lower quality than were his later works.

Hayes extended his catalogue method to examine the masterwork production of seventy-six of the composers discussed in Harold Schonberg's *Lives of the Great Composers* for whom enough information was available to determine when they began to study music. Only three produced a masterwork in fewer than ten years of musical preparation. Composers who started in music relatively late in life took at least as long to produce a masterwork as did those who started much earlier, indicating that the younger composers were not simply "maturing," but that both young and old were developing some rather specific musical skills.

Hayes also carried out a parallel study of the development of painters, with a masterwork defined as a work listed in one of eleven art-reference books. The results were similar to musical composition, with an early period of low productivity, followed by a rapid increase to the mature level, followed after a number of years by a slow decline. The same is true of development of poets, as examined by a student of Hayes, who again found an initial period with little or no work of note, followed by a period of increasing production, a leveling off, and a late decline. Hayes speculates that other areas, among them fiction-writing, science, and athletics, may also require major amounts of skill, and may also show similar patterns of development. Hayes's results provide confirmation that the study of expertise can be extended beyond areas that are characterized by "problem solving" to those requiring "creativity."

The two case studies of Picasso's paintings also provide information concerning changes that occur over an artist's career. In both cases, we see the use of external sources, although that seems to have been more extensive in *Les Demoiselles*. *Guernica* can be seen as following Picasso's own work, with *Minotauromachy* being the most important of a long series of works containing similar characters in similar organizations. The early version of *Les Demoiselles* is more directly related in style to Picasso's earlier work, especially that of the Iberian period, than is the final version, because of the intervention of outside influences.

Based on this artist, one might hypothesize that a young artist is more susceptible to outside influences, because he or she has a less established individual style, and therefore would be less able to deal with new artistic problems by using previous work as a base. This may also mean that the younger artist is more likely to show radical stylistic shifts.

Conclusions

This chapter has surveyed a wide range of creative thinking in the arts. The results provide further support for the conception of creative thinking as ordinary. Even the most radical advances began in continuity with the past, as variations on old themes. Discontinuity, or movement away from the past, came about through reasonable processes: critical analysis on the part of the artist, or as the result of external triggers. These findings support those from the case studies examined in earlier chapters, as well as the findings from the study of laboratory problem solving. In the next chapter, I will use these results as the basis for developing a theory of creative thinking.

CHAPTER 8

A New Understanding of Creative Thinking

This book began with a consideration of two ways of viewing creativity: the "genius" view, which conceives of creativity as the result of extraordinary thought processes; and the "ordinary" view, in which creativity is seen as resulting from thought processes possessed by all of us, seen most clearly when we solve problems (see Chapter 4). Ordinary thought begins in continuity with the past, which means that creative thinking begins with what we know, but it also goes beyond the past, based on new information arising out of the situation.

"Genius" theorists have postulated many different types of thinking as underlying creativity (e.g., lateral thinking, divergent thinking, unconscious thinking, incubation, insight, remote associations), the assumed purpose of which is to allow the creative thinker to "break set," and go beyond past experience. However, research has not provided support for these extraordinary modes (see Chapters 2 and 3), and neither did the broad survey of case studies in Chapters 5 – 7.

We can now move beyond the concept of genius and toward an "ordinary" theory of creative thinking, which will be done in three steps. First, in light of the case studies, I will reconsider the definition of creativity and related concepts, such as whether "novel" works are merely new combinations of old ideas, or if there is such a thing as creating something that is really new. I will then consider whether all creative thinking can be looked upon as problem solving. Finally, I will return to the three general issues posed in Chapter 1: (1) the origins and development of creative works; (2) the differences between creative individuals and others; and (3) why some works are more valued and influential than others.

Defining Creativity

As mentioned in Chapter 1, I have elsewhere used as the definition of creativity the production of novel works that are of value, but more recently I have come to the conclusion that the definition is at once too broad and too narrow. It is too broad because it includes as creative *any* novel product, so long as it is of value, without considering how that product came about; not all valuable novel products are creative. It is too narrow because it excludes works that are novel but of little value or even, if such are possible, works with no value whatever; a novel work without value can be creative.

"Accidental" Creativity

Consider an artist who, while painting, accidentally knocks over a can of paint, which produces a splattering of paint on the canvas. The artist keeps the canvas, say because it can be painted over and used again, but, before the "spill-painting" is covered over, it is seen and positively valued by others. I would not call that painting creative, because for a product to be called creative, it must be the novel result of *goal-*

directed activity; novelty brought about by accident would not qualify as creative, no matter how valuable the outcome. It is interesting to contrast this hypothetical accident with Jackson Pollock's development of his "allover" pouring technique (see Chapter 7). At first glance, Pollock's method seems accidental, but it was not, because from the beginning, he was using techniques of spilling and pouring in a purposeful manner.

On the other hand, assume that the hypothetical artist had examined the spilled "painting" and decided that it had artistic value, and kept it for that reason. Under those circumstances, one could talk about the artist's creativity, at least as exhibited through his or her judgment.

There have been creative "discoveries" that have come about through accidents, such as Alexander Fleming's discovery of penicillin, which is reported to have come about because a mold spore was blown in an open window in his laboratory. However, the discoverer who is remembered for an "accidental" discovery did more than just stumble across something and present it to the scientific community as a *fait accompli*. No one knows the names of those who discovered the Dead Sea scrolls, because those individuals brought nothing of their own to those discoveries. Fleming took his accidental discovery and subjected it to thorough investigation, so that he was able to make use of it.

Creativity is thus exhibited in accidental discoveries when the individual realizes that the accident could be plumbed further. Here, one recalls Louis Pasteur's statement that chance favors the prepared mind. This is no different than when an individual attempting to solve a problem receives unexpected feedback that a proposed solution does not work, which triggers a re-analysis of the situation and leads to a new solution. In the case of an accidental discovery, the trigger comes from outside rather than directly from the individual's action, but the thought processes and result are the same: the individual must know enough to see the possibilities, and then must make something of the accident.

From this perspective, the scribblings with crayon on paper of a monkey or the random banging on a piano of an infant are not creative works of art because they are not goal-directed, although they may be novel, and the latter may be valuable to parents. (This assumes that the infant is not banging on the piano to make music.) In the same way, the free-associational "word-salads" of the schizophrenic are excluded.

Of course, the simplest way to determine whether some product is the result of goal-directed activity is to ask the individual who produced it, but this method leaves out animals and nonverbal humans. One can through careful observation of nonverbal organisms determine whether the outcome of some action was goal-directed or an accident. For example, one can look for evidence of surprise when it occurs, which would indicate that the outcome was accidental. Wolfgang Kohler's analysis of insight in chimpanzees was based on observation, and it was possible to determine the goal-directed nature of the animals' behavior (see Chapter 2).

I would thus propose that the conventional definition of creativity be changed to require the production of goal-directed novelty. John Hayes has reached a similar conclusion regarding the need to eliminate accidents from the definition of creativity, and has proposed that a creative product must reflect the intelligence of the thinker—which is equivalent to its being a result of goal-directed activity. Hayes also retains the criterion of value or appropriateness in his definition, which, as is discussed in the next section, may not be necessary.

Creativity and Value

Should the designation of a product as creative depend on whether it is successful and/or positively valued by others in the field? Positive evaluation seems to me not necessary for creativity to exist. If Watt's steam engine had been ignored by succeeding generations, say because a cheaper and more efficient source of power had been invented shortly thereafter, the invention would surely still qualify as creative, because of its relation to what was then in existence: Watt produced a new kind of engine. The fact that — in this hypothetical example — it was soon surpassed is not relevant to the judgment of its creativity, although under these altered circumstances there would be no encyclopedia entries about Watt and the steam engine. In the same way, if Impressionistic painting had been initially rejected by most critics (which it was) and if it had been ignored by succeeding generations of artists and critics (which it was not), the creativity of the style and its developers would in my opinion be intact, although their positive evaluation would not be.

Mihalyi Csikszentmihalyi has recently proposed a provocative reconceptualization of the concept of creativity, with an increased emphasis on the role of societal judgments of value. Consideration of his view can make clear some of the difficulties that arise when one includes the criterion of value in the definition. Csikszentmihalyi has developed a multicomponent model of creativity (see Chapter 6), in which a cyclical process is proposed. Assume that an individual produces some new work; before that work can be deemed creative, it must be examined by the other members of the "field." In art, this consists of critics, gallery owners, patrons, and other artists; in science, it consists of other scientists.

If the members of the field find value in the work, it then becomes incorporated in the "domain," which is the accumulated work that has been found to be worth preserving and passing on to the next generation (the domain of painting, say, or the domain of molecular biology). According to Csikszentmihalyi, this entire process defines creativity, so that if one produces something novel that is not accepted by the field, and therefore does not become part of the domain, neither the work nor the person can be called creative. Conversely, if a previously ignored work now becomes valued in the field, the work and the person who produced it become creative.

Csikszentmihalyi's emphasis on the different sorts of processes, individual and social, that must be taken into account when attempting to understand creativity and related concepts is important. However, if one makes the definition of creativity depend on the evaluation by the field, the term may lose much of its meaning. Chapter 3 presented a number of cases in which changes occurred over time in the value attributed to the work of a scientist or artist. If value is included in the definition, these cases leave one in the awkward position of having to change the judgment of creativity, which may make the concept vacuous. If this view is carried further, it may mean that one will never be able to tell whether or not some person or product is creative, since an evaluation can change significantly over the years. This seems to go against what is generally meant by the term, and leads me to believe that evaluation may not be helpful in defining creativity.

Even if a novel product of goal-directed activity fails to accomplish the task for which it was made — that is, even if it is unsuccessful — it should still in my view be called creative, because from a cognitive perspective, success and failure are equivalent. An inventor might design a device to pick fruit off trees, say, but it turns out not to work; perhaps it crushes the fruit. Since the inventor was working on a complicated novel device, there are aspects of its performance that could not be predicted. However, this should not count against the invention's being creative, because the ultimate success or failure depends on factors that come into play after it is produced. During the creative process, all rational inventors attempt to use their knowledge to anticipate and to deal with any negative outcomes. In some cases they may be correct, and in others not, but in terms of cognitive processes the two situations are equivalent. I would therefore propose that if an inventor, in a goal-directed attempt to devise a machine to carry out some task, produces a novel device, then — even if that device is a failure — it, and the inventor, should be called creative.

In science, the issue of success is similar. A new theory might be shown by experiment to be incorrect, but since the outcome of the experiment was not known by the theorist, it has nothing to do with the determination of the creativity of the theory. Similar issues arise when one considers the success of a work of art. If an artist paints a portrait and decides afterward that it is not successful, that is no different in cognitive terms than if the artist had judged the outcome positively.

I would, therefore, propose to limit the term *creativity* to an individual's goal-directed production of novel work; the result of the assessment by members of the field would be the *value* of the product. A work of value can also have *influence*, if it is incorporated in the works of others, and I would use the term *genius* to refer to the individual who produces work of exceptional value and/or influence. The creativity of an individual would therefore not change with variations in the judgments given his or her work.

One may thus be able to simplify the definition of creativity by using only the criterion of goal-directed novelty, and separating creativity from value and influence, i.e., from genius. I am not proposing that value plays no role in creative thinking, because when an individual is working toward a goal, the evaluation of progress plays a role at every step, as was shown again and again in the case studies. The evaluation of a product after it is produced should not, however, play a role in our designation of that product as creative.

Social Factors Creativity

A student in class recounted the story of an artist she knew who destroyed what he considered to be his best work just after he produced it, before anyone else could see it. Is that artist creative? The work is obviously goal directed; and it would seem to be straightforward for the artist to determine novelty, but that is more complicated than it first appears. He might without realizing it be repeating himself or producing work that was very similar to that of someone else, with which he had been familiar. Judging novelty thus can run into possible memory problems, and an isolated individual cannot judge that his or her memory is accurate, and therefore cannot judge whether or not he or she is creative.

The same need for external examination is true for science. The complexity of ideas in scientific theorizing requires that others judge their implications, because the theorist might have made a mistake in reasoning that renders the work inadequate on logical grounds. Assessment of novelty is a problem in scientific theorizing as well, because the scientist may not realize that a "new" theory is very similar to the work of another, even work with which he or she may have been familiar. The same is true in invention: a person may have "in vented" something that he or she was exposed to before, but may not recall now. In order for any product to be labeled creative, then, it must be exposed to external inspection and judgment, if only to judge its novelty.

The Question of Novelty

Although novelty is at the core of creativity, there is no agreement on what novelty is: some believe that creative thinking produces works that are truly new (see quotations at the beginning of Chapter 1, on Watt's invention of the steam engine and the discovery of DNA). Others, including many psychologists, have argued that creating something "new" involves putting together old ideas in new combinations. We have seen an example of this thinking in Lowes's analysis of Coleridge's creative imagination (see Chapter 7); and this view has been widely advocated over the years by, among others, Poincaré; Koestler; J. B. Watson, the founder of American behaviorism; as well as by modern psychologists. In this view, nothing is really new: we have a stock of ideas that we keep combining in different ways.

Based on the case studies, these perspectives — novelty as the truly new and novelty as combinations of the old — are both too extreme. Creative products, even the most novel, are related to what came before, but are also more than simply new combinations of old ideas.

The view of novelty as completely new runs into several problems. First, if creative products come out of nothing, one is left enthralled in mystery, which precludes the scientific study of the creative process. There is, as well, much empirical evidence that contradicts the idea that any human creation comes into existence without antecedents, since antecedents can be found for even the most radical creative products in the arts, science, and technology. The case studies given earlier described works that were at the highest level of achievement in a broad range of domains; if antecedents and continuity of thought can be found for those examples, they can probably be found for any product.

Rejecting the idea that creative products spring from nothing does not mean, however, that one must accept the opposite view, that there is nothing novel in any creative product. As an example of this view, Poincare argued that creative thinking in mathematics involved combining ideas ("hooked atoms") until some combination was formed that was relevant to the problem at hand. This "combining-ideas" view is also problematic, in several ways: it ignores situations in which genuine novelty is produced, and it does not specify the "ideas" that are being combined.

An example of true novelty is the distorted faces in Picasso's *Les Demoiselles* (see Chapter 7). Those striated faces were not without antecedents, since Picasso in his work had previously used striations as shading. But in this particular painting they were made into something new: simple shading was transformed from a representation of an aspect of reality (shadow) into a medium for expression of emotional content almost without any relation to reality.

Also, the term "idea" leaves much unclear. As an example, Watson and Crick used Pauling's helical structure, which can be called an old idea, but they did not simply combine it with the "idea" of DNA. Rather, they took the helical structure and used data of various sorts to reason out what the specific new parameters were, which seems to have required production of something new, rather than just combination of the old.

How Many Kinds of Creativity Are There?

I have emphasized the parallels among creative processes in several domains and their common "problem solving" aspects. However, theorists have made a number of distinctions among processes that raise questions about the generality of any such conclusions. One distinction centers on the creative product: in the arts and in invention, creativity brings new objects into existence; in science, creativity results in the discovery of already existing things. A second distinction is between problem solving and problem finding (see Chapter 5 – 7). For example, James Watt came to the conclusion that the Newcomen engine he had repaired was unacceptably inefficient; this led him to a new problem: increasing the engine's efficiency. Thus, Watt first *found* a new problem, and then set out to solve it.

In science, problem finding occurs in several ways. A scientist may examine a theory and find a conceptual difficulty in it that must be rectified, and the resulting new theory then opens new areas for investigation. Or a scientist may develop a new way of analyzing some phenomenon, which would open the way for other scientists to test that analysis through devising specific experiments, which is a type of problem solving. In the arts, problem finding is seen, for example, when a composer makes the decision to work in a new style, which sets the stage for subsequent problem solving, as the composer works out the specific possibilities.

Creativity and Discovery

When Picasso painted *Les Demoiselles d'Avignon*, it has been argued, he created a unique product, which did not exist before he carried out the act of painting, and which would not have come into existence had he not lived. Similarly, if the Wright brothers had not lived, when an airplane had been invented by someone else, it would not have been the same as the Wrights'. The use of the word "creation" to describe the production of such works stems from the use of the term to describe God's creation, and in discussions of artistic creativity especially, the parallel between divine and artistic creation is sometimes emphasized—most particularly, the bringing forth of something from nothing.

In contrast, according to this proposed distinction between creating and discovering, when Watson and Crick discovered the structure of the DNA molecule, they were not creating something from nothing. The structure of DNA already existed, waiting to be found, independently of the state of scientific knowledge, and even independently of humans, like America "waiting" for Columbus. If Watson and Crick had not lived, the structure of DNA would still have been discovered (or uncovered), and that structure would have been identical to that found by Watson and Crick.

However, this proposed distinction between creation and discovery is not as clear-cut as it seems. The artist or inventor is not totally free to create from nothing, and the scientist is not totally constrained by the to-be-discovered object.

As we have seen in numerous cases, including the case of *Les De-moiselles*, even the most radical artistic works are related to what came before; earlier works, by the artist in question and by other artists, influence the structure and content of later works. The same is true of inventions (see Chapter 5). Furthermore, several individuals may independently converge on similar styles of painting, based on similar social and intellectual influences and subject matter, such as the paintings of the early Impressionists. Artists and inventors thus do not work independently of the external context; art, invention, and science are — in at least this aspect — more similar than at first they might seem to be.

Much of the scientific enterprise involves the development (creation) of theories, and such activity is far removed from the discovery of previously existing objects (see Chapters 2, 3, and 6). As an example, Charles Darwin, Alfred Russell Wallace, and Patrick Matthew formulated the theory of evolution, they did not discover anything. Indeed, evolution is a *process*, which it may be impossible to observe in action in any simple sense. The same is true of Allen Newell and Herbert Simon's groundbreaking advocacy of information processing by computer as a metaphor for human thinking. The formulation of theories is closer to the "artistic" end of the scale than the term "scientific discovery" may lead one to believe.

One can also question whether scientific discovery involves already existing objects. The discovery of DNA was not the same as the discovery of America, because the structure was not simply "waiting" to be found (see Chapter 6). When one discovers a new continent, say, or a dollar on the street, the discovered object is perceived directly through the senses. What was available to Watson and Crick, on the other hand, was a set of very indirect clues, such as the results of chemical analyses and X-ray diffraction experiments. Only those who had a theoretical basis for interpreting X-ray diffraction patterns could, at the time, carry out the complicated reasoning process required in order to *deduce* that the structure of DNA is helical. Watson and Crick, without being able to see DNA, had to *devise* a structure that would account for these and many other results.

The achievement of Watson and Crick is like that of a paleontologist who, based on the discovery of a few fossilized bones, reconstructs the skeleton of an immense dinosaur. In such a case, the facts must be interpreted by the scientist. Discovery in this sense turns out to have much in common with development of scientific theory, which in turn has similarities to artistic creativity.

A further similarity between science and art is seen in the role of "style" in science. As discussed in Chapter 6, it was Crick's opinion that, had he and Watson not discovered DNA, the correct structure would have come out in bits and pieces over several years. He believed that such an uncovering of the structure would have resulted in a much less revolutionary influence than that of his and Watson's production of the complete structure at once. Thus, although the *objective* result of a scientific discovery not depend on the discoverers, the *psychological* results of a scientific discovery are not inevitable. The same discovery can have very different effects depending on the manner in which it is originally presented, and the scientific enterprise is not nearly so cut-and-dried as the notion of discovery would lead one to believe.

Problem Solving and Problem Finding

The distinction between problem solving and problem finding is also not sharp. First, problem finding sometimes occurs as the result of problem solving. For example, Watson and Crick's discovery redefined much of biology, and set a new class of problems to be solved, but it was the result of problem solving. In addition, the processes underlying problem finding may be a subset of those underlying problem solving. When a scientist makes a critical analysis and reformulation of assumptions underlying some area, for example, he or she is using the same skills of critical analysis used in examining one's own work. This suggests that problem finding occurs in the course of ordinary problem solving, when one sees difficulties in what one has produced and decides to modify it; this, of course, occurs in science, art, and invention.

One area in which creativity would seem to be based more on problem finding than problem solving is the arts, as when a poet is stimulated to write a poem based on some event he or she has witnessed. However, when one examines problem finding of this sort in the broader context of an artist's career, it too may be a form of problem solving. As Colin Martindale comments about taking up poetry, one does not do it in the hope of being mediocre. Anyone who decides to become an artist of any sort, makes a commitment to produce a body of original work in that field. Using an external event as the basis for a new project is a solution to the problem of production of a significant body of original work. Put another way, the artist is trying to solve the problem of what to do next. In this view, problem finding is problem solving, which leaves us with only one process or set of processes to deal with.

The Central Questions of Creativity Revisited

In Chapter 1, three general questions of creativity were posed:

1. Where do new ideas come from. Can one trace the antecedents of novel works? Are new works conceived whole, or do they undergo changes from the original conception to the final form?
2. Why might one individual make a creative discovery, while another individual, seemingly just as knowledgeable and motivated, does not do so?
3. Why are some works broadly valued and influential, while others are not?

Where Do Novel Ideas Come From?

In the cases considered in Chapters 5–7, we saw that—in each instance—novel ideas came from the past; that is, creative works began in continuity with the past, as summarized in the table on the facing page. Based on the wide range of domains examined, and the high levels of performance, it may be hypothesized that one can always find antecedents to any creative product. But the task remains to specify in as many cases as possible the sources for a given work, and then, if possible, to specify in greater detail how the antecedent was used. A beginning was made for some case studies in the earlier chapters, but the surface has barely been scratched.

One important component of this continuity in creative work is that a new situation is dealt with either as a near analogy (i.e., this new situation is like that old one) or as what could be called an identity (e.g., cognitive "transfer" from an earlier cotton gin to Whitney's—see the accompanying table). Not all creative works must begin with transfer of knowledge based on near analogies, but it is a reasonable working hypothesis, based on the case studies examined in this book.

A variety of artists, especially musicians and poets, report that they sometimes experience inspirations on a small scale — such as the

Examples of Continuities

Example	Source
Invention	
Watt's engine	Newcomen's engine
Whitney's cotton gin	Older gin
Edison's kintoscope	Edison's phonograph
Wrights' biplane	Chanute's biplane
Science	
Watson & Crick's helix	Pauling's alpha-helix
Darwin's monad theory	Lamarck & E. Darwin; monad concept
Arts	
Calder's mobiles	Calder's earlier moving sculpture
Picasso's *Les Demoiselles*	Ingres, Cézanne, Delacroix, Matisse, etc.
Picasso's *Guernica*	Picasso's *Minotauromachy* and other works
Pollock's poured paintings	Siquieros workshop, Hayter, Klee
Dostoyevsky's *The Idiot*	Dickens's Pickwick; Cervantes's Don Quixote; Jesus
Coleridge's *Kubla Khan*	Purchas's *Pilgrimage* and numerous other sources
Mozart's early works	His father's music exercises; works of other composers

spontaneous occurrence in consciousness of a line of poetry or a fragment of melody — which is then used as the basis for conscious elaboration of a composition. These reports are unlike those of Coleridge and of "Mozart's letter," in that they do not involve finished works, and are so frequent that they bear consideration.

Such inspirations do not, however, necessitate the postulation of extraordinary thought process, because even if they are truly "spontaneous," with no traceable conscious antecedents or specifiable external stimuli, they would still be no different than the more prosaic thoughts that constantly spring to mind during our ordinary activities. As an example, one may be driving to work when a thought of a planned vacation may suddenly occur, without any antecedent that

Examples of Transfer in Creative Thinking

Invention

Whitney:	Old gin; not remote
Edison:	Kinetoscope based on phonograph; not remote
Wrights:	Wing-warping based on birds; not remote
	Other transfer came from aviation; not remote

Science

Darwin:	Lamarck and Erasmus Darwin; not remote
	Monad; not remote
	Artificial and natural selection; not remote
	Malthus; not remote
Watson & Crick:	Pauling's alpha helix; not remote
Wilkins:	Analyze DNA as had been done for other molecules, stretching, changing humidity, etc., not remote

Arts

Calder:	Abstraction in sculpture from Mondrian; not remote
Picasso:	*Demoiselles*, Iberian faces, flat noses, scrolled ears; not remote
	Guernica, structure of *Minotauromachy*; not remote

one can trace. There is a long history in philosophy and psychology that explains such thoughts as the result of a string of associations. It could therefore be assumed that something either in one's previous thoughts or in the environment is likely to have set off an associative chain that resulted in thinking about the vacation. (Of course, Freud also assumed that a string of associations was involved in such spontaneous thoughts, although the associative links might be unconscious and unavailable to the thinker.)

This view can be elaborated to explain "spontaneous" thoughts (and therefore "inspirations"): a string of associations is set off by an environmental event, and the thinker can reconstruct neither the initiating event nor the string of associations, because of the speed of the associative chain and the disruptive effect of the outcome. That is, if one has been working for a significant amount of time on a problem, and a solution is finally worked out, the emotional response could easily disrupt the ability to reconstruct the process leading to the solution. In addition, in most cases the product is more important than the intermediate steps, so that they would receive little or no attention, making it difficult at a later time to reconstruct what had happened. Furthermore, for a musician or poet, with a highly developed skill, "spontaneous" thoughts might involve music or poetry, just as our ordinary thoughts can involve speech or visual imagery. Thus, there is no need to postulate a unique mechanism to explain spontaneous "creative" inspirations.

How Do Creative Works Achieve Final Form?

As mentioned in the discussion of Mozart in Chapter 7, perhaps simple products with which the individual has extensive experience can be conceived whole and/or brought forth without revision; but for larger-scale works, creation begins with only a glimpsing of the final product — in musical composition, for example, a snatch of melody and perhaps an idea of the overall structure (see Chapter 7). On the basis of the case studies in Chapters 5 – 7, it can be hypothesized that creative works of any scale always undergo revision and modification between their initial and final form. The examined cases never reached finished form without extensive refinement, often over significant periods of time.

The changes from initial idea to final work occur first because an individual can anticipate and respond to difficulties with a work before it is actually produced; and second, the work-in-progress can be judged inadequate, in which case attempts will be made to modify it. Because these modifications depend at least in part on the critical judgment of the individual, logical reasoning can play a role, as well as analogical thinking. Change in a work can also occur as the result of external events triggering a shift in direction. In such a case, chance would play a role in the creative process. The following table summarizes the development of several creative examples and how the components interact with each other.

These processes — continuity based on near analogies, and discontinuities based on reasoning and sensitivity to external events — are components of ordinary thinking. Therefore, the conclusions here support the claim that creative works — even the most radical — are the result of ordinary thinking processes.

Examples of Discontinuities and Their Sources

Example	Source
Invention	
Wrights:	
Prone operator	Reasoning: less resistance
1902: vertical tail	Reasoning
Science	
Darwin:	
Rejection of monads	Discovery of unicellular fossils — some organisms stay simple
Superfecundity	New data in literature
Watson & Crick:	
3→2 strands	X-ray data; new density and water-content data; reasoning
Backbone outside	X-ray data; reasoning
Anti-parallel chains	Unit cell
Mg ions to H bonds	No magnesium present; evidence for H bonds in DNA
Base Pairing	Like-with-like "torn to shreds"; complementary pairs: trial and error
Arts	
Calder:	
Move to abstraction	Mondrian and Miro
Use of wind	Repetitiveness of motors; reasoning
Picasso:	
Les D: 7→5 characters	Artistic judgment
Distortions	Primitive art

Individual Differences and Creativity

If ordinary thought processes underlie creative thinking, then we are all capable of producing novel works. This does not mean, however, that we are all equal in our potential: there are differences among us that may constrain the areas in which we can work, and other differences that affect the influence that our work will have.

Domain-Specific Skills

Possession of a high degree of domain-specific skill allows an individual to perform at a high level of competence within some domain. Skills in prose writing, for example, allow the writer most effectively to transmit to a reader what the writer wishes to convey. These skills may be very domain-specific, so that a writer of short stories may possess skills somewhat different from those of a novelist, just as Pollock surely possessed somewhat different skills than did Picasso. A helpful analogy here may be to athletic skills, where a football quarterback and a lineman may have little in common in the way of skills.

These skills may be innate and/or acquired, but there may be some biological limitations on what we can acquire. Some of us are better equipped for some domains others are; and each of us is better equipped for some domains than for others.

For example, we can all learn to draw, but there may be differences in the accuracy with which we can learn to record on paper what is in front of us, and also in the accuracy with which we could reproduce some object previously seen. Only those who could draw accurately could produce important work in an era that valued "realism" in art, but individuals without this reproductive ability might succeed in an era that favored abstraction. Thus, not only are different skills important for creativity within subdomains, but as changes occur in style and taste, the characteristics required of those who would excel within the domain probably also change.

Evidence for the inherited nature of skills such as those involved in artistic fields comes from studies of two groups of extraordinary individuals, savants and prodigies. Savants are individuals who possess to a high degree one isolated skill, which is accompanied by an overall intellectual capacity at the level of retardation. A graphic description of a savant tells of a man who can barely speak, is almost totally nonsocial, but who can play the piano marvelously, with a detailed memory of many works, both classical and popular. Prodigies, such as Mozart and Picasso, are individuals who possess a high degree of skill in a specific area at a very early age, and who are normal or above normal in other areas.

The existence of such individuals provides evidence that the specific skills for various domains are to some degree innate, although recent research indicates that — at least, in the case of the prodigy — these skills will not express themselves without strong support from the environment, especially the family, as we saw also in the cases of Mozart and Picasso. Thus, even the most talented must have the right environment if their talent is to bear fruit.

Examination of the skills required in the various areas in which individuals exhibit creativity could provide a basis for a deeper understanding of how novel works are produced. Psychologists have made little attempt to analyze in depth many of the tasks in which humans exhibit creativity, although some "task analysis" has been carried out by Newell and Simon (1972) for several different types of problem-solving situations, such as proving theorems in logic. Similar analyses in a variety of domains would seem to be a prerequisite for understanding the creative imagination.

Domain-Specific Expertise

Even the most talented individuals, in order to produce influential work, must acquire expertise in a domain. This acquisition serves the creative process as the basis for continuity in thinking, raising the question if, in order to begin to do innovative work in a domain, one must know what came before. Perhaps not. Perhaps, on the basis of limited knowledge, one may be able to produce work that is goal-directed and novel for oneself, and that thus would be creative.

In order to produce *influential* work in a field, however, one may have to know what came before. If one does not know the domain, there is always the possibility of reinventing the wheel, and not going beyond what had been done long before. In this context, it would be interesting to examine case studies of untutored or self-taught individuals of established reputation, such as Grandma Moses, to determine how closely their work was related to that of others.

Motivation and Commitment

The individual who would produce influential work must be willing to work on a problem for a long time, if only because influential work deals with important, often extremely complex, problems (see Chapter 5). As one works for a long time on a specific problem, there is an increasing possibility of something new developing out of that work, since small steps taken over a long period of time can add up to a relatively radical advance. Working for a longer time also increases the chances of feedback and of outside triggers, which can stimulate discontinuity.

A high level of motivation and commitment is more than simply putting in long days. Individuals who produce world-class work are totally absorbed in their careers. An example is Watson's description of his and Crick's work habits as they worked on the structure of DNA. In *The Double Helix*, Watson presents himself as a bit of an adolescent more interested in parties and playing tennis than in research. However, several incidents, that he describes in passing, present a different description of his attitude and commitment toward his work. In one case, he describes climbing over the fence to get into the lab at night after a party, so that he could carry out an analysis. On another occasion, Watson comments that Crick was late in coming into the lab because it was Saturday. However, Crick had spent the morning before he came in reading *Nature*, a scientific journal. Also, from Watson's description of that Saturday morning in the lab, one gets the impression that everyone was working.

R. E. Ochse has hyposthesized that childhood social difficulties can lead an individual to emphasize the importance of work. Such individuals feel that they must make their mark in the world by themselves, using intellectual skills, and that other avenues are closed to them. Supporting evidence comes from studies showing creative individuals are much more likely than are matched controls to have suffered trauma in childhood — such as loss of a parent — that might make it more likely for them to withdraw from social contacts and emphasize personal intellectual activities.

Recent research by Teresa Amabile and her colleagues has argued that "intrinsic motivation" (interest in a task for its own sake) is more important in fostering creative work than is "extrinsic motivation" (carrying out the task to achieve some extrinsic gain such as money or prestige). In Amabile's studies, young people ranging in age from grade school to college were asked to carry out tasks that can result in creative products, such as writing a poem or constructing a collage. One group was promised a monetary reward (an extrinsic reward), while another group was not. The promise of an extrinsic reward consistently resulted in lower quality of product. Also, if individuals were told that their work would later be judged by others, the quality was lowered.

These results contrast with reports of creative individuals concerning their motivation, as well as studies of their personality characteristics (see Chapter 3). Creative scientists possess a strong need for professional recognition by their peers, which is an extrinsic motivational characteristic. Watson's report of his and Crick's motivation in pursuing the structure of DNA also indicates that individuals at the highest levels of creativity are motivated by extrinsic concerns: Watson says that he and Crick wanted to win the Nobel prize. There have also been many instances of conflicts in the scientific community about who was first in making some discovery, which also indicates that scientists are not carrying out research only for its intrinsic interest.

Similar extrinsic motivational considerations play a role in artistic creativity. Many works were produced either as part of one's employment or for independent commissions (see Chapter 7). The fact that Mozart left a number of works unfinished has been attributed to the withdrawal of a commission, indicating clearly that his interest in those works was — at least, in part — extrinsically motivated. In addition, much great music has been produced with the express purpose of selling copies of the compositions to interested amateurs, who would play the music in their homes. Mozart produced almost all of his mature works, including many of his greatest, either under commission or for "academies" — concerts produced by Mozart himself, which featured new works composed for the occasion.

The same is true in other arts. Many great novels, including those of Charles Dickens and of Mark Twain, were produced one chapter at a time, for publication in monthly serials. Many great paintings, such as Leonardo da Vinci's *Mona Lisa* and *Last Supper*, as well as Michelangelo's ceiling for the Sistine chapel, were the result of commissions, as were many other great works of sculpture and architecture. In many cases, creative products have been fueled by funds from a prosperous audience.

Amabile has tried to deal with the apparent contradiction between her studies and the historical evidence by noting that individuals at different levels of expertise in a domain may be differently affected by external rewards. The individuals who are renowned within a domain are deeply knowledgeable within it (see Chapter 7). The young people in Amabile's studies were not, and perhaps external factors interfered with their performance because it gave them something else to think about, and thus overwhelmed their processing capacities. An individual established in a field can rely more on expertise developed over years of work, and thus would have more capacity available to deal with — and even, perhaps, be positively affected by — external factors such as rewards.

Why Do Only Some Individuals Succeed?

Watson and Crick were the first to formulate the double helix because they were the first to have available all the components needed to specify it in sufficient detail to develop a model (see Chapter 6). Thus, the various groups of investigators working on DNA, while undoubtedly competent, were not equal. Furthermore, the success of Watson and Crick was not due to their ability to break away from past experience (i.e., some "set-breaking" skill—see Chapters 1–3), while Wilkins and Franklin were locked into theirs. Rather, Watson and Crick used their past experience, and it led them in the correct direction from the very beginning.

In conclusion, there are multiple reasons why one individual succeeds while another does not. First, one individual may be better suited to function within a given domain, which means that he or she would be more likely to produce works in that domain. Second, one individual may be more motivated, increasing the chances that he or she will acquire needed expertise and persevere in working on a difficult problem. Both these factors will increase the likelihood of a truly novel product. Finally, one individual may succeed over another because he or she produces great works, which, as discussed in the next section, is independent of the creator.

Why Are Only Some Works Judged to be Great?

The greatness of a work is not intrinsic to it, and is independent of the creator, except in a case where an individual tailors a work to satisfy some audience. To become great, a work must be judged positively by those within the field. It must thus match the taste of those in the field. These judgments are not absolute, since there can be large changes over time in standards in art. Thus, a work that is judged at one time to be great might have been ignored or even actively rejected at another. Also, there are in science major changes that occur over time in the way problems are approached (e.g., the cognitive versus the behavioral perspectives in psychology), and individuals differ greatly in the ways in which they approach problems in science. So here, too, for a person to produce work of influence, his or her approach to scientific problems must be compatible with that of other scientists, so that they can understand it and build on it.

Some works, then, are considered greater than others because they fit the taste of the field at a given time. As we have seen, creativity and greatness are different things: the former depends on the individual, the latter on the judgment of others.

Ordinary Thinking and Creative Output

How do we increase creativity? As noted in Chapter 2, one of the assumptions of the genius view is that creative thinking is a special skill, possessed by only a few of us. From this perspective, opportunities exist to teach people how to think creatively, a concept that has provided for numerous training programs. If — in place of the genius view — we adopt a conception of creative thinking as ordinary, it changes the approach to maximizing individuals' creative output.

First of all, concept of creative thinking as ordinary leads one away from the view that we must teach people to think creatively, because in one sense this is not necessary, since we all are already able to think creatively. This does not mean, however, that we cannot increase the probability that people will better solve problems, because solving problems depends on more than just the ability to think. In the same way, the fact that ordinary thinking is creative at its base does not mean that we cannot increase the probability for people to produce significant works in the sciences and the arts, because here, too, creative output depends on more than the ability to think.

Based on the discussion in this book, there are two ways in which we can increase people's performance in these areas: provide an environment that encourages them to develop expertise, and maximize their motivation. Of these two components, motivation may be the more important, because one needs motivation to acquire expertise in the first place, and one needs it to stay at the task so to produce innovation.

As an example of how, from an "ordinary" perspective, one might approach the issue of increasing creativity, consider a situation in which a person is facing a problem. The person considers the problem and draws a blank — no solution comes to mind. Based on the notion of continuity of thought, an inability to think of a solution in the first place probably would arise because the person has no information in memory that can be matched to the problem. Thus, as a first step in making it more likely that this individual could begin to solve the problem, we should provide more information.

In contrast to methods based on the genius view, which attempt to teach general "creativity-enhancing skills" (e.g., "set-breaking" — see Chapter 2), the conclusions from this book indicate that we should emphasize development of deep expertise in a particular domain. As was shown in Chapter 4, the transfer of one's knowledge to a new problem depends first on the two situations having "surface" elements in common, such as using rays to destroy a tumor; in this way, the new situation can remind the person of the previously-experienced problem. In addition, in order for the old situation to be useful in dealing with the new problem, old and new must have analogous structures, so that the old solution can, with modification, be applied.

This leads to the expectation that experience with a wide range of problems will facilitate transfer. In addition, individuals should probably be explicitly instructed in the use of past experience to deal with new problems, because research has shown that instruction can increase transfer, and can result in people developing general skills relevant to broader classes of problems. Also, without such instruction, "spontaneous" transfer may be minimal.

In addition, it might be useful to instruct would-be problem solvers in the role of analogies in creative thinking, as well as instructing them in devising general descriptions to summarize their experiences, as well as new problems they encounter, since such generalizations may facilitate remote transfer. We could also provide individuals with instruction in how external triggers have in the past facilitated creative solutions to problems in various domains, although without some breadth of examples, the students might not get much from such demonstrations.

The second issue in increasing creative output revolves around motivation: How do we keep individuals motivated, so that they develop expertise and grapple over the long term with problems of significance? If we are dealing with professionals, then they are already motivated and there would not be a problem. With young people who have not yet embarked on a career, we must get them interested in the first place, and keep them so. Exposure at an early age to subject matter in the arts and sciences, structured in such a way as to appeal to the young, can result in a child's naturally developing an interest in some area.

At a later age, exposure to mentors can play multiple roles. A mentor, someone totally immersed in a career, provides a role model, and some of the enthusiasm is contagious, as evidenced by reports from creative individuals of the influence of their "teachers." In addition, exposure to a mentor allows the learning of "tools of the trade," and provides evidence that the domain is worthy of life-long commitment. It might thus be possible to increase creative output in various ways, although none of these ideas are short-term, or simple to implement.

Conclusion

If ordinary thought processes serve to bring about creative advances, then we do not need a special theory to explain how they are brought about; we simply need a complete theory of thinking, *per se*. If, and when, we can understand how our ordinary thinking brings about the most mundane of outcomes — how we decide that it is time to pull weeds from our garden and then go about doing it; how we put together dinner from what happens to be on hand in the refrigerator; how one is able to answer a question or give directions — then we will understand the thought processes underlying the most momentous works humans can produce.

Reference Notes

CHAPTER 1

Page 3

The genius view has existed in Western society for thousands of years: Murray (1989).

Don Giovanni quote: Dormen & Edidin (1989, 49).

Page 4

Definition of creativity: e.g., Amabile (1989), Ochse (1990), Rothenberg (1979), Weisberg (1986, 1988).

Degree of transformation: Jackson & Messick (1967)

Differing degrees of creativity: e.g., Amabile (1983), Boden (1991).

Pages 4-5

Value of invention: see also Basalla (1988).

Page 5

Value of work of art: see also Csikszentmihalyi (1988).

Page 7

Individuals simply serve as vehicles through which divine ideas are expressed: Murray (1989).

Page 7

"Breaking the set": Amabile (1989), Luchins & Luchins (1959), Matlin (1989).

Page 8

Personality structure which allows special mode of thinking to flourish: Martindale (1989), Ochse (1990), and Woodman & Schoenfeldt (1989).

Extraordinary sensitivity and flexibility: Rogers (1954).

Pages 8-9

"Problem finding": Runco (1992).

Artists have more insight into, or are closer to, their own emotional experiences: Freud (1908/1959).

Page 10

If a creative product has extraordinary effects, it must have come about in extraordinary ways: see also Brown (1989).

Pages 10-11

We use the old to generate the new: Basalla (1988), Weisberg (1986).

Reasoning and the accumulation of new pieces of information: Weisberg (1986).

Page 12

Case studies used to great advantage by Howard Gruber and his students: e.g., Gruber (1981), Wallace and Gruber (1989).

Page 12

For additional case studies, see Basalla (1988), Aris, Davis, & Stuewer (1983), and Wallace & Gruber (1989).

Each case of creative thinking may be unique: Gruber (1981).

Page 13

For more details on Calder's development: Lipman (1976/1989), Marshall (1987).

Page 18

Edison's use of analogy: Jenkins & Jeffrey (1984).

Page 19-20

Earliest version of kinetoscope based on phonograph; Edison quote: Jenkins and Jeffrey (1984).

Page 21

Edison's small number of ideas: Jenkins (1983).

Pages 23-24

Specific skills, motivation, and knowledge: see also Amabile (1983, 1889), Perkins (1981), and Simonton (1984, 1988).

Page 24

Commitment to one's chosen field: Mansfield and Busse (1981), Ochse (1990).

Pages 24-25

Study by Hayes: Hayes (1989).

General skills relevant to all creative work: see Amabile (1989) for a variant of this view.

CHAPTER 2

Page 28

The method of psychobiography: Freud (1910/1964), Stannard (1980).

Page 29-30

Further discussion of primary process thinking in creativity: Koestler (1964), Ochse (1990), Rothenberg (1979), Suler (1980).

Pages 30-31

Neo-Freudians: e.g., Kris (1952), Rothenberg (1979); see Suler (1980) for summary of neo-Freudian view.

Page 31

Associational thinking as primary process: Martindale (1989); see also Simonton (1988).

Page 31

Mechanisms of primary-process thinking: Koestler (1964), Suler (1980).

Page 31

Recent psychobiographies: Solomon (1977), Gedo (1980).

Page 32

Rothenberg (1979).

Page 34

Analysis of daydreams: Ochse (1990).

Page 34

Newspaper accounts of bombing of Geurnica: Chipp (1988).
Earthquake as exciting experience: Richardson (1991).

Page 35

Collaboration of Picasso and Braque on cubism: Rubin (1989).

Pages 35-36

Accuracy of Freud's case studies: Stannard (1980).

Page 36

Kraepelin (1921/1976).

Page 37

Jamison's studies: Jamison (1989), Jamison, Gerner, Hammen, & Padesky (1980); Goodwin & Jamison (1990).

Page 37

Andreasen (1987).

Page 38

Bipolar affective disorder and suicide in poets: Goodwin & Jamison (1990).

Page 38

Robert Schumann's bipolar disorder: Henahan (1986), Slater & Meyer (1959).

Page 38

Schumann's mood and output: adapted from Slater & Meyer (1959).

Pages 38-39

Question of causal relationship: see also Richards (1981).

Page 39

Stressful events in childhood and creativity: Ochse (1990).

Page 40

Hayes's study of musical composition: Hayes (1989).
Constancy of probability of great works: Dennis (1966), Simonton (1988).

Page 41

Comparison group of biographers: Jamison (1989).
Poetry as refuge for manic-depressives: Richards (1981).

Pages 41-42

Virginia Woolf's use of her experiences: Caramagno (1988).

Page 42

Poincaré (1908/1952).

Page 42

Koestler (1964).

Page 43

Mozart's letter: reprinted in Ghiselin (1952, 44-45, emphases original.

Pages 43-44

Coleridge's report: reprinted in Ghiselin (1952, 84-85).

Pages 44-45

Poincaré's observation of his own unconscious at work: Poincaré (1908/ 1952), Hadamard (1954), Simonton (1988), Wallas (1926).

Page 45

Four stages of creativity: Wallas (1926).

Pages 45-46

Creative worrying: Olton (1979).

Page 46

Mozart's composing: Sloboda (1985), Tyson (1987).
Questions about "Kubla Khan": Schneider (1953).

Page 46

Darwin's notebooks versus his autobiography: Gruber (1981).

Pages 47-48

Study of incubation: Patrick (1935).

Page 48

Study of incubation: Eindhover & Vinacke (1952).

Pages 48-49

Olton's studies of incubation: Olton (1979), Olton & Johnson (1976).

Pages 49-50

Use of self-reports: Ochse (1990); there are similarities here to Koestler's [1964] notion of bisociation. See also Martindale (1989) and Simonton (1988).

Difficulty in reporting on one's own cognitive processes: Nisbett & Wilson (1977).

Page 50

Gestalt psychologists on trial-and-error versus insight: e.g., Kohler (1927); see also Holyoak (1990), Matlin (1989), Metcalfe (1986a, b), Sternberg & Davidson (1982), Weisberg (1992).

Pages 50-51

Reproductive versus productive thought: Wertheimer (1982).

Page 51

Kohler's study of apes: Kohler (1927/1976).

Page 52

Studies of apes raised in captivity from birth: Birch (1945), Epstein (1991).

Pages 52-53

Development of insight: Harlow (1949).

Pages 54-55

Nine-dot problem: Scheerer (1963), Burnham & Davis (1969), Weisberg & Alba (1981).
Nine-dot problem "strategy" instructions: Lung & Dominowski (1985).

Pages 55-56

Studies of intuition: Bowers, Regehr, Balthazard, & Parker (1990).

Pages 56-58

Remote associations: Simonton (1988), Campbell (1960), Mednick (1962).

Pages 57-58

RAT not successful in predicting creative ability: Mansfield & Busse (1981).

Pages 58-60

Guilford's theorizing: Guilford (1950).

Pages 60-61

Lateral thinking: deBono (1968, 1985); for citations, see e.g., Adams (1979), Amabile (1989), Bransford & Stein (1984), Halpern (1989), Levine (1988).

Pages 61-62

Literature on divergent thinking: Mansfield & Busse (1981), Torrance (1988).

Lack of predictive validity of creativity tests: Kogan & Pankove (1974).

Creative individuals do not necessarily score high: Segal, Busse, & Mansfield (1980).

Scientists' descriptions of how they think: Mansfield & Busse (1981).

Darwin's notebooks: Gruber (1981); Watson's report on DNA: Watson (1968); Picasso's preliminary sketches: Glimcher & Glimcher (1986); Edison's notebooks: Jenkins & Jeffrey (1984).

Page 62

Brainstorming: Osborn (1953).

Importance of deferring judgment: Adams (1979), Amabile (1983, 1989), Bransford & Stein (1984), Halpern (1989), Levine (1988).

Pages 63-64

Adams (1979).

Pages 64-65

Adams's influence: e.g., Amabile (1989, 48-49).

Pages 65-66

Bransford & Stein (1984), Levine (1988).

Page 67

Does brainstorming work? Gerlach, Schutz, Baker, & Mazer (1964), Johnson, Parrott, & Stratton (1968).

CHAPTER 3

Page 70

Voluminous literature in this area; for reviews: Mansfield & Busse (1981), Ochse (1990).

Pages 70-71

Characteristics cause creativity: e.g., Barron (1955).

Pages 70-71

Economic differences: Ochse (1990).

Pages 72-73

Small number of characteristics shared by all creative individuals: see Simonton (1988) for review.

Page 73

Aesthetic feelings of scientists: Mansfield & Busse (1981), Ochse (1990).
No surprises: Barron & Harrington (1981).

Page 73

Critical note: Busse & Mansfield (1981).

Pages 73-74

Personality inventories versus mailed questionnaires: Mackinnon (1962).

Page 74

No control group: for review, see Ochse (1990).

Pages 74-75

Lack of close match between creative and noncreative groups: for review see Mansfield & Busse (1981).

Pages 74-75

Mackinnon (1962).

Page 76

Aesthetic sense in scientists: Busse & Mansfield (1981).

Page 76

Flexibility versus rigidity in scientists: Mitroff (1974).

Page 77

High degree of motivation present early: Segal, Busse, & Mansfield (1980).

Pages 77-78

Getzels & Csikszentmihalyi (1976); see also Segal, Busse, and Mansfield (1981).

Pages 78-79

Csikszentmihalyi follow-up (1990).

Similar results: Segal, Busse, and Mansfield (1981).

Pages 79-80

Assumed sensitivity of scientific genius: Guilford (1950).

Pages 80-81

Study of Leonardo: Hope (1990).

Page 81

Newton, Darwin, Gall, and Le Verrier: Broad (1983).

Pages 81-82

Einstein: Clark (1972).

Page 82

"Old museum piece": Clark (1972, 648).

Page 83

Dennis (1966).

Page 83

Simonton (1988).

Page 84

Genius is not a psychological characteristic: Csikszentmihalyi (1988), Weisberg (1986).

Pages 84-85

Bach's genius: Weisberg (1986).

Page 85

Rembrandt and Botticelli: Csikszentmihalyi (1988).

Page 85

Basalla (1988).

Page 86

Mendel's genius: Csikszentmihalyi (1988).

Page 86

Bartlett (1932).

Page 88

Haydn on Mozart: Blume (1956, 10).

CHAPTER 4

Page 92

E.g., Newell, Shaw, & Simon (1962), Newell & Simon (1972); on cognitive revolution, see Lachman, Lachman, & Butterfield (1979).

Creative thinking as problem solving: Langley, Simon, Bradshaw, & Zytkow (1987).

Page 94

Problem space: Newell & Simon (1972).

Page 94

Searching problem space: Duncker (1945), Newell and Simon (1972), Polya (1957).

Pages 94-96

GPS: Newell & Simon (1972).

Page 96

Creativity as "better ways of searching": Newell, Shaw, & Simon (1962), Perkins (1981).

Page 96

Expertise: Glaser & Chi (1988).

Pages 96-98

Candle problem: Weisberg & Suls (1973).

Pages 98-99

Analogical transfer: Spencer & Weisberg (1986).

Page 99

Carrying out solution in imagination: Weisberg (1980), Weisberg & Suls (1973).

Pages 99-100

Development of box solution: Weisberg & Suls (1973).

Pages 100-101

Interest in box solution: Duncker (1945), Glucksberg & Weisberg (1966), Weisberg & Suls (1973).

Pages 101-104

Charlie problem: Weisberg & DiCamillo (1992).

Page 105

Analogies in creativity: see Koestler (1964) for review.

Pages 105-106

"most important dream . . .": Koestler (1964, 118).

Types of analogies: for further discussion see Vosniadou & Ortony (1989).

Pages 106-107

Investigations of analogical transfer using radiation problem: Gick & Holyoak (1980, 1983), Keane (1985), Spencer & Weisberg (1986).

Pages 107-108

Simultaneous convergence solution: Gick & Holyoak (1983), Holyoak & Koh (1987).

Pages 109-110

Pioneering studies of transfer: Gick & Holyoak (1980, 1983).

Pages 110-111

Role of context in transfer: Spencer & Weisberg (1986).

Page 111

Other studies of context: Catrambone & Holyoak (1989), Keane (1987).
Keane's further study: Keane (1987).

Page 111

Holyoak & Koh (1987).

Page 112

Ross (1987).

Page 113

Additional negative conclusions concerning role of analogy in creativity: Perkins (1985).

Was Kekulé dreaming: Rothenberg (1991).

Page 113

Expertise: Glaser & Chi (1988).

Expertise in domains such as musical composition and painting: Hayes (1989), Weisberg (1986).

Pages 113-115

Early work in problem solving skills in chess: DeGroot (1966).

Pages 114-115

"Chunks" and replication of DeGroot: Chase & Simon (1973).

Pages 115-116

Studies of expertise: Chi, Glaser, & Farr (1980), Greeno (1980).

Expertise in physics: Chi, Feltovich, & Glaser (1981).

Pages 116-117

Studies of expertise in radiology: Lesgold (1988).

Page 117

Greeno (1980).

Pages 117-119

Soar: Newell (1990).

Page 118

Thorndike's "identical elements": Thorndike (1913).

Page 120

Teaching "critical thinking": see summaries in Halpern (1989), and discussion in Bransford, et al. (1985) and Polson & Jeffries (1985).

Page 120

No evidence for remote transfer without overlap of surface information: e.g., Holyoak & Koh (1987), Spencer & Weisberg (1986).

Radiologist's large data base: Lesgold (1988).

Page 120

Hintzman (1986).

Pages 121-122

Difficulties in teaching thinking: Hayes (1985).

CHAPTER 5

Page 126

Information about flight available: cf. Csikszentmihalyi (1988).
Watt's hero's status: Basalla (1988).

Pages 127-128

Watt's engine: Rolt & Allen (1977).

Page 129

"long line of . . . connections": Basalla (1988, 40).

Page 129

The price of coal and Watt's genius: Rolt & Allen (1977).

Page 130

Problem finding: Getzels & Csikszentmihalyi (1976), Runco (1992).
Watt not first to be impressed by inefficiency: Robinson (1969).

Pages 130-132

Whitney: Basalla (1988).

Pages 132-145

Wright brothers discussion: Howard (1987), Walsh (1975).

Pages 139-140

Walsh's oservations of birds: Walsh (1975).

Pages 148-149

"Naturfacts": Basalla (1988).

CHAPTER 6

Page 152

Scientific revolutions: Kuhn (1978).

Pages 152-168

Historical background for Watson and Crick, discussions of Wilkins, Franklin, and Pauling: Olby (1974), Watson (1968/1980).

Page 154

Watson's postdoctoral fellowship: Watson (1968/1980).

Page 157

Franklin's notes: Olby (1974).

Page 160

Structures of bases: Olby (1974), Watson (1968).

Page 163

Report of Franklin's work: Olby (1974), Watson (1968/1980).

Page 164

Like-with-like "torn to shreds": Watson (1968/1980).

Page 168

Crick's beliefs about discovery: Olby (1974).

Page 169

Selective combination in Darwin: Davidson & Sternberg (1986); see also Koestler (1964).

Pages 170

Darwin formulated and rejected a theory: Gruber (1981).

Pages 170-177

Historical background: Eiseley (1961).

Page 172

Lamarck: Sheppard (1960).

Pages 177-179

Monad theory: Gruber (1981).

Pages 179-181

Monads to natural selection: Gruber (1981).

Pages 181-184

Computer models: Langley, et al. (1987).

Page 185-186

Are the models creative? Csikszentmihalyi (1988).

Pages 186-187

Revolutionary science: Kuhn (1978).

Pages 186-187

Problem solving versus problem finding: Runco (1992).

Page 187

Scientific change is smooth: e.g., Lakatos (1970).

Page 187

Role of mentors: John-Steiner (1985).

Pages 187-188

Darwin's social network: Eiseley (1961).

CHAPTER 7

Page 192

Genesis of *Kubla Khan*: Lowes (1927/1964).

Page 193

The most important painting: e.g., Rosenblum (1976).

Pages 197-201

Background for *Les Demoiselles*: Golding (1968), Rubin (1984).

Page 196

Another possible source for faces: see Richardson (1991).

Page 198

Specific primitive masks: Golding (1968).

Such masks not available in Paris: Rubin (1984).

Page 199

Picasso reacting to Matisse: Rubin (1984).

Pages 202-209

Background for *Guernica*: Chipp (1988).

Pages 203-204

Ambiguity of location: Chipp (1988); see also Rothenberg (1979).

Page 206

Late revision: Blunt (1969).

Pages 206-207

Continuity with Picasso's career: Chipp (1988).

Pages 206-207

Light-bearing girl: Kimmelman (1989).

Page 208

Historical antecedents: Chipp (1988), Blunt (1969).

Pages 209-215

Pollock historical background: Landau (1990).

Page 210

Pollock as the first great American painter: Rubin (1967).

Pages 210-211

Benton's influence: Polcari (1979).

Page 211

Siqueiros workshop: Laundau (1990).

Pages 214-215

Benton's analysis: Polcari (1979).
Pollock's decision-making process: Rubin (1967).

Pages 215-216

Reports of poets: Abrams, et al. (1968).
Perkins (1981).

Pages 216-218

Coleridge's imagination: Lowes (1927/1964).

Page 217

More than dreamwork in *Kubla Khan*: Schneider (1953).

Page 218

Revision in poetry: Abrams, et al. (1968).

Pages 218-221

New York Public Library exhibit: Mitgang (1984).

Pages 221-223

Musical composition as problem solving: Sloboda (1985).

Pages 223-224

Mozart background: Sadie (1983), Zaslaw (1989).

Page 224

First great symphony and concerto: Sadie (1983).
Compositions without sketches? Hertzmann (1963).
Extant sketches: Sloboda (1985).

Pages 224-225

Compositional difficulties exhibited in sketches: Tyson (1987).

Pages 225-226

Jupiter finale: Sherman (1990), Wollenberg (1975).

Pages 225-226

Rosetti's horn concertos as influence: Robbins-Landon (1956).

Pages 226-227

Discontinuities in symphonic style: Zaslaw (1989).

Pages 227-228

Beethoven's notebooks: Solomon (1977).

Pages 228-229

Bach's background: Emery, Wolff, & Temperley (1983).

Bach's duties: Marshall (1972).

Page 229

Rules of composition: Einstein (1945).

Rhetoric and music: Bettmann (1985 – 1986), Buelow (1980).

Pages 229-230

Bach as borrower: Carrell (1967).

Handel as borrower: Dean (1982).

Beethoven as borrower: Derr (1984).

Page 230

Folk melodies: Baker (1982).

Pages 231-232

Notebooks for *The Idiot*: Boell (1983), Wasiolek (1967).

Pages 232-233

Sources for *Crime and Punishment*: Mochulsky (1967).

Page 233

Stevenson: Finch (1958).

Pages 233-235

Chaplin background: Robinson (1985).

Pages 235-236

Critical analyis: Getzels & Csikszentmihalyi (1976).

Pages 236-237

Mozart's early symphonies: Zaslaw (1989).

Pages 237-238

Expertise in creating art: Hayes (1989).

Page 237

Schonberg (1970).

CHAPTER 8

Page 242

My use of definition: Weisberg (1986, 1988).

Page 243

Accidental discoveries: see Austin (1978).

Page 244

Hayes's definition: Hayes (1989).

Pages 244-245

Csikszentmihalyi's reconceptualization: Csikszentmihalyi (1988).

Page 246

Use of *genius*: See also Albert (1975).

Page 247

Old ideas in new combinations: e.g., Martindale (1989).

Pages 248-249

Artistic creativity brings new objects into existence: May (1975), Ochse (1990).

Page 249

A work of art as unique: Ochse (1990).

Page 250

Radical works related to what came before: see also Basalla (1988).
Impressionists converge on style of painting: Herbert (1988).

Page 250

Newell & Simon (1972).

Pages 251-252

Martindale (1989).

Page 252

Origins of novel ideas: see also Basalla (1988).

Pages 252-253

Spontaneous occurrence of lines of poetry or fragment of melody: for examples, see Ghiselin (1952).

Page 255

Creation begins with a glimpse: Sloboda (1985).

Chance in creative process: Austin (1968).

Page 257

Savant: Treffert (1988).

Prodigies: Feldman (1988).

Task analyses in a variety of domain: e.g., Sudnow (1978).

Page 259

Totally absorbed: Ochse (1990).

Childhood social difficulties: Ochse (1990).

Page 259

Intrinsic motivation: Amabile (1983), Hennessey & Amabile (1988).

Pages 259-260

Conflicts over who was first: Simonton (1984).

Page 260

Prosperous audience: Csikszentmihalyi (1988).

Page 263

Surface elements in reminding: Ross (1987).

Instruction in the use of past experience: Ross & Kennedy (1990).

Page 263

Influence of "teachers": John-Steiner (1985).

Bibliography

Abrams, M. H., Donaldson, E. T., Smith, H., Adams, R. M., Monk,
    S. H., Ford, G. H., & Daiches, D. (Eds.) (1968). *The Norton
    anthology of English literature.* (rev. cd.) New York: Norton.
Adams, J. L. (1979). *Conceptual blockbusting.* 2d ed. New York: Norton.
Albert, R. S. (1975). Toward a behavioral definition of genius.
    American Psychologist, 30, 140–151.
Allport, G. W. (1965). *Pattern and growth in personality.* New York:
    Holt, Rinehart, & Winston.
Amabile, T. (1983). *The social psychology of creativity.* New York:
    Springer-Verlag.
Amabile, T. (1989). *Growing up creative. Nurturing a lifetime of
    creativity.* New York: Crown Publishers.
American Psychiatric Association. (1987). *Diagnostic and statistical
    manual of mental disorders.* (3d ed., rev.). Washington, D.C.:
    Author.
Andreasen, N. (1987). Creativity and mental illness: Prevalence rates in
    writers and their first-degree relatives. *American Journal of
    Psychiatry, 144,* 1288–1292.
Aris, R., Davis, H. T., & Steuwer, R. H. (Eds.) (1983). *Springs of
    scientific creativity. Essays on founders of modern science.*
    Minneapolis: University of Minnesota Press.
Austin, J. H. (1978). *Chase, chance, and creativity.* New York: Columbia
    University Press.
Baker, R. (1982). *Mozart.* London: Thames and Hudson.
Barron, F. (1955). The disposition towards originality. *Journal of
    Abnormal and Social Psychology, 51,* 478–485.
Barron, F., & Harrington, D. M. (1981). Creativity, intelligence, and
    personality. *Annual Reviews of Psychology, 32,* 439–476.
Bartlett, F. C. (1932). *Remembering.* Cambridge, England: Cambridge
    University Press.
Basalla, G. (1988). *The evolution of technology.* New York: Cambridge
    University Press.

Bettmann, O. L. (1986, Winter). Bach the rhetorician. *American Scholar*, 113 – 118.

Birch, H. (1945). The relation of previous experience to insightful problem solving. *Journal of Comparative Psychology, 38*, 367 – 383.

Blume, F. (1956). Mozart's style and influence. In H. C. Robbins Landon & D. Mitchell (eds.), *The Mozart companion.* New York: Norton, 10 – 31.

Blunt, A. (1969). *Picasso's "Guernica."* New York: Oxford University Press.

Boden, M. A. (1991). *The creative mind.* New York: Basic Books.

Boell, J. (1983). Dostoyevsky and the creative process in The Idiot. Unpublished manuscript, Temple University.

Bowers, K., Regehr, G., Balthazard, C., & Parker, K. (1990). Intuition in the context of discovery. *Cognitive Psychology, 22*, 72 – 110.

Bransford, J. D., & Stein, B. S. (1984). *The IDEAL problem solver. A guide for improving thinking, learning, and creativity.* New York: Freeman.

Bransford, J. D., Stein, B. S., Arbitman-Smith, R, & Vye, N. J. (1985). Improving thinking and learning skills: An analysis of three approaches. In S. Chipman, J. W. Segal, & R. Glaser (eds.), *Thinking and learning skills,* vol. 1, Hillsdale, NJ: Erlbaum, 133 – 206.

Briggs, J. (1984). The genius mind. *Science Digest, 92,* 74 – 78.

Broad, W. J. (1983, February 1). What happens when heroes of science go astray? *New York Times,* pp. C1, C2.

Brown, R. (1989). Creativity. What are we to measure? In J. A. Glover, R. R. Ronning, & C. R. Reynolds (eds.), *Handbook of creativity.* New York: Plenum, 3 – 32.

Buelow, G. J. (1980). Rhetoric and music. In S. Saide (ed.) *The new Grove dictionary of music and musicians.* New York: Norton, 793 – 803.

Burnham, C. A., & Davis, K. G. (1969). The 9-dot problem: beyond perceptual organization. *Psychonomic Science, 17,* 321 – 323.

Busse, T. V., & Mansfield, R. S. (1981) The blooming of creative scientists: Early, late and otherwise. *Gifted Child Quarterly,* 63 – 66.

Campbell, D. T. (1960). Blind variation and selective retention in creative thought as in other knowledge processes. *Psychological Review, 67,* 380 – 400.

Canaday, J. (1980). *What is art? An introduction to painting, sculpture and architecture.* London: Hutchinson.

Caramagno, T. C. (1988). Manic-depressive psychosis and critical approaches to Virginia Woolf's life and work. *Publications of the Modern Language Association, 103,* 10 – 23.

Carrell, N. (1967). *Bach the borrower.* London: George Allen & Unwin.

Catrambone, R., & Holyoak, K. J. (1989). Overcoming contextual limitations on problem-solving transfer. *Journal of Experimental Psychology: Learning, Memory, and Cognition, 15,* 1147 – 1156.

Chase, W. G., & Simon, H. A. (1973). Perception in chess. *Cognitive Psychology, 4,* 55 – 81.

Chi, M., Feltovich, P. J., & Glaser, R. (1981). Categorization and representation of physics problems by experts and novices. *Cognitive Science, 5,* 121 – 125.

Chi, M. T. H., Glaser, R., & Farr, M. J. (1988). *The nature of expertise.* Hillsdale, NJ: Erlbaum.

Chipp, H. B. (1988). *Picasso's "Guernica:" History, transformations, meanings.* Berkeley: University of California Press.

Clark, R. W. (1984). *Einstein: The life and times.* New York: Avon Books.

Colcridgc, S. T. (1952). Prefatory note to Kubla Khan. In B. Ghislein. (ed.) *The creative process.* New York: Mentor, 84 – 85. (Original work published 1816).

Csikszentmihalyi, M. (1988). Society, culture, and person: a systems view of creativity. In R. J. Sternberg (ed.), *The nature of creativity. Contemporary psychological perspectives*, Cambridge: Cambridge University Press, 325 – 339.

Csikszentmihalyi, M., & Getzels, J. W. (In press) Creativity and problem finding in art. In F. H. Farley & R. W. Neperud (eds.), *The foundations of aesthetics, art, and education.* New York: Praeger.

Davidson, J. E., & Sternberg, R. E. (1986, summer). What is insight? *Educational Horizons,* 177 – 179.

Dean, W. (1982). *The New Grove Handel.* New York: Norton.

deBono, E. (1968). *New think.* New York: Basic Books.

deBono, E. (1985). The CoRT thinking program. In S. Chipman, J. W. Segal, & R. Glaser (eds.), *Thinking and learning skills.* (Vol. 1). Hillsdale, NJ: Erlbaum, pp. 363 – 388.

DeGroot, A. (1966). Perception and memory versus thought: some old ideas and recent findings. In B. Kleinmuntz (ed.) *Problem Solving: Research, method, and theory*, New York: John Wiley, 19 – 50.

Dennis, W. (1966). Creative productivity between the ages of 20 and 80 years. *Science, 123,* 724 – 725.

Derr, E. (1984). Beethoven's long-term memory of C. P. E. Bach's rondo in E-flat, W. 61/1 (1787), manifest in the variations in E-flat for piano, opus 35 (1802). *Musical Quarterly, 70,* 45 – 76.

Deutsch, O. E. (1964). Spurious Mozart letters. *Music Review, 25,* 120 – 123.

Dorman, I., & Ediden, P. (1989, July, August). Original Spin. *Psychology Today,* 46 – 52.

Duncker, K. (1945). On problem-solving. *Psychological Monographs, 58,* no. 5, whole no. 270.

Eindhoven, J. E., & Vinacke, W. E. (1952). Creative processes in painting. *The Journal of General Psychology, 47,* 139 – 164.

Einstein, Alfred (1945). *Mozart: His character, his work.* London: Oxford University Press.

Eiseley, L. (1961). *Darwin's century. Evolution and the men who discovered it.* New York: Anchor Books.

Emery, W., Wolff, C., & Temperley, N. (1983). Johann Sebastain Bach. In C. Wolff, W. Emery, E. Helm, R. Jones, E. Warburton, & Derr, E. S. (eds.), *The New Grove Bach Family*, New York: Norton, 44–237.

Epstein, R. (1991). Skinner, creativity, and the problem of spontaneous behavior. *Psychological Science, 2,* 362–370.

Feldman, D. H. (1988). Creativity: dreams, insights, and transformations. In R. J. Sternberg (ed.), *The nature of creativity. Contemporary psychological perspectives*, Cambridge: Cambridge University Press, 271–297.

Finch, H. R. (1958). Introduction. In R. L. Stevenson, *Kidnapped.* New York: Washington Square Press.

Freud, S. (1959). Creative writers and day-dreaming. In J. Strachey (ed.), *Standard edition of the complete psychological works of Sigmund Freud*, (vol. 9), London: Hogarth Press, 143–153. (Work first published 1908).

Freud, S. (1964). *Leonardo da Vinci and a memory of his childhood.* New York: Norton. (Original work published 1910.)

Gedo, M. M. (1980). *Picasso. Art as autobiography.* Chicago: University of Chicago Press.

Gerlach, V. S., Schutz, R. E., Baker, R. L., & Mazer, G. E. (1964). Effects of variations in test directions on originality test response. *Journal of Educational Psychology, 55,* 79–83.

Getzels, J., & Czikszentmihalyi, M. (1976). *The creative vision: A longitudinal study of problem finding in art.* New York: John Wiley.

Ghiselin, B. (ed.) (1952). *The creative process.* New York: Mentor.

Gick, M. L., & Holyoak, K. J. (1980). Analogical problem solving. *Cognitive Psychology, 12,* 306–355.

Gick, M. L., & Holyoak, K. J. (1983). Schema induction and analogical transfer. *Cognitive Psychology, 15,* 1–38.

Glaser, R., & Chi, M. T. H. (1988). Overview. In M. T. H. Chi, R. Glaser, & M. J. Farr (eds.), *The nature of expertise*, Hillsdale, NJ: Erlbaum, xv–xxvii.

Glimcher, A. & Glimcher, M. (1986). *Je suis le cahier. The sketchbooks of Picasso.* Boston: The Atlantic Monthly Press.

Glucksberg, S., & Weisberg, R. W. (1966). Verbal behavior and problem solving: Some effects of labelling in a functional fixedness task. *Journal of Experimental Psychology, 71,* 659–664.

Golding, J. 1968. *Cubism. A history and analysis. 1907–1914.* London: Faber and Faber.

Goodwin, F. K., & Jamison, K. R. (1990). *Manic-depressive illness.* New York: Oxford University Press.

Greeno, J. G. (1980). Trends in the theory of knowledge for problem solving. In D. T. Tuma, & R. Reif (eds.), *Problem solving and education: Issues in teaching and learning*, Hillsdale, NJ: Erlbaum.

Gruber, H. (1981). *Darwin on man*. (2d ed.) Chicago: University of Chicago Press.

Guilford, J. P. (1950). Creativity. *American Psychologist, 5*, 444–454.

Guilford, J. P. (1959). Traits of creativity. In H. H. Anderson (ed.), *Creativity and its cultivation*, New York: Harper, 142–161.

Hadamard, J. (1954). *The psychology of invention in the mathematical field*. New York: Dover.

Halpern, D. (1989). *Thought and knowledge. An introduction to critical thinking*. 2d ed. Hillsdale, NJ: Erlbaum.

Harlow, H. (1949). The formation of learning sets. *Psychological Review, 56*, 51–65.

Hayes, J. R. (1981). *The complete problem solver*. Philadelphia: Franklin Institute Press.

Hayes, J. R. (1985). Three problems in teaching problem solving skills. In S. Chipman, J. W. Segal, & R. Glaser (eds.), *Thinking and learning skills*, vol. 2), Hillsdale, NJ: Erlbaum, 391–406.

Hayes, J. R. (1989). Cognitive processes in creativity. In J. A. Glover, R. R. Ronning, & C. R. Reynolds (eds.), *Handbook of creativity*, New York: Plenum, 135–145.

Henahan, D. (1986, July 20). Pondering the link between genius and madness. *New York Times*, p. H21.

Hennessy, B. A., & Amabile, T. M. (1988). The conditions of creativity. In R. Sternberg (ed.), *The nature of creativity. Contemporary psychological perspectives*, Cambridge: Cambridge University Press, 11–42.

Herbert, R. (1988). *Impressionism. Art, leisure, and Parisian society*. New Haven, CT: Yale University Press.

Hertzman, E. (1963). Mozart's creative process. In P. H. Lang (ed.), *The creative world of Mozart*. New York: Norton, 17–30.

Hintzman, D. L. (1986). "Schema abstraction" in a multiple-trace memory model. *Psychological Review, 93*, 411–428.

Holyoak, K. J. (1990). Problem solving. In D. N. Osherson. & E. E. Smith (eds.), *An invitation to cognitive science. Thinking*, vol. 3, Cambridge, MA: MIT Press, 117–146.

Holyoak, K. J., & Koh, K. (1987). Surface and structural similarity in analogical transfer. *Memory & Cognition, 15*, 332–340.

Hope, C. (April 12, 1990). The real Leonardo. *New York Review of Books*, 41–43.

Howard, F. (1987). *Wilbur and Orville. A biography of the Wright brothers*. New York: Knopf.

Jackson, P. W., & Messick, S. (1967). The person, the product, and the response: Conceptual problems in the assessment of creativity. In J. Kagan (ed.), *Creativity and learning*, Boston: Houghton Mifflin, 1–19.

Jamison, K. R. (1989). Mood disorders and patterns of creativity in British writers and artists. *Psychiatry, 52,* 125–134.

Jamison, K. R., Gerner, R. H., Hammen, C., & Padesky, C. (1980). Clouds and silver linings: Positive experiences associated with primary affective disorders. *American Journal of Psychiatry, 137,* 198–202.

Jenkins, R. V. (1983). Elements of style: Continuities in Edison's thinking. *Annals of the New York Academy of Sciences, 424,* 149–162.

Jenkins, R. V., & Jeffrey, T. E. (1984). Worth a thousand words: Nonverbal documents in editing. *Documentary Editing, 6,* 1–8.

John-Steiner, V. (1985). *Notebooks of the mind. Explorations of thinking.* Albuquerque: University of New Mexico Press.

Johnson, D. M., Parrott, G. L., & Stratton, R. P. (1968). Production and judgment of solutions to five problems. *Journal of Educational Psychology Monograph Supplement, 59,* no. 6, part 2.

Keane, M. (1987). On retrieving analogues when solving problems. *Quarterly Journal Experimental Psychology, 39A,* 29–41.

Kessel, N. (1989). Genius and mental disorder: A history of ideas concerning their conjunction. In P. Murray (ed.), *Genius. The history of an idea,* Oxford: Blackwell, 196–212.

Kimmelman, M. (1989, February 10). 'Guernica': Few ripples at first, many since. *New York Times,* p. C33.

Koestler, A. (1964). *The act of creation.* New York: Macmillan.

Kogan, N, & Pankove, E. (1974). Long-term predictive validity of divergent-thinking tests: Some negative evidence. *Journal of Educational Psychology, 66,* 802–810.

Köhler, W. (1976). *The mentality of apes.* New York: Liveright. (Original work published 1927).

Kraepelin, E. (1976). *Manic-depressive insanity and paranoia.* New York: Arno Press. (Original work published 1921).

Kris, E. (1952). *Psychodynamic explorations in art.* New York: Wiley.

Kuhn, T. (1978). *The structure of scientific revolutions.* (2d ed.). Chicago: University of Chicago Press.

Lachman, R., Lachman, J. L., & Butterfield, E. C. (1979). *Cognitive psychology and information processing: An introduction.* Hillsdale, NJ: Erlbaum.

Lakatos, I. (1970). Falsification and the methodology of scientific research programmes. In I. Lakatos & A. Musgrave (eds.) *Criticism and the growth of knowledge.* Cambridge: Cambridge University Press.

Landau, E. G. (1990). *Jackson Pollock.* New York: Abrams.

Landon, H. C. R. (1956). *The Mozart companion.* New York: Norton.

Langley, P., Simon, H. A., Bradshaw, G. L., & Zytkow, J. M. (1987). *Scientific Discovery. Computational explorations of the creative process.* Cambridge, MA: MIT Press.

Lesgold, A., et al. (1988). Expertise in a complex skill: Diagnosing X-ray pictures. In M. T. H. Chi, R. Glaser, & M. J. Farr (eds.), *The nature of expertise*, Hillsdale, NJ: Erlbaum, 311–342.

Levine, M. (1988). *Effective problem solving*. Englewood Cliffs, NJ: Prentice-Hall.

Lipman, J. (ed.) (1989). *Calder's universe*. Philadelphia: Running Press. (Original work published 1976).

Lowes, J. L. (1964). *The road to Xanadu*. Boston: Houghton Mifflin. (Original work published 1927).

Luchins, A. S., & Luchins, E. H. (1959). *Rigidity of behavior*. Eugene, OR: University of Oregon Press.

Lung, C. T. & Dominowski, R. L. (1985). Effects of strategy instructions and practice on nine-dot problem solving. *Memory & Cognition, 11*, 804–811.

Mackinnon, D. W. (1962). The personality correlates of creativity: a study of American architects. In G. S. Nielsen (ed.), *Proceedings of the 14th International Congress of Applied Psychology*, vol. 2, Copenhagen: Munksgaard, 11–39.

Mansfield, R. S., & Busse, T. V. (1981). *The psychology of creativity and discovery*. Chicago: Nelson-Hall.

Marshall, R. (1987). *Alexander Calder. Sculpture of the nineteen thirties*. New York: Whitney Museum.

Marshall, R. L. (1972). *The compositional process of J. S. Bach: A study of the autograph scores of the vocal works*. (2 vols.) Princeton, NJ: Princeton University Press.

Martindale, C. (1989). Personality, situation, and creativity. In J. A. Glover, R. R. Ronning, & C. R. Reynolds (eds.), *Handbook of creativity*, New York: Plenum, 211–232.

Matlin, M. (1989). *Cognition*. (2d ed.) New York: Holt, Rinehart, & Winston.

May, R. (1975). *The courage to create*. New York: Norton.

Mednick, S. A. (1962). The associative basis of the creative process. *Psychological Review, 69*, 220–232.

Metcalfe, J. (1986a). Feeling of knowing in memory and problem solving. *Journal of Experimental Psychology: Learning, Memory, and Cognition, 12*, 288–294.

Metcalfe, J. (1986b). Premonitions of insight predict impending error. *Journal of Experimental Psychology: Learning, Memory, and Cognition, 12*, 623–634.

Miller, R. F. (1981). *Dostoyevsky and The Idiot: Author, narrator, and reader*. Cambridge, MA: Harvard University Press.

Mitgang, H. (1984, January 3). Library displays the poet's search for perfection. *New York Times*, p. 21.

Mitroff, I. I. (1974). Norms and counter-norms in a select group of the Apollo moon scientists: A case study of the ambivalence of scientists. *American Sociological Review, 39*, 579–595.

Mochulsky, K. (1967). *Dostoyevsky: His life and work.* M. A. Minihan, trans. Princeton, NJ: Princeton University Press.

Mozart, J. C. W. A. (1952), a letter. Reprinted in B. Ghiselin, B. (ed.), (1952), *The creative process.* New York: Mentor, 44–45.

Murray, P. (1989). *Genius. The history of an idea.* Oxford: Blackwell.

Newell, A. (1990). *Unified theories of cognition.* Cambridge, MA: Harvard University Press.

Newell, A., Shaw, J. C., & Simon, H. A. (1962). The process of creative thinking. In H. E. Gruber, G. Terrell, & M. Wertheimer (eds.), *Contemporary approaches to creative thinking,* New York: Atherton Press, 63–119.

Newell, A., & Simon, H. A. (1972), *Human problem solving.* Englewood Cliffs, NJ: Prentice-Hall.

Nisbett, R. E., & Wilson. T. D. (1977). Telling more than we can know. Verbal reports on mental processes. *Psychological Review, 84,* 231–259.

Ochse, R. E. (1990). *Before the gates of excellence. The determinants of creative genius.* Cambridge: Cambridge University Press.

Olby, R. (1974). *The path to the double helix.* Seattle, WA: University of Washington Press.

Olton, R. M. (1979). Experimental studies of incubation: Searching for the elusive. *Journal of Creative Behavior, 13,* 9–22.

Olton, R. M., & Johnson, D. M. (1976). Mechanisms of incubation in creative problem solving. *American Journal of Psychology, 89,* 617–630.

Osborn, A. (1953). *Applied imagination.* (Rev. ed.) New York: Charles Scribner's Sons.

Patrick, C. (1935). Creative thought in poets. In R. Woodworth (ed.), *Archives of Psychology, 178.*

Patrick, C. (1937). Creative thought in artists. *Journal of Psychology, 4,* 35–73.

Perkins, D. N. (1981). *The mind's best work.* Cambridge, MA: Harvard University Press.

Perkins, D. N. (1983). Novel remote analogies seldom contribute to discovery. *Journal of Creative Behavior, 17,* 223–239.

Poincaré, H. (1952). Mathematical creation. In *The foundations of science.* G. B. Halsted, trans. New York: The Science Press. Reprinted in B. Ghiselin (ed.), *The creative process,* New York: New American Library, 33–42. (Original work published 1908).

Polcari, S. (1979). Jackson Pollock and Thomas Hart Benton. *Arts Magazine, 53,* 120–124.

Polson, P. G., & Jeffries, R. (1985). Instruction in general problem-solving skills: An analysis of four approaches. In S. Chipman, J. W. Segal, & R. Glaser (eds.), *Thinking and learning skills,* vol. 1 Hillsdale, NJ: Erlbaum, 417–455.

Polya, G. (1957). *How to solve it.* (2d ed.) New York: Doubleday.

Popper (1968). *The self and its brain.* New York: Praeger.

Richards, R. (1981). Relationship between creativity and psychopathology: An evaluation and interpretation of the evidence. *Genetic Psychology Monographs, 103,* 261–324.

Richardson, J. (1991). *A life of Picasso. vol. 1. 1881–1906.* New York: Random House.

Robinson, D. (1985). *Chaplin. His life and art.* New York: McGraw-Hill.

Robinson, E. (1969). Commemorative lecture. James Watt, engineer by act of parliament. In R. Donaldson (ed.), *Bicentenary of the James Watt patent for a separate condenser steam engine,* Glasgow: University of Glasgow, 9–26.

Rogers, C. R. (1954). Toward a theory of creativity. *ETC: A review of general semantics, 11,* 69–82.

Rolt, L. T. C. & Allen, J. S. (1977). *The steam engine of Thomas Newcomen.* New York: Science History Publications/USA.

Rosenblum, R. (1976). *Cubism and twentieth-century art.* New York: Abrams.

Ross, B. H. (1987). This is like that: The use of earlier problems and the separation of similarity effects. *Journal of Experimental Psychology: Learning, Memory, and Cognition, 13,* 629–639.

Ross, B. H., & Kennedy, P. T. (1990). Generalizing from the use of earlier examples in problem solving. *Journal of Experimental Psychology: Learning, Memory, and Cognition, 16,* 42–55.

Rothenberg, A. (1979). *The emerging goddess.* Chicago: University of Chicago Press.

Rubin, W. (1967). Jackson Pollock and the modern tradition. *Art Forum, 5,* 14–22.

Rubin, W. (1984). Picasso. In W. Rubin (ed.), *"Primitivism" in 20th century art,* Vol. 1, New York: Museum of Modern Art, 241–343.

Rubin, W. (1989). *Picasso and Braque: Pioneering Cubism.* New York: Museum of Modern Art. Distributed by Bullfinch Press, Boston, MA.

Runco, M. (1992). *Problem finding.* Norwood, N.J.: Ablex.

Sadie, S. (1983). *The New Grove Mozart.* New York: Norton.

Scheerer, M. (1963, April). Problem-solving. *Scientific American, 208,* 118–128.

Schneider, E. (1953). *Coleridge, opium, and Kubla Khan.* Chicago: University of Chicago Press.

Schonberg, H. C. (1979). *Lives of the great composers.* New York: Norton.

Schrodinger, E. (1944). *What is life? The physical aspect of the living cell.* Cambridge: Cambridge University Press.

Segal, S. M., Busse, T. V., & Mansfield, R. S. (1980). The relationship of scientific creativity in the biological sciences to predoctoral accomplishments and experiences. *American Educational Research Journal, 17,* 491–502.

Sheppard, P. M. (1960). *Natural selection and heredity*. New York: Harper & Row.

Sherman, C. H. (1990). Notes to *Michael Haydn: 8 symphonies*. H. Farberman, Conductor/Bournemouth Sinfonietta. VoxBox CDX 5020.

Simonton, D. K. (1984). *Genius, creativity, and leadership*. Cambridge, MA: Harvard University Press.

Simonton, D. K. (1988). *Scientific genius. A psychology of science*. New York: Cambridge University Press.

Slater, E., & Meyer, A. (1959). Contributions to a pathography of musicians: 1. Robert Schumann. *Confinia Psychiatrica, 2,* 65–94.

Sloboda, J. (1985). *The musical mind*. New York: Oxford University Press.

Smith, E. T. (1985, September 30) Are you creative? *Business Week,* 80–84.

Solomon, M. (1977). *Beethoven*. New York: Schirmer Books.

Spencer, R. M., & Weisberg, R. W. (1986). Context-dependent effects on analogical transfer. *Memory & Cognition, 14,* 442–449.

Stannard, D. E. (1980). *Shrinking history. On Freud and the failure of psychohistory*. New York: Oxford.

Sternberg, R. J., & Davidson, J. E. (1982, June). The mind of the puzzler. *Psychology Today,* 37–44.

Sudnow, D. (1978). *Ways of the hand. The organization of improvised conduct*. Cambridge, MA: Harvard University Press.

Suler, J. R. (1980). Primary process thinking and creativity. *Psychological Bulletin, 88,* 144–165.

Thorndike, E. L. (1913). *Principles of teaching*. New York: Seiler.

Torrance, E. P. (1988). The nature of creativity as manifest in its testing. In R. J. Sternberg (ed.), *Creativity. Current psychological perspectives*, Cambridge: Cambridge University Press, 43–75.

Treffert, D. A. (1988, January/February). An unlikely virtuoso. Leslie Lemke and the story of savant syndrome. *The Sciences,* 28–35.

Tyson, A. (1987). *Mozart. Studies of the autograph scores*. Cambridge, MA: Harvard University Press.

Vosniadou, S. & Ortony, A. W. (1989). *Similarity and analogical reasoning*. New York: Cambridge University Press.

Wallace, D. B., & Gruber, H. E. (1989). *Creative people at work. Twelve cognitive case studies*. New York: Oxford University Press.

Wallas, G. (1926). *The art of thought*. New York: Harcourt Brace.

Walsh, J. E. (1975). *One day at Kitty Hawk*. New York: Crowell.

Wasiolek, E. (ed.) (1967). *The notebooks for The Idiot*. K. Strelsky, trans. Chicago: University of Chicago Press.

Watson, J. D. (1968). *The double helix*. New York: Signet.

Watson, J. B. (1958). *Behaviorism*. Chicago: University of Chicago Press.

Weisberg, R. W. (1980). *Memory, thought, and behavior*. New York: Oxford University Press.

Weisberg, R. W. (1986). *Creativity: Genius and other myths*. New York: Freeman.

Weisberg, R. W. (1988). Problem solving and creativity. In R. J. Sternberg (ed.), *The nature of creativity. Contemporary psychological perspectives*, Cambridge: Cambridge University Press, 148–176.

Weisberg, R. W. (1992). Metacognition and insight during problem solving: Comment on Metcalfe. *Journal of Experimental Psychology: Learning, Memory, and Cognition, 18*, 426–431.

Weisberg, R. W., & Alba, J. W. (1981). An examination of the alleged role of "fixation in the solution of several "insight" problems. *Journal of Experimental Psychology: General 110*, 169–192.

Weisberg, R. W., & DiCamillo, M. A. (1992). Multiple memory searches as the basis for restructuring in an insight problem. Unpublished manuscript, Temple University.

Weisberg, R. W., & Suls, J. M. (1973). An information-processing model of Duncker's candle problem. *Cognitive Psychology, 4*, 255–276.

Wertheimer, M. (1982). *Productive thinking*. (Enlarged ed.) Chicago: University of Chicago Press.

Wollenberg, S. (1975). The Jupiter theme: new light on its creation. *Musical Times, 66*, 781–783.

Woodman, R. W., & Schoenfeldt, L. F. (1989). Individual differences in creativity. An interactionist perspective. In J. A. Glover, R. R. Ronning, & C. R. Reynolds (eds.), *Handbook of creativity*, New York: Plenum, 77–91.

Zaslaw, N. (1989). *Mozart's symphonies. Context, performance practice, reception*. New York: Oxford University Press.

Name Index

Subject Index